IN PRAISE OF HELEN M. LUKE

"Helen M. Luke became an embodiment of the wise woman archetype in her later years and was a major figure among American Jungian authors whose books drew from her life and analytic work."

Jean Shinoda Bolen, M.D., author of *Crossing to Avalon*

"The maps and metaphors of the inner cosmos have rarely been so richly drawn."

Jean Houston, author of *A Mystic Life*

"Helen Luke's warm and very human book resonates with the archetypal struggles of all who seek to become the unique individuals they are meant to be and provides us with hope for our own journey to wholeness."

Dr. Robert A. Johnson, author of *Contentment*

"Helen Luke courageously gives us her life to look upon as a road map for living without losing the presence of soul."

Reverend Rosalyn L. Bruyere, author of *Wheels of Light*

ALSO BY HELEN M. LUKE

Kaleidoscope: The Way of Woman and Other Essays

Dark Wood to White Rose: Journey and Transformation
in Dante's *Divine Comedy*

Old Age: Journey into Simplicity

The Way of Woman: Awakening the Perennial Feminine

SUCH STUFF AS DREAMS ARE MADE ON

The Autobiography and Journals of

HELEN M. LUKE

Introduction by Charles H. Taylor

Journals edited by Barbara A. Mowat

A PARABOLA BOOK

BELL TOWER NEW YORK

Grateful acknowledgment is made for permission to quote the following: Excerpts from "East Coker" in *Four Quartets*, copyright 1940 by T. S. Eliot and renewed 1968 by Esme Valerie Eliot, and "Little Gidding" in *Four Quartets*, copyright 1942 by T. S. Eliot and renewed 1970 by Esme Valerie Eliot, reprinted by permission of Harcourt, Inc., and Faber and Faber Ltd. Excerpt from "Oedipus at Colonus" in *Sophocles, The Oedipus Cycle: An English Version* by Robert Fitzgerald, copyright 1941 by Harcourt, Inc., and renewed in 1969 by Robert Fitzgerald, reprinted by permission of the publisher. Excerpts from Charles Williams, *All Hallow's Eve* (Grand Rapids, Mich.: Wm. B. Eerdmans Publishing, 1981), reprinted by permission of David Higham Associates Limited, London. Photographs courtesy of the Apple Farm Community, Three Rivers, Michigan; Mr. and Mrs. Robert Luke; and Mr. Nicholas Luke.

Published by Bell Tower, New York, New York. Member of the Crown Publishing Group. Random House, Inc. New York, Toronto, London, Sydney, Auckland www.randomhouse.com

Bell Tower and colophon are registered trademarks of Random House, Inc.

Originally published in hardcover by Parabola Books in 2000. First paperback edition published in 2001.

Printed in the United States of America

Library of Congress Cataloging-in-Publication Data
Luke, Helen M., 1904–1995
Such stuff as dreams are made on: the autobiography and journals of Helen M. Luke / introduction by Charles H. Taylor; journals edited by Barbara A. Mowat—1st pbk. ed.
"A Parabola book." Originally published: New York: Parabola Books, c2000.
1. Dreams.   2. Dream interpretation.   3. Spiritual life.   4. Jungian psychology.
5. Luke, Helen M., 1904–1995   I. Mowat, Barbara A.   II. Title
BF1091.L82 2001
150.19'54'092—dc21   00-062120

ISBN 0-609-80589-4

10 9 8 7 6 5 4 3 2 1

First Paperback Edition

CONTENTS

We are such stuff
As dreams are made on, and our little life
Is rounded with a sleep.

THE TEMPEST
ACT 4, SCENE I

INTRODUCTION

WE LIVE IN A TIME when neurobiologists are making immense advances in our understanding of the human brain. Yet few scientists agree on the nature and function of dreams. Few believe that dreams can offer meaningful guidance to the consciousness that remembers and reflects on them. Now Helen M. Luke, who died in 1995 at the age of ninety, brings us a posthumous book that illuminates the function of dreams by offering us an intimate account of her own dreams and how they contributed to the unfolding of her life. It is the internal story behind her mature work at Apple Farm (the spiritual community she helped to establish and direct in Michigan) and behind the writing that distinguished her last three decades.

Following the autobiography, written at seventy, are substantial selections from almost twenty years of subsequent handwritten journals that Luke entrusted to Barbara Mowat, Director of Academic Programs at the Folger Shakespeare Library in Washington, D.C., to select and prepare for posthumous publication. They reflect intimately, often self-critically, on the ongoing dialogue she had with her dreams and creative life, and provide a rich perspective on what can be learned by keen attention to the psyche's offerings that come in sleep. In sleep, there is a kind of "non-ego knower" who repeatedly widens and deepens our understanding of ourselves and our relation to the transpersonal world. The evidence of this is a great gift of Helen Luke's extraordinarily faithful, candid, and honest account.

Luke was a generation younger than the Swiss psychiatrist C. G. Jung and half a generation younger than most of the followers who knew him well. She describes her one interview with him with candor and humor, noting his seemingly irrelevant observations that puzzled and even irritated her at the time. Even though she soon came to realize how he had hit the mark, she never took up any personal communication with him. She did substantial analytic work with two of the earliest Jungian analysts, one in London and the other in Zurich, but never enrolled in the formal training programs that were just being organized. Her reading of Jung's published works as they appeared was both wide and deep, and her clinical orientation follows closely Jung's own preoccupation with the individuation process and the psychological meaning of religious literature and sacred symbolism.

Both in her own life and in her work with others she sought to heed the call of the larger personality, whose "center and circumference" is often termed the Self by Jung to distinguish it from a view of personality defined only by daylit ego-consciousness. Luke's therapeutic perspective is close to the classical Jungian tradition. It is concerned especially with development of a whole personality potentially able to contain and use creatively the conflicts between instinct and intention that afflict every person. Insight into these conflicts often comes from noticing analogies to patterns of meaning expressed in the wide range of mythic, sacred, and psychological symbolism that religious and literary tradition reveals across the ages and around the world. Her books, frequently drawing on major works of literature such as Dante's *Commedia*, Shakespeare's *The Tempest*, or T. S. Eliot's *Four Quartets*, explore metaphors of enduring meaning for those who seek psychological maturity today.

Consistent with her "classical" orientation, her work has little to say concerning the preoccupations of clinical theory with reductive analysis of childhood wounds, intense exploration of object relations, or the study of transference interactions. Jung wrote less of child development than many later psychologists, and Luke is in that tradition. Yet what is striking about her autobiography, and especially the later meditations of her journals, is that she returns repeatedly to reflect anew on her relationships to her mother, her father, and her early history. The seriousness with which Luke studies the events of history and the phenomena of inner life is deeply provocative. Examining intimate experiences, reflections, and images from within, she searches for their application, symbolically understood, to her lifelong quest for understanding. And in the process, the reader is drawn to reflect on layers of meaning in his or her own story that may have been neglected or misunderstood.

Luke's autobiographical writing and reflections give an unusually honest, subtle example of how a life's self-analysis may go forward. Not only does she seek what is new and creative for her development, but she also goes back to reflect on how intimate wounds and fateful events have been part of her becoming. One is reminded that Dante places in the Earthly Paradise, at the top of the Mountain of Purgatory, two rivers that must be crossed: first, Lethe, of ancient heritage, in which the injuries, injustices, and passions of the past must be forgotten or surrendered, and second, Eunoe, Dante's own invention, in which one must gather together, remember, in the river of "good mind," all that comes from one's past and has contributed to who one essentially is.

The autobiography, Luke makes clear, was written with the expectation that it might one day be published, but the journal was intended from the beginning as a private diary of her inner life. With characteristic honesty, when first remarking on the impetus from a dream, she observes, "how always I have a care to a hypothetical reader. . . . Life is a drama and no drama is complete without the participation of an audience . . . even if the listener is 'the companion' in oneself." Her writing is at once intensely private and introverted and yet also often has the eloquence of a lover of language who chooses every word with care: "I see this diary as a means to awareness of the 'ruthless task' of individuation in the patterns of my privacy."

In both the autobiography and the journal, Luke's debt to Jung is clear. So too is her engagement with the Anglican church as well as the Bible and other religious literature. After her marriage, she had given up her mother's Christian Science faith and was later baptized in the Church of England. During her work in California she was associated for a time with a particular church and priest, but as the church shifted its focus from the spirit within to social action without, she became unable to identify with the institution. When in a dream a Catholic friend told her that she hated Protestant tracts, she found herself responding, "I hate *all* tracts." Although she kept her attachment to the church alive in years of friendship with certain priests and orders, even working for some years as a therapist for members of one order and for persons unsure of their cloistered vocation, she made it clear that her loyalty to the individual's own calling came first. Over time she came to feel that formal association with any particular order or declaration of traditional creed was impossible. For her, as for Jung, much of the literature and ritual of the Christian tradition held rich symbolic and psychological meaning, but never in a literal or doctrinaire way. While the milieu of Apple Farm has the interiority of a religious retreat, its devotion is to the symbolic life, lived in incarnate closeness to the earth and open to psychological and sacred symbols from across the worlds of space and time.

Throughout Luke's mature writing, both for the public and in her journals, we feel a tremendous sense of the mystery of an inner life deeply lived. The power of the Other, the source from which her images derive, is presented with a respectful awe that allows for both the mysteries and the uncertainties of interpretation. Even treasured and recurring personal images are received with gratitude, not possessiveness. While she welcomes several visions of being merged with the stem of a beloved water lily flowering in the sunshine above her, she concentrates, as a mystic might, on the wonder of the experience rather than interpreting its affirmation of her ability, like that of the stem, to mediate the essential flow between the flower in the sun and its roots in the dark mud below.

In attempting to suggest the authenticity of Luke's revelation of her life's journey, it is easy to make it sound universally optimistic—but it is not so. She assures us in a variety of ways that "I have been subject to all the ups and downs of the lesser dreams from the level of the personal unconscious and the usual goings on of shadow and animus" and notes how they keep the ego "firmly on the earth." Her confessions that it is hard for her not to need the affirmation of others are convincing. At times she suffered feelings of substantial depression or of boredom as she got older and had less energy. Always her creative work on herself or her writing recovered her essentially life-affirming attitude, in which "one is filled with awe before the mystery."

Two of her dreams from early childhood recur thematically in many mature reflections. In the first, she is terrified as she is swept along in a great rainbow, differentiated in all its colors, but moved by a power before which she is helpless. By the end of her journal, we know that the fearful power which forces her through the sufferings of her personal journey has enabled her to develop the finely differentiated feeling that the rainbow's spectrum represents and that her writing richly displays. In the second early dream, she sits on a stone, a milestone at the edge of a village, and is told by a hard-faced woman that she must leave the village and go away down the lonely road, in fear. And we accept, as she does, that the hard-faced agent of destiny, so seemingly unloving, has made possible the conscious evolution of her life.

This combination of personal autobiography, written at the culmination of seventy years of life, and of an intimate diary from two succeeding decades, provides both an engaging life story and ever more probing insights into the assimilation of that story's meanings. The regular arrival of new dreams and the recurring presence of older ones makes a counterpoint between fresh understandings provided by new material on the one hand and by deeper explorations of earlier material on the other. Barbara Mowat has done a masterful job of selecting from more than fifty volumes of journal entries to focus steadily on Luke's account of psychic development in maturity and old age. Her story both feeds us in itself and stimulates us to reconsider our own life.

And always it keeps before us the question of our own relationship to the great transpersonal powers that cause a life to evolve in such unpredictable, often painful ways. We are increasingly aware of Luke's engagement with a numinous source within, a palpable contact beyond description, beyond images, less finite than any state of maturity or individuation. Yet her intimate diary of doubts and insecurities—compensated for by a consistently faithful effort to look within for the meaning and delights of each step along the way—gives us a powerful example of how life may be explored with an attitude toward sacred paradox that can bear to live with mystery.

CHARLES H. TAYLOR
Jungian Analyst

PART I

THE AUTOBIOGRAPHY

Such Stuff as Dreams Are Made On

CHAPTER ONE

———

PRELUDE

In looking back over the dreams of a considerable period a man
may sometimes discover in tiny scraps and fragments, even in
single images, meanings to which he was utterly blind at the time.
They were parts of a pattern that was slowly being woven. . . .

HAROLD C. GODDARD
The Meaning of Shakespeare, P. 16

AS I READ these words I remembered a dream that *The dream* came to me about fifteen years ago. In this dream I held in my hands a *of the* piece of midnight blue material, of heavy silk perhaps, square, about ten *golden* inches by ten inches. Fine gold threads were woven into the dark back- *pattern* ground in what seemed an entirely haphazard way, making no coherent pattern, having, it appeared, no meaning. Yet I knew in my dream that a woman had written here in gold thread the story of her life, if I could but know how to read it. I interrupt the dream to explain that this woman was an old friend of mine in actuality. She was older than myself, and had meant a great deal to me since my youth, had been in fact the one who first opened the doors for me to the wisdom of C. G. Jung. Yet outwardly her life had appeared a complete failure. None of her great artistic gifts had matured, she was crippled by illness, her husband was dead, she had barely enough to live on. A few days before my dream I had had a letter from her expressing her sense of ultimate and irremediable failure. As I read the letter and looked back over the many years of our friendship, I was flooded with a sense of gratitude to this woman, remembering her indomitable courage in the face of every kind of suffering and how my every contact with her as a girl and all through the years had jerked me out of triviality and subservience to collective opinion and reconnected me with a sense of the meaning and dignity of life. In the dream, as I tried to decipher the jumble of threads, I suddenly knew that I was looking at it from the wrong angle and I gave the cloth in my hand a quarter turn clockwise. Immediately I saw a beautiful and coherent golden pattern, and in the center, exquisitely embroidered, was the figure of a woman holding a child, and her robe flowed out from her shoulders like a river of gold. "House of Gold"—the image came to me from the Litany of Loretto. In wonder I questioned in the dream how my friend could possibly have created this lovely, intricate thing, when, as I knew, she had simply been trying to write the story of her failed life, and the result had seemed to her a meaningless jumble. And the answer came to me as clearly as though I had heard it spoken, and with a sense of profound joy. She had done nothing but choose a direction for each line of stitching, with all the consciousness and integrity possible to her, and the pattern had emerged and the picture had been woven, to be seen in all its beauty by those who would learn to make the "quarter turn."

The quarter turn

New "meanings to which [we are] utterly blind at the time. . . ." A new meaning was dawning for me many years after this dream, as I grew old. The pattern of my life too had been "slowly woven" through the years as I tried to choose consciously the "direction" at each stage of the journey, and perhaps now it was time for me to attempt the quarter turn and to endeavor to see from a new angle, and as a whole in the making, the "tiny scraps and fragments" of the past.

What is the meaning of the *quarter* turn? This is not the only dream in which that image has appeared. The psyche may be imagined as a circle, and if a line is drawn bisecting it horizontally with the half circle below the line dark and the half circle above it light, one may see in it an image of the collective attitude of most people. Everything unconscious, instinctive, dark, of the earth is *lower* than the clear light of the conscious mind—devalued, pushed down, and ignored as men go their way, trying to banish all shadows with the light of pure rationality, walking on the bisecting line of the circle without a glance downward. This attitude, persevered in, leads inevitably to the *half* turn, the circle turned upside down, with the dark uppermost—violence, sensuality, ignorance, and superstition trampling upon and excluding all the order and clarity of consciousness. But if one can make the *quarter* turn, if one can bring up the dark things and give them equal status with the light, while at the same time the light descends into the dark, then earth is raised to heaven, and heaven descends to earth, and the holy marriage  may be consummated not only in the pleroma but here and now. "In my flesh shall I see God." There is a final symbol of that which is beyond the quarter turn—the yin-yang fishes of China. In this we feel the unity of stillness and movement, the eternal dance of dark and light in which, though order and pattern are never lost, there is a constant fluidity. The seed of the light is seen in the dark, the seed of the dark in the light, and all the "scraps and fragments," so meaningless in isolation, so incoherent in the light of unshadowed reason, are revealed as the significant threads of a great pattern, with which the ego must never identify but of which it is an essential part.

Earth raised to heaven, heaven descending to earth. Another dream of many years ago returns to me. I dreamed that a child, my son, had had a dream in which he was given a spade and told that his work was to dig the dust of earth and lift it to heaven, and for every shovelful of earth he lifted up he was to dig a shovelful of the dust of heaven and bring it down to earth. So it is in the life of time—every up followed by a down and every down by an up. I remember a woman new to the ritual of the Catholic Mass saying to me, "The thing that struck me most powerfully about it was the constant rhythm of up and down movements." In the life of time the ascent and descent are known as a constant repetition, an alternation of this and that, but beyond time in the totality we shall know them as one. "The above is as the below."

CHAPTER TWO

EARLY DREAMS

THE THEME, the myth, of an individual life is often, as Jung has said, foreshadowed in the dreams of childhood. Four of my dreams as a child have remained with me through the years. Two of them were recurrent dreams, and though I have no memory of how often or over how long a period they came, I am fairly sure that they had ceased by the time I was seven or so. The third came only once, but also, I believe, before I was seven. The fourth was an image from a series of unremembered nightmares from which I suffered soon after I went to boarding school.

The earliest of these was a dream which certainly came more than once and from which I would awake terrified. In it there was a kind of mist of many colors, as it were a great rainbow, and I, tiny and alone, was carried helplessly at enormous speed along in its stream. I saw no earth nor sky— nothing but the all-enveloping colors—and I knew in the dream that there was no possible escape from this inexorable wheel.

The earliest dream

Some weeks before beginning to write down these things I had a dream which I believe may have unconsciously pushed me into this beginning of a journey in search of the origins of my personal imagery. I did not at the time associate it with the earliest dream of my life, but as I wrote these pages the connection hit me with a sense of wonder, for in this recent dream I saw the rainbow colors once more—not misty this time, but for an instant clear and distinct. I glimpsed a rainbow river of life, in which I was not swept away afraid and unknowing, but which flowed within, flowed without, and which seemed to me to "resound" with beauty. I woke with this strange word in my mind—sound and vision in one image.

The milestone and deserted village

The second recurrent dream came several times, or so it now seems to me. It is as vivid to me in old age as ever it was, and only now do I begin to realize the fullness of its prophetic meaning; it was the beginning of the myth behind my life. In the dream, I sat on a stone. It was an old milestone such as still exist, or existed in my youth, along many of the roads of England. They always fascinated me: ancient, grey, rounded at the top, telling the miles to the city. The stone of my dreams was a milestone set opposite the last house in a small town or village. It was dusk, the light was grey, the street was completely empty of life, and the windows of the houses were blank. Then an upper window in the house opposite me was thrown open and a hard-faced woman spoke to me in an icily cold voice. She pointed to the desolate road which stretched to my right away from the village. "Get out," she said, "go—you are forbidden to stay here." I looked along the road which ran on a sort of causeway and was lost in the mist, and I knew that I must walk along it alone. I woke in great fear.

I see now how the theme of this dream has recurred at many milestones along the road of my life. I have never been allowed to settle for long in a protected situation with those I have loved. Always I have been driven out again onto the lonely road. At the time of the dream I was a child surrounded by warmth and protected by devoted love, and all my life I have yearned for this safety. But the first agonizing separation from my mother when I was sent to boarding school at eight years old was not far ahead. Looking back at the dream, I know that it was the fact that I was sitting on the ancient stone that enabled me to face the unknown. Granite-hard, earth-rooted, the Stone has always been there when I have been confronted with the things I have most feared—coldness of heart and the lonely, unprotected road. In these later years many images both of the Road and of the Stone have appeared in my dreams, and of these I shall write later.

I return now to the third dream of my childhood. I stood alone a little way along the causeway road of the earlier milestone dream. Evidently I had already set out. The road was raised about eight or ten feet above the surrounding land. Down below the road, on the left, I saw a fire burning and was horror-struck as I realized that the fire was licking the feet and legs of my mother, who stood with her back against a wooden cross, her arms outstretched on the crosspiece. She was not nailed to it, nor, I think, tied, but somehow supported by it.

The crucified mother

I feel sure that this dream must have come after one of my most intense childhood experiences. I had been questioning my mother about my father, who died when I was eight months old, and she told me then of her suffering when she lost him. I can still hear the catch in her voice as she spoke. Child though I was, I believe I first touched at that moment the agony of compassion. I entered emotionally and imaginatively into my mother's suffering and the impact went very deep. I remember that moment as something beyond tears or words, and it seems to me that it was more than a simple identification with my mother. The terrible pain of separation touched me for the first time. The dream would bear this out. It was also perhaps an image of the actual fire of suffering through which my mother passed not only through her loss, but much later too before her death in 1949. Moreover, I am aware of two other associations which probably contributed to the imagery of the dream. Both concern the great symbol of fire.

My favorite story as a small child was of Shadrach, Meschach, and Abednego and the burning, fiery furnace. I remember the actual street in London along which we were walking when my grandmother told me the story. She loved all the Bible stories and on our walks in the then-quiet street off St. John's Wood she would tell them. The image came alive of the three (with those glorious names!) walking in a great sheet of flame with the fourth who was the Son of God. I saw them and still see them walking unafraid. The second fire association must have been Joan of Arc—a story that awed me from a very early age, so that I surely was aware without words of the transforming fire. I dreamed of myself entering it consciously much later on the road, at the great turning point of the second half of life.

The last of my childhood images from the unconscious is the only "scrap" that remains from a series of nightmares which were so terrifying that I remember trying desperately to stay awake at all costs. Finally they had to send me home from school for a while. I believe the immediate cause was the cruelty and hardness of a woman who was at that time in charge of the smallest little girls in the school. Her cruelty was not often directed at me, but I saw it with the horror which that kind of thing always awoke in me. I do have an image of her standing over me and jeering as I sobbed and cried out in that awful half-conscious stage of a nightmare. Whether it was a fact or not, I am not sure. Her expression was like that of the hard-faced woman in my earlier dream.

The Hind   The one memory of the content of the nightmares is a most curious image. I would awake screaming that the Hind was after us—an odd word for a child of nine to use. It is impossible, of course, to know what my childish associations would have been, but the most likely conscious knowledge of the word would have come from the story, well known to all English children, of Drake's ship "The Golden Hind" in which he sailed the oceans of the world, and the meaning of the word "hind" would certainly have been explained in history lessons. That pursuit by a deer, a typically timid and gentle animal, should have caused so much terror seems inexplicable, but when we remember the archetypal meaning of the deer as a symbol of Christ, the image takes on a depth of meaning which links it to that other dream of the milestone. The hard-faced woman inwardly, the cruel woman outwardly—the polar opposites of my loving mother—may be seen as the deadly attacks from the shadow which force one onto the lonely road, and which in spite of terror and flight lead finally to the acceptance of the pursuing "Hound of Heaven," which in my imagery was the "Hind." As I look back now it moves me greatly to think that, like Drake in his "Golden Hind," I too would be carried through the storms, inwardly and outwardly, over the ocean to find a new world, to find in America the great adventure of my later life. The deer, too, appeared again about ten years ago in several dreams and fantasies, so that I now discover in all those early images meanings which reveal the beginnings of the slowly woven pattern, of which Goddard so beautifully wrote.

CHAPTER THREE

CHILDHOOD AND
THE MOTHERS

MY PARENTS had been married for a little over two years when my father, Kenneth Reinold, died in 1905 at the age of twenty-nine. I was, as I have said, eight months old. He was an officer in the Bombay Police in India, and he died there while my mother was in England with me. She was not physically strong and had come home for her confinement. My father had been to England on leave after my birth, so that briefly he had known me, and after he returned to India we were to have joined him soon. But he died after a short illness, and my mother came near to drowning in her grief. The marriage had been supremely happy, and she told me later how she rejected God and life itself in those days, and how frequently I was brought to her as she lay in bed. Only because of me, she said, did she hold on to her will to live.

Curiously, the image she evoked in me, and which remains vividly in my memory, of myself as a baby sitting on her bed in a darkened room, does not include a physical embrace, and it occurs to me how accurate symbolically this detail is. Images do not lie, in spite of our misreadings. I do not mean that my mother was not affectionate and demonstrative to me as a child, but that never in all the years did she cling to me in any outer sense. No matter how much she suffered from physical separations, nothing was allowed to interfere with what she felt right for me as a child, or with my freedom to go where I would as I grew up. The inner tie was proportionately greater, both in a positive and negative sense.

My mother's intense devotion to me lasted to the end of her life, and my identification with her came near to crushing me. From babyhood through all my early years the fear of losing her was a dark shadow in my life, and I did not begin to realize even the need of breaking my tie to her until my mid-twenties and after I was married. There were none of the usual incentives to rebellion, no visible curbs on my freedom of thought or action. I was bound by the unconscious inability to think in opposition to my mother on any matter of real importance.

Nevertheless, my mother was a person of such integrity and courage that her suffering forged in her the real selflessness of mature love, and therefore, when I had finally broken the crippling unconscious identification and was in search of my own identity, I was able to recognize that her gift of love to me had been an inestimable strength. At the last, as she drew near to her death, she affirmed my freedom in full awareness and with all her heart. Of this I shall write later in its place.

Some of the paradoxes of my nature in my childhood and youth—indeed all through life—spring surely from this double nature of my mother's love and its overwhelming, all-pervasive importance to me. On the one hand was the integrity and truth of her conscious love, on the other her unconscious projection of her emotional life onto me. My visible personality had a kind of happy freedom and sureness in some areas which won me many friends; and yet I suffered always from hidden fears and anxieties, centering around the great fear of losing my mother. Thoughts of illness and death in any form were a terror to me. I could not endure even a scene in a movie involving a hospital and had to shut my eyes. This, I am sure, came from a *participation mystique* with my mother's experience of loss, and I also believe that I carried an unconscious weight of guilt for my father's death. Unconsciously I may have been convinced that if I had not been born my mother would have been in India with my father, and he probably would not have died.

This guilt came to the surface during analysis many years later, and, when in addition to this, one remembers how great must have been the pressure of having to *deserve* the admiration and love which flowed from my mother, it is not surprising that I have had a life-long struggle with a besetting conviction of worthlessness which is of course a compensation for the unconscious demand to excel. No amount of outer success, no tribute from friends and admirers, can do more than temporarily lift such a conviction and ease the constant yearning for reassurance. There is no true relief from this miserable sense of "nothing but" through any of these props. It is the cross the ego carries to the end but more and more willingly as consciousness grows, and the only cure, as I very well know, lies in the creative act, the imaginative thought or feeling whereby the ego becomes a channel, not an autonomous obsession, and its worth or worthlessness are no longer relevant in the light of the true center of life. I believe that in rare moments even as a child I was wordlessly and intuitively aware of the difference between this freedom and the escape into exuberance brought by success and praise.

The second powerful feminine influence in my childhood came from my maternal grandmother. I lived with her whenever my mother was away and I loved her greatly. She was of pure Scottish descent; her father was of Lowland stock, a Presbyterian missionary in India, but her mother had ancestors from the Outer Hebrides and this great-grandmother was, I am told, a very remarkable woman with ideas ahead of her time. My grandmother had suffered much in her childhood, as had also my mother, from having been left for years with strangers or in schools in England. In those days of sailing ships the men and women who served in India could only come home at rare intervals; and even later, when my mother was a child, fares were not often paid for home leave. An English edu-cation, however, was considered absolutely essential for the children of their class. Each of my parents and both my grandmothers had suffered from these agonizing separa-tions, for my father's grandfather likewise was a missionary in India—an Anglican priest. Perhaps these wounds account for an extra charge of emotion in the clinging of mothers to daughters in my family, for my grandmother's absorption in my mother was as great as was my mother's in me and considerably less conscious. Everything her daughter did or thought was perfect in her eyes and she adopted at once all the passionately held convictions of my mother such as the suffragette's creed and Christian Science—much to the fury of my grandfather.

She was small, quick, and vigorous, her white hair (which had been red) piled high on her head, and she had a quality which is hard to define. There is a word much despised in these days which in its true sense describes her—she was a "lady," outwardly to her fingertips and inwardly in the immense and simple generosity of her heart which flowed out to everyone who came near her from the greatest to the humblest. She no doubt added greatly to the atmosphere of "spoiling" which surrounded me—I was the adored and special child to her as to my mother, but my mother remained always first for her. She had an extremely nervous and restless temperament and was racked by anxieties of all kinds. She told me once she had never quite got over her fear of the image, implanted in her by her dour Scottish school mistresses, of the Devil with horns and tail lurking round every corner to catch her for the least fall from goodness. Nevertheless she was gay and full of humor and a rock of safety to me in my mother's absences, which were frequent enough. Apart from her work—she was trained as a midwife—my mother was often ill in those early years and was also several times arrested, and was in prison once for a whole month, for her part in suffragette activities. (I was, of course, very proud of this.) At the outbreak of war she became first a munitions worker and then joined the newly founded women's police force, in which she rose by the end of the war to be a Chief Inspector in charge of the force of police women at a huge munitions factory at Gretna on the Scottish border.

Earliest memories

I return now to my own earliest memories. My very first is of standing at the top of a flight of wooden stairs (I was about three years old) and hearing a crash which frightened me very much. My grandmother had fallen downstairs and her arm was broken. I can see the closed door of my grandmother's room and the image in my mind of her lying in there with straw sticking out of her broken arm such as I had seen in the arm of one of my dolls! I remember my acute feelings of fear and pity, and I am struck by the fact that so many of my early memories involve agonizing feelings of pity.

Soon after this my mother and I must have moved to London from my grandparents' house in Sevenoaks, Kent. We stayed at first in lodgings near Baker Street and later had a flat in St. John's Wood not far to the north. From this time I became a city child, and we stayed in this area of London until my mother went north to Gretna in 1916 or so.

The city children of those days, however, do not have the same memories of noise and turmoil as do those today. I see the streets around my home as relatively empty, enlivened by the milk cart, the muffin man, and the occasional "four wheeler" or hansom cab—and how I loved those fascinating hansoms! It was the greatest treat to be taken for a ride in one with its smell of horse and leather—the dark interior, and the doors that folded back and then shut one into that small private place with the trap door in the roof through which the cabby, mounted high in his glory above the horse, would occasionally shout down a question or comment. On the main roads were the huge horse buses with their open top decks to which I would insist on climbing, looking anxiously to see whether the front seats were vacant where one sat just behind the driver on his lofty perch above the great strong horses. Long after the motor buses began to appear, I would beg to wait for a horse bus, so inferior did the horseless vehicle seem to me.

Looking back I realize that nearly all the really intense memories of my early childhood are of people and of animals—very few of places or things. The streets of London are filled with horses in my memory; particularly I loved the teams of great draught horses drawing the brewers drays in the City of London.

Then there was my dog—the first of many to whom through the years I would give my "heart to tear." *

She was an ugly, fat, black mongrel called Flo, with Schipperke blood, and she bared her teeth and grinned when pleased, which placed her far above all other dogs in my mind! I literally adored her, and although I remember the agonizing loss of later dogs, I have no memory of her death. Perhaps it was an experience so painful I have blocked it out, for it seems to me that there is something about the suffering and death of animals that brings a kind of pain which, though of course much less deep and long-lasting than the pity and grief engendered by human suffering and loss, is in one way more acutely agonizing for a short time. I believe it has something to do with our responsibility for animal suffering—particularly that of domestic animals with their dependence upon man. Even a child is potentially a person in whom the seeds of conscious independence are present. Perhaps the passionate concern of the English over cruelty to animals—a concern often ridiculed by other nations, and indeed sometimes degenerating into sentimentality—is rooted in the national myth of the "gentleman," the courteous man and chivalrous knight who is responsible for rescuing the weak and helpless and for the welfare of all who depend on him. However this may be, the love of dogs, and, at a greater distance, of horses, runs like a thread through my life. In my teens I was determined to be a farmer, to breed horses and spend my life with them, and the rare occasions when I had an opportunity to ride were happy indeed. One ecstatic summer only I spent on a farm. I learned to milk a cow, I collected eggs, and I was in heaven. The war put an end to such things, and I never had the fortune to own a horse—except in dreams!

---

* "Brothers and sisters I bid you beware / Of giving your heart to a dog to tear." Rudyard Kipling.

My imagination at this time was already eager for stories. By the age of five I could read for myself and I spent much time oblivious of the outer world and absorbed in the fairy stories I loved so much. It is significant to me that the image from all my reading which remains clearest and most numinous to this day is of Curdie, in George MacDonald's *The Princess and Curdie*, kneeling beside the fairy godmother's fire which burned and did not consume, and thrusting his hands into it at her bidding. They emerged from the fire with the power to recognize, when they touched another's hand, the essential nature of that person. For sometimes Curdie felt a tiger's claw, sometimes a dog's paw or a bird's talon, and once the slithering of a snake. He could know his friends when he found a true human hand in his own. This is another strong fire image to add to those already mentioned.

At four years old I was taken to my first play, *Peter Pan,* and after this the Christmas weeks in London, with the children's plays and pantomimes, was a time of delight each year. I greatly preferred a play with a real story to the irrelevancies of pantomime. My reaction to my first visit to *Peter Pan* at the age of four was typical. The pirates, the fighting, the poison I enjoyed without a qualm, but I burst into broken-hearted sobs and had to be taken out of the theater for a while when Mr. Darling, who, it will be remembered, greatly disliked Nana, the dog-nurse, fed her a bowl of medicine after luring her to drink it with promises of delicious food! It was a dirty trick in the feeling area, a betrayal of the dog's trust, which was a horror to me.

One other important thread in my life appeared also in these very early years. When I was five my mother took me to France to a small village on the Brittany coast for the month of August and continued to do so each year until 1914. Here in a simple French pension I first began to hear, to speak, and to love a foreign language, and here we made some life-long French friends.

I am struck by the fact that almost all my vivid memories of people before I went to boarding school are of women: my mother, my grandmother, our marvelous down-to-earth cook-housekeeper (another adoring mother to me), and a girl cousin ten years older than myself who seemed to me to be the most beautiful person in the world. I also loved my father's gentle, quiet mother, whom I visited from time to time, first in her old house in the village of Downton, near Salisbury, where I had been born, and later in London. I was also attached to two girls four years older than myself, who with their mothers and grandmothers spent holidays with us, but I remember no children of my own age.

It was not until I went away to school that any man made more than a superficial impact on me. My grandfather, of much importance later, was at that time a hazy figure on the periphery of my world and I certainly sensed already my mother's and my grandmother's resentment of him. My other grandfather died when I was very small; my mother's only brother, a soldier, I remember vaguely from his brief visits. He also died when I was six and, again, I have a clear memory of my mother's grief. My father had one brother in the Navy and I hardly knew him, though I developed a romantic attachment to the idea of a sailor uncle and longed to be a boy so that I might go to sea.

From age five to eight I attended a girls' day school, where I learned well, I believe, but my main memory of it is of my desperate shyness, the agony I went through at having even to answer to my name in a large gathering of girls. It may therefore be imagined how tremendous was the change from the wholly feminine and protected atmosphere of those years to a co-educational boarding school where I knew nobody at all; I was eight years old—and the memory of my first day and night and of the awful loneliness is vivid indeed. It was surely a first living out of the dream of the hard-faced woman and the lonely road;  but I sat upon the stone—the first milestone of my life—and drew from it, unconscious child that I was, the strength to face and accept unalterable facts. On that first day I neither cried nor showed my misery, and not until I was alone in bed that night did I shed silent tears into my pillow.

———

SCHOOL AND THE FATHER

IT MAY SEEM to many that it was a cruel thing to send so young and shy a child away from home. To Americans especially, such a thing seems horrible, but it must be remembered that in England the tradition of boarding school is an accepted thing. Eight was young, it is true, for most girls but the usual age for boys. It was, I now believe, my salvation, and I cannot be sufficiently grateful to my mother for having done it. I know how much it must have cost her, but she recognized the danger of allowing me to continue in my safe nest, an only child surrounded by adoring "mothers" with no father and no brother; moreover, she herself was at that time often sick and in bed or in hospital.

For the first months, I went home each weekend, which at first made the new life endurable for me, but after a while it became clear that the frequent breaks were making me homesick all over again on each Monday morning; therefore the weekends were stopped and I soon settled down. However, it was to these weekly train journeys that I owed my first truly emotional and numinous attachment to a man.

The father image   There was an art master at the school at this time whose name was Wilfred Walter. He later went on the stage and became a well-known Shakespearean actor. (Thirty years later I met him in Los Angeles, and something of the mana of my feeling for him as a child still hung about him.) In his classes I did not shine, but I had a particular relationship with him not shared by the other children, for he, too, went to London for the weekends and he took charge of me on the train every Saturday. He was a big, strong man with dark curly hair and a vivid personality, and he gave me his whole attention on those journeys. Starved as I was for a father, I loved him.

It is interesting that, although of course I have many memories of woman teachers, yet—with the exception of a great affection for the "Matron," the school nurse, who was a warm down-to-earth, motherly woman—I do not remember loving any of them. I had plenty of numinous mothers already! But there were two other masters at St. George's who carried the father image for me, and their influence on me, with that of Wilfred Walter, was incalculable. Looking back I can feel the impact of their personalities on the then-latent world of my mind and spirit, and their legacy to me was great indeed. If I had stayed at home for my school days or gone to the usual girls' school, the only powerful masculine image in my unconscious would have been my mother's animus—or the animus of such woman teachers as I would have encountered. This might easily have crippled all my future relationships with men and of course with my own animus. I had a hard struggle as it was, but without the masters and the boys at St. George's it would have been immeasurably harder.

Wilfred Walter was an artist through and through; the Rev. Cecil Grant, headmaster of St. George's school, was a priest of passionate faith with a flavor of Old Testament prophet, who inspired the deepest respect and awe, but not often, I imagine, love. Mr. Howe, the Classics and English master, was a lover of learning, a lover of the beauty of the word, and most rare of all, a truly great teacher. These were the three masters who stand out like beacons in my memory—an artist, a priest and a lover—and all three of them "poets" in the inner sense. I was indeed blessed.

Cecil Grant was a small slender man, with a black beard and piercing black eyes which struck terror and respect into his pupils (and into their parents!). I remember his delicate, almost feminine hands. He had a fat, sugar-coated wife, and, with the perception of children, we all knew that in some areas he was under her thumb, but in the realm of the mind and spirit there was no question as to who was the master. His authority was unquestioned even when violently disagreed with—and the mark of its validity was that he would always listen to sincerely stated opposition in the larger questions. It is this that distinguishes authority from mere power.

There was however a dark underside to his influence, of which I was somewhat aware. He was fundamentally a Jehovah-like figure, and it is of the Old Testament prophets that I think when I remember his beautiful voice reading the King James version of the Bible. (Thank heaven we were nurtured on no other translation in those days!) To him I owe the inestimable gift of an imaginative knowledge of the Bible and love of its poetry. But his religion and morality were black and white, and the sacramental paradox of essential religion was obscured, or so it seems to me now.

The third master, Mr. Howe, did not teach me until I was about twelve years old. His subjects were English, Latin, and, most important of all to me, Greek. There were only four of us in that class beginning the study of Greek—three boys and myself—and I can feel the excitement of it now, for Howe awoke in me the first tiny spark of an objective love of learning. As a schoolgirl I worked hard because of my pressing need to excel, but, being female, my first concern from the earliest years was with people, with the emotional situations around me. In Howe's classes, however, I began to respond to his burning love of the classics and of poetry and language, and I caught from him my first glimpse of the Logos. Such things are always "caught," not taught, and the "infectious" people, not the merely learned, are the great teachers. Howe evoked the creative spirit, not the drive for information. Of the four in that class, one of the boys, Rex Warner, became a well-known classical scholar, poet, and mythologist; another, Stephen Luke, later my husband, grew into a person of sensitive intelligence and rare compassion combined with practical wisdom; the third boy never caught any spark, it seemed, and I fear we gave him a bad time! The fourth was myself, and my tribute is that it fires me again just to remember the atmosphere in that classroom. One of my regrets is that I did not maintain the study of Greek when I decided to read modern languages instead of the classics at Oxford.

There was one other class that I loved with the same kind of delight as was evoked by those of Howe. We were taught Dalcroze eurythmics by a fine woman teacher whose name eludes me. It seems at the opposite pole outwardly, and yet I can see the affinity—for Howe brought love and imagination to the study of the classics, and eurythmics combined imaginative dance with the precisions of musical harmony and body movements. Perhaps these hours of eurythmics were the happiest and freest of all my school activities.

To return to my "fathers," here is perhaps the place to say more of the one family father-figure in my life—my mother's father.

My grandfather had very little significance for me as a small child. I must have hurt his feelings often, unconsciously identified as I was with my mother's hostility. I remember shrinking from his rather clumsy efforts at showing his deep affection for me.

He was a thorough Victorian in the best and worst senses of the word. He was descended on his father's side from French Huguenots, called Philpin, and on his mother's from Sir Peter Lely, the seventeenth-century painter whose family were for generations squires in East Anglia. My grandfather legally took his mother's name of Lely as soon as he was twenty-one—partly I am sure from snobbery and partly because he loathed his father. He joined the Indian Civil Service on coming down from Oxford. He had become Sir Frederic Lely and was Governor of the Central Provinces before I was born. His career in India had been distinguished by his integrity and courage—he had even risked his whole career once by fighting the authorities in support of the needs of the people in his district. He was the best type of British civil servant in those days—by our standards narrow and conservative, but incorruptibly just and dedicated to his job. It was typical of him that while he did much to encourage the entry of women in India into the professions (he himself always went to a woman doctor), his attitude to his own wife and daughter was completely Victorian; especially in money matters he was secretive and suspicious. With me he swung to the other extreme. He paid for my education; as I grew up, he handed out money without asking questions whenever I needed it; and he lavished all his warmth on me. I came to respect him and to feel great affection for him, but I remember very little of him before my Oxford days.

CHAPTER FIVE

GROWING UP

I SEE MYSELF during those school years—first the excessively shy and timid child, terrified of a rough word or of any kind of disapproval, then gradually acquiring assurance outwardly and a shell behind which I hid my anxiety and extreme sensitivity. I threw myself wholeheartedly into everything I undertook, and it was this quality I suppose which brought me success in many areas. I was among the first in work, and also in the athletics which in English schools brought so much prestige even to girls, and I won popularity with old and young. These things kept at bay the fears and feelings of inadequacy which were never far below the surface.

I was born under Libra, and the necessity for harmony in personal relationships was very strong in me; and my life-long struggle with the tendency to seek peace at any price had already begun. Libra, however, also bestows on its nativities the passionate love of justice, and added to this in my small self was the obvious dominance of the feeling function, which gave me a sureness in feeling areas which I altogether lacked when it came to thinking. I did not begin to trust my own thoughts until I was well over fifty; but the most powerful memories of my schooldays are of the occasions when, against all the tendencies of my usually obedient, peace-loving, and timid nature, I rose up to tackle what I considered to be gross injustice, and stood to my feelings.

My earliest experience of senseless injustice and cruelty did not involve an outward confrontation with authority, but it stands out in my memory as my first awareness of how a passionate feeling could take hold of me as an individual, no matter what anyone else might feel or think.

World War I

I was nine years old when the war broke out in August 1914. School began in September and we still had with us a German Fräulein who was in charge of the little girls. I suppose that the authorities had not yet completed the internment of Germans. The hysteria of bitter hatred of everything German was sweeping the country. I was sitting at one of the long refectory tables in the dining hall; Fräulein at one end presided, and a small boy, whom I particularly disliked, made loud, sneering, and cruel remarks about Germans directed at her. She sat silent and withdrawn, and I sensed her intense unhappiness, alone and rejected. It seems a small incident but my reaction was not small; I remember to this day the sick horror and anger which possessed me. To torment a person whom we all knew and loved because she belonged to an enemy race seemed to me a most horrible thing. I truly suffered, and I suffered alone.

Fräulein X left soon afterwards and it was her successor who gave me my first direct contact with physical cruelty. I think now that this woman must have had a serious neurosis with a streak of real sadism. She could charm us with the fascination of a snake hypnotizing its victim, and yet we knew that at any moment she might turn on us with senseless rage. I have already written of this woman in relation to the nightmares which came at this time.

I myself was only occasionally the butt of her worst tyranny, but there was one child whose parents were away in China, and I remember thinking even at the time that for this reason the woman knew she could safely ill-treat her. One day when she was angry I saw her drag this child along by the hair, and it was this that roused me to my first act of lonely self-assertion in the face of the gods of my childish world. In spite of my quaking heart, in spite of my fear of disapproval and of the particularly terrifying headmistress whom we little ones rarely dared to speak to, I was so horrified by what was going on that I made myself confront the head-mistress in order to protest the cruelties. I can remember screwing up my courage and dragging with me a most reluctant small sympathizer. After this and my nightmares, the cruel woman did not reappear the following term.

This was the first of several such situations of cruelty or injustice dur-ing my school years which I refused to accept in silence. In spite of the fact that in my teens I was certainly a horrible little prig, I was surpris-ingly held in respect and even love by the worst and most rebellious characters among my peers. I had some kind  of innate authority which I suppose sprang from the passionate, not theoretical, sense of justice that possessed me, and it was probably this that evoked response among the bold, bad children. We were not beset by the enormous problems of today such as drug-taking and sexual promiscuity, but the rebellions were dif-ficult enough. In English schools the prefects and in particular the head girl (as I became in my last year and a half) had a great deal of authority delegated to them. The headmaster once sent for me and told me that the behavior of one or two of the elder girls and one boy was causing despair in the teachers and he was handing them over to me in the hope that I could do something about them. I talked to those girls and the boy with extraordinary confidence, I remember. I liked them so much better than the good ones, in spite of my own "over-good" tem-perament—and they responded. A sense of humor must have redeemed my priggishness. Was it a sort of foretaste of my second-half-of-life vocation?

I do remember one strong, if disguised, direct intuition of this work that lay far in the future, which came to me suddenly in my teens as I stood in a London square of big white painted Regency houses. How often such moments carry with them forever a visual image of the place! Suddenly I knew what I wanted to do when I grew up. I would be a Christian

Science practitioner! I was, following my mother, an ardent Christian Scientist at this time, and therefore the intuition of a healing profession took this form. This momentary certainty I never really forgot, though it sank down into the unconscious for many years.

The influence of Christian Science in my childhood, was, like most things, double-sided. My mother converted to it in 1914, and like all her big life commitments it was a whole-hearted, total involvement. She quickly recovered her health, but she was no fair-weather Christian Scientist; from 1914 to the end of her life in 1949, when she died of cancer, she never took so much as an aspirin. For me as a child the creed came as a reprieve, and although it delayed for so long the final confrontation with evil and with the body's ills and undoubtedly increased my anxieties in the unconscious, I wonder whether without that reprieve I might not have gone under to my overwhelming fears of illness.

There is moreover another side to Christian Science. At its root is a great truth which Mary Baker Eddy unquestionably experienced, but, like so many others after a profound vision, she went on to a mistaken interpretation of it. She had recognized that flesh and spirit are one reality, not two, but she could not grasp the paradox that the flesh remains real as flesh in the transcending reality. Rejecting paradox, the experience meant to her that all fleshly, evil, dark things were illusions to be banished by "spiritual right thinking." It is the age-old heresy that refuses the Incarnation.

This truth of the oneness of the outer and the inner life had a very strong hold on me, even in my child's conscious mind. I have thought that perhaps it is to this that I owe the immediate sense of absolutely certain recognition that took hold of me when I opened the first book about Jung that came my way when I was thirty-nine and changed my life.

Like my mother's, my commitments, however much they were collectively determined, were never lukewarm. I stood by my Christian Science beliefs in a Church of England school, for the most part quietly, but openly when they were challenged. I discovered at least how to think differently from my environment, though not how to disagree with my mother. In this context another small indication of the future arises in my memory. I see

Mr. Howe towering over me at my desk with one of my essays in his hand and a curious look on his face. Most of these essays of mine were hash-ups of other people's points of view, and he must have been surprised by this one because he said, "Where did you find these thoughts?" I answered, "I just had them." The essay's subject was "Courage," and what Jung calls the "natural feminine mind" must have been aroused in me, since I remember my strong feeling involvement with the subject. I even remember something of what I wrote. I argued that physical courage was often not in reality courage at all when it was a substitution for moral courage—that is, that real courage might sometimes lie in facing the appearance of cowardice. Something like that! I smile at the thought because there is such a flavor of the kind of subject I love to write of now!

The memory is solitary in the years of my intellectual growth. I had a clear and reasonably quick mind, but, as I have said, no faith in my thinking judgment, therefore no intellectual originality. I could never have risen to a first-class degree at Oxford, for which original thought is a necessity, though I easily achieved a good second.

As I look back over my childhood and my school days there is one constant in the changing scene. It seems to me I was always "in love" with somebody or something with all the attendant pangs of anxiety and delight—with my mother all the time, with successive dogs, with friends, with stories, with one older girl after another—but not until I was seventeen did I fall in love with a boy.

This boy was not at St. George's. I kept the boys there at a safe distance when they approached me, though I already had a rare kind of friendship with Timmy Luke. We lived in a cottage, a converted Oast house, on a farm in Kent after the war, and at the farmhouse (so old that it was mentioned in Doomsday Book in 1086) lived a family who took in boys whose parents were abroad, or foreign boys, and gave them a home. My relationship with these boys had an entirely different flavor. They taught me to dance and to respond to the male in a feminine way, and I grew a little out of my tomboy phase. Then I fell deeply and truly in love with one of them.

I am not about to write of the beauty and the pangs of first love. Suffice it to say that I did know something of that which Charles Williams has

called "the Beatrician experience," but as time passed and I felt the unspoken disapproval of my mother, for whom a mere kiss outside marriage was almost a sin, I spoiled things by my prudery. Then I went up to Oxford and he went off to work his way round the world. He later became an impassioned Catholic convert. At Oxford there were other men, but none got very far with me. Timmy Luke was up at the same time, but it was not until after he graduated that the relationship with him blossomed into love. (Timmy was his nickname from early childhood, and universally used. His full name was Stephen Elliott Vyvyan Luke.)

I left St. George's in a blaze of glory. I was "Captain of the school," as it was called, and highly "successful" in all areas of work, play and relationship. I have never forgotten the astonishment I felt at the final assembly at school, when the headmaster spoke about my personal qualities in terms I could never have imagined. I thought "he can't have realized all the fears and anxieties underneath!"

From this dizzy height, I went on to Oxford where of course I was very small beer—a beneficially corrective state of affairs, and one which caused me no suffering. I was happy there, discovering the interior rewards of study and the delights of discussing everything under the sun with friends, playing lacrosse with success as at school (I became a Blue), and spending vacations in Italy or France. Between school and Oxford I had spent some months abroad, and had begun to have love affairs with places. The English countryside, Florence, Paris, and finally, after my marriage, my own native city of London, became for me places of mana, the mere thought of which, after so many years in the New World, can bring a lump to my throat. To these loves were added later the wilderness of Judaea, the desert beyond Jordan, the Parthenon, and Delphi.

At Oxford I read Dante and sat at the feet of another great teacher and scholar, Professor Cesare Foligno. My gratitude to him equals my feeling about Mr. Howe. I was at Somerville College, and two of the dons there also gave me much. The vice principal, the Hon. Alice Bruce, was tutor in my special subject of Molière and she taught me a great deal. My love of languages grew apace. Vera Farnell, then Dean and Librarian, was a fascinating figure to me with her dry humor, her self-possession and intellectual integrity, and her interest in persons.

I remained throughout my Oxford years emotionally immature. I both looked and was very young for my age, and I was frightened of anything unconventional. I was to remain arrested in this area until such time as I could face a break from the spell of my identification with my mother. After leaving Oxford I worked for a time in an antique shop, then went through a secretarial training course. I somehow knew that I could not carry a job requiring real independent judgment, such as befitted my education, though I did not then know why. I finally became private secretary to Sir Aubrey Smith, a retired Admiral and a director of his family business at Hay's Wharf beside London Bridge.

Meanwhile Timmy Luke and I were deeply in love and, on his passing the extremely difficult competitive examination of the Administrative Branch of the Civil Service, we were married on December 21, 1929. I was twenty-five.

CHAPTER SIX

MARRIAGE

THE YEARS OF MY MARRIAGE brought to me one of the most exquisitely beautiful things in human life—the experience of a love encompassing friendship, companionship, and absolute trust between a man and a woman. Those who take the whole question of women's liberation out of its proper sphere of social and economic justice and prate about psychic equality between man and woman as though it could be collectively imposed must never have known the tender subtleties of a relationship in which equality of value in man and woman is so obvious as never to be even thought of, while differences of quality between the essential male and female in each personality are a perpetual joy.

My husband and I could not have consciously defined such things during those years, but already, before we left school at St. George's, the foundations of this kind of relationship were there in the respect and honesty that lay between us and in the seeds of love for that which is beyond the personal. For without that "third thing" there is never any true meeting between two people—only a mixing.

Perhaps the very strength of our early friendship, added to the problems which sprang from our mother complexes (for Timmy too grew up without a father), may have been in part a cause of our ultimate separation. I do not mean that we were not deeply and truly in love, but there were areas where I could not in all those years fully meet his needs, areas in which I won freedom only when it was too late for him. This is a fact to be accepted without bitterness, for it carried in the end great meaning for us both. His love and support were with me through the years of painful awakening which brought me finally to analysis and to confrontation with the unconscious. I, too, it may be, gave to him the same kind of gift, for a very close and wise friend of us both said to me when the time of parting came, "You have opened doors in him, which, for that very reason, you yourself cannot pass through."

However that may be, the truth I want to affirm here is that *friendship* between a man and a woman may have an intensity, may bring an ecstasy even, which is not dependent on physical union, though the difference of sex is an essential ingredient. I experienced it before marriage and our coming together sexually, and I experienced it after our marriage was over. It glowed when we were young in our sharing of the simplest things, such as walking in the countryside, or exploring the empty streets of the City of London on a Sunday; but the culmination of this soaring joy of friendship came, after eighteen years, at the very end of our marriage, when physical desire had no part in our relationship. It came in the midst of our greatest suffering, after we had agreed on the rightness of a divorce. In the weeks that remained before we actually parted, this fruit of our long trust and companionship came to its ripeness, and I am sure that my husband also felt that extraordinary ecstasy in which we knew that, however widely our lives might diverge and even if we never met again, yet the truth of our years together with all their ups and downs, successes and failures, was "laid up in Heaven." The word "ecstasy" means the state of being outside the ego. It is an exact description of this experience—to know freedom from the ego's demands through unity with another beyond desire, in the joy of that which is neither and both.

For the first two years or so of our marriage I remained on some levels in the same state of arrested development of which I have written. The breakthrough came on a dull cold Christmas day. I had gone for a walk in the afternoon with an older woman whom I greatly loved, and who had been to me that transitional mother figure who is so often a godsend to young people on the threshold of self-discovery. She was a person of much wisdom and individual strength, and through her I not only awoke to my dependence on my mother, but was able to find courage to free myself also from simply transferring my dependence onto her.

A break-
through

On that Christmas day we walked together along the sidewalk outside Kensington Gardens—the park railings on our left, the overcast sky, the street empty of people, are still clear. The exact words spoken have gone, but the sense of shock remains. I suddenly understood the threat to my marriage which lay in my closeness to my mother. The outer symbol of it was the help I was allowing her to give me—cleaning house, etc.—because I had a full time job as well as my husband. Once aware, I did not hesitate, and within days had told her she must not do these things for me. It was the first time I had been adamant in the face of her distressed failure to understand, and I date the small beginnings of my conscious individuation from that act of standing by my new insight.

I had remained, since coming down from Oxford, in my job as private secretary to the director of Hay's Wharf beside London Bridge. The office overlooked the river, and ships came from all over the world, passing through the "gateway" of Tower Bridge to unload at our wharves. It was a fascinating place. However, as soon as it was possible financially for me to leave my job, we wanted to have a child. I soon became pregnant but miscarried at the third month.

In 1936 Timmy was seconded to the British Administration in Palestine (The League of Nations Mandate*) for two years. It was the policy in the Colonial Office at that time to send the young administrative officers

---

* The Palestine Mandate was a territory that included Jordan, Israel, and a portion of Palestine. It was one of several territories overseen by the Supreme Council of the Allies under the Treaty of Versailles, with Great Britain appointed as its mandatory power.

abroad for a period of experience outside England. To us it was a most exciting adventure. Slowly I had been discovering in myself thoughts and feelings that at first frightened me very much, upsetting all the rocks of conviction which had upheld me though my childhood and youth, and the move out of England precipitated my open recognition of these things. I was able to tell my mother that I could no longer accept Christian Science; I was able to go to a doctor without almost fainting from fear; all my attitudes to life began to expand tentatively, and new friendships blossomed for us both with people of rare quality.

Thus the first months passed in Jerusalem with the sense of the rising of new life, and to my joy I became pregnant again. I was to learn now the enormous strength of that which I later came to recognize as the resistance in my unconscious to the terror of taking up full responsibility for my own life and my own motherhood. *Palestine and illness*

All seemed well until the fifth month of pregnancy, when I began to have a discharge that worried me. At this time we were on holiday in Lebanon and the doctor there ordered me to stay in bed until the discharge should cease. My husband had to return to his job and leave me with strangers in a pension high about Beirut, and lying there in a tiny room under a mosquito net, I began to discover what real loneliness was, accompanied by constant anxiety about the child. After I had endured a week or so of deepening depression and misery, two English women, Quakers who lived near, came and rescued me, taking me to their house and installing me in a comfortable bed on a screened veranda overlooking the glorious view to the sea. I have seldom been more grateful. I was supposedly better though still greatly depressed, and finally my husband got leave, hired a big, well-sprung car, and came to fetch me.

In Jerusalem they found the child was dead in my womb; I was rushed to hospital and it was removed. There followed thrombosis in one leg. Many weeks later it spread to the other leg. I lay on my back and grew

weaker and weaker. There were no drugs in those days to help. They practically gave up hope for me, and warned my husband that I would probably
die. My mother came from England. For the first time I could hardly bear
to see her, though I did not realize why. Then came the turning point—
the first remembered truly conscious awareness of my own psychic
processes. I suddenly knew that I had not, through all those months,
wanted to get better. I had been, as it were, retreating further and further
into the "womb" of the hospital. I realized that in spite of the misery,
depression, and fear, I had been enjoying my absolute helplessness and the
"mothering" of the nurses. It was as though my psyche sat up and shook
itself and said, "No more of that nonsense!" That very night a hemorrhage
began. The blockage broke physically as well as psychically; the doctor
rejoiced, my husband was radiant, my mother went home happy, and slowly
I returned to life. I was four months in that hospital, and one memory is
pure joy—the beauty of the pre-dawn light over the mountains of Moab
which I could see from my bed. It was often a pale translucent green which
is indescribable. When I emerged, we went to Amman in Transjordan and
spent some immensely happy weeks on the edge of the desert that I loved
so much.

I have told of this experience in detail because of its crucial inner significance. At an equally powerful and much more conscious turning point
of my life, ten years later in Zurich, the same tremendous resistance to the
way that led towards individuation would have to be met. Again it attacked
me through the body and again I emerged by a hair's breadth from the
threat.

Beginnings
of a
conscious
approach to
the psyche

That first descent into the dark that I experienced in Palestine in 1937
marked the real end of my childhood and of my dependence on my personal mother. The deeper unconscious levels of the mother complex could
not, of course, be confronted until much later. Meanwhile we returned to
London; the black year of the Munich disaster and the certainty of
approaching war was upon us. In my personal life, however, the first beginnings of a conscious approach to the psyche began to emerge. I was urged
by a friend to go to a Freudian analyst she knew in order to work out the

psychological reasons for my miscarriages. I owe to that analyst a much freer relationship to the instinctual side of life, but we did not get near the root of the matter. Years later through Jungian analysis I was able to see the connection between the miscarriages and my tie to my mother, who made no secret of the fact that she hoped very much that I would not have

any children. A career was her great ambition for me—a career in the masculine sense. Outwardly, I felt entirely free of subservience to her point of view. I longed for a home and children, and when, in 1939, just before war broke out, I again lost a baby after six months of pregnancy, we decided to adopt children. We bought a house in the country some thirty miles outside London—far enough for the children to be relatively safe from the  bombing, near enough for my husband to join us for weekends or whenever he could get there. Bombs on the railway lines were frequent and anxiety great, but the home was there and by 1941 two babies. I began to learn how to be a mother myself. (Incidentally, my mother, once the children were there, became a devoted grandmother.)

I remember that my mother, in her very last conversation with me on the day of her death, said to me, "I am so happy that you are going to America. You will have the career I have always wanted for you," and I am hit once more with profound wonder at the mysterious working of the Self in our lives. Superficially many might say, "You see how this tremendously powerful urge from your mother has dominated your life; it forced you, through the unconscious, to reject your pregnancies; it finally brought your marriage to shipwreck; and it has had its way with you at the last." Such a judgment leaves out all the mystery which lies at the heart of life and all the meaning which springs from the choices of the individual. My mother's intuition that I had work to do other than the work of wife and mother was entirely right, however wrongly she interpreted it. If, however, I had not found the courage to rebel—to insist on having children and remaining at home for those years, my efforts at a career would have remained conventional and wholly uncreative. As it was, when my love for the psychology of Jung was born and a career did open for me, it was the very last one my mother could understand or would have chosen for me. The end of my marriage was a great grief to her, too. Being the fine person she was, she accepted all this out of respect and love, but I know how deeply she suffered.

For her suffering I bear guilt, of course—the Promethean guilt which every step on the way to consciousness carries with it. Moreover, who knows how much I owe to the very fact of her passionate though premature and seemingly mistaken belief that I was meant to have a "career." When people's lives are intertwined, they are bound to hurt each other grievously—but provided always that neither one betrays the deepest of his or her conscious values, no matter how great the outer damage brought by such loyalty seems, then out of that hurt is forged the pure gold of the love that sets each one free to seek the Self. I dare to think that the great "injuries" which were mutually inflicted by my mother, my husband, and myself on each other carried this mysterious power. That which wounds and that which heals are one.

CHAPTER SEVEN

THE FORTIES

THE FIRST FIVE YEARS of the forties brought the
darkness and the fire, the destruction and the heroism of the world at war.
For me, the second five years, 1945 to 1950, were the years of my own great
darkness, my own destructive yet purging fire, and the beginnings of the
inner struggle which demands all the same qualities of courage, endurance
and loyalty as a battle to the death in the outer world. Collectively, of
course, a war is either won or lost; the forces of destruction, of regression
into barbarity, may be temporarily halted, but there can never be any resolution of the struggle in collective terms. It sinks into the unconscious to
rise again. The outer darkness, however, may constellate the inner confrontation in many individual souls, and it is on the response of individuals
that the future depends—on their ability to find, beyond the battle of the
opposites, that which neither wins nor loses but transcends and unites.

I suppose there are few people in Europe or England who, having lived
through those days leading up to the outbreak of war, do not retain a highly
charged memory of them. I had gone away by myself for a brief holiday
to recuperate in mind and body from the loss of my baby. I stayed at the
ancient inn, the Swan, in the beautiful Suffolk village of Lavenham, with
its great church and bell tower standing high above the village on a small
hill. Everyone had been practically certain that war would come, but, as it

became clear that the moment indeed was upon us, the shock was still great. I got into my car and drove home to London.

All of us were certain at that time that, the moment war was declared, the Germans would bomb London in an immediate attempt to destroy us, and we knew we had no defenses. So as I drove, the fear was cold in my

heart. I came to Ely—and here I turned aside on my journey on an impulse and went into the Cathedral. I suppose it is because of that day's experience that Ely has remained to me the most numinous of all the great English cathedrals that I have known and loved. Walking down the nave with its immense Norman arches, standing at the meeting place of nave and transept, the center of the cross, and gazing up into that glorious octagonal lantern tower, peace flowed into me, and for a moment I felt an impact of eternity in this place of worship built with love eight hundred years before to the glory of God. I emerged from the half-dark into the daylight and stood for a while looking up at the huge grey pile and drinking in the sense of permanence. Many wars had come and gone, but still it stood serene. Bombs of course could soon destroy even this mighty frame, but nothing could destroy the spirit that built and maintained it. The war ceased to fill the whole horizon, and I saw it for an instant in its true proportions, a small part of the immense pattern of history, of the story of man's spirit. I went on to London; the fear was still there but something transcendent held and contained it through the days to come.

The "phony war" brought us a reprieve, and in November we bought a little Regency period house in the village of Binfield in Berkshire, and settled into it in preparation for the hoped-for baby. The old man who sold the house to us had left all his simple but beautiful antique furniture there for us. A huge wisteria vine, a glory in spring, grew over the front of the house. Beside it was a noble lime tree. There was a small stone barn with a stable nearby, and a good-sized garden with an apple orchard. Through those meager years we had fruit and vegetables (preserved for the winter), eggs from our chickens and honey from our bees. These things mean comparatively little today, but in that time of rationing and extreme shortages they meant treasure beyond price. And another treasure was ours in Binfield—a village woman who was one of the best cooks it has been my fortune to know, and a rock of support in all our troubles. I should have said three treasures—for a pearl of a handyman and gardener (unfit for active service) worked for us part-time, and later a young girl who helped with the two babies and whose simplicity and earthy maturity are a joy to remember.

The house in Binfield is in retrospect the most loved of all my English homes. We lived there for seven years only, yet this was a long time in my experience, which had been for the most part of frequently changing London flats. The few years we spent in Kent in the Oast house cottage were the only exception, but even there the house was not our own. Moreover, the time in Binfield cannot be measured by ordinary standards. The danger that surrounded us intensified every experience, and time was somehow no longer measured in months and years. We lived with a greatly heightened awareness of the beauty and value of all simple things, which especially in 1940 and 1941 we knew might soon be lost to us in the Nazi horror. The stripping of pettiness from life in those early days of the war, the sense of unity and mutual help among all sorts and conditions of people, was a thing no one who was in England at that time could ever forget. There was an atmosphere of *forgiveness* everywhere, that most rare of human qualities. There was not even much bitterness against the enemy, in striking contrast to the 1914 war. One opposite constellates the other, and when the danger was past the old trivial hostilities took over again; but nevertheless such moments reveal the beauty hidden in the most unlikely persons and affirm the truth, "what a piece of work is a man!"

Few villages near London entirely escaped the bombs. In Binfield two sticks fell in 1940 in one week, sending villagers to sleep under their tables for the next years though no more bombs came our way for the rest of the war. The sound of the guns in London, however, and the sight of the glow in the sky when fires were burning in the massive raids brought the war

Bombs in Binfield

very near, and there was constant anxiety for those we loved. My closest Oxford friend was killed in the first week of the Blitz, and later two others. My mother, typically, insisted on remaining in London doing war work, and Timmy of course was there most of the time. Refugees filled the village in 1940; cheerful, indomitable, many of them had lost everything. For a while we all had mothers and children sleeping on the floor in every spare corner until homes could be found for them.

Later we would hear with dread the roar of the bombers going north to the Midlands and returning in the small hours. Later still, during the last year of war, we would see in the summer dusk the whole sky, it seemed, filled with our own planes on their way to Germany.

We were allowed no cars in those days. On the nights when Timmy was due home from London, I would ride my bicycle in the black-out the three or four miles to the station, pushing his with me. Sometimes I would have to wait with others in the pitch dark for one or two hours; the station-master would bring us news from the signal-box of the progress of the train through a raid. Then would come the relief and joy of his arrival—and a quiet day with him and the children. No wonder that the little house took on so much mana!

Last, I want to mention another memory—the sound of Churchill's voice over the radio in those terrifying days of 1940, when it seemed that nothing but a miracle would save us, and the extraordinary courage, serenity almost, that flowed into us from his indomitable spirit. It was not so important any more whether the Germans came or not; the only thing that mattered was our refusal collectively and individually to run away from whatever might happen. It was a taste of the sine qua non of the individual "quest."

Close upon the joy of the ending of the war came the beginning of our personal tragedy. Timmy did not tell me of his conflict until 1945, but already in 1943 I had sensed half-consciously that all was not well, and it was in that summer that a friend gave me a little book about a Jungian analysis. I was staying with my children at the time in a house by the sea with no electricity, and I remember finishing the book by candle light in bed. I slept then and dreamed. In the dream I fell slowly, slowly down into darkness and death as though into a pit; for an infinitesimal moment I seemed to touch the bottom which was death itself and then I began to rise, as though on successive waves, each one carrying me further up towards the light and then receding a little; and at each upward surge I was filled with joy and the words came to me with a quiet certainty, "Now I shall know, now I shall know." I was thirty-eight years old; it was the first dream I had remembered since childhood.

At home again, I began to read everything of Jung's that I could lay hands on. I read and read far into the nights, absorbed as I had rarely been since I read adventure stories in childhood. I understood little with my head, but it was as though my whole being *recognized* and responded to his words.

Meanwhile, trouble was brewing in the unconscious. I was not well physically; all of us were exhausted after the long years of acute strain. In the autumn of 1944 the old friend who had given me the little book about Jung, and who was herself undergoing analysis, made an appointment for me to see Mrs. Toni Sussman, her ana- lyst. I was astounded, having no recollection of having asked for this, being sure Mrs. Sussman would not find me interesting enough. However, my friend was vehe- ment in her certainty that I had made the request. Anyway, I kept the appointment; the inner journey began and the outer suffering was not long delayed.

From 1945 to 1947 we tried, Timmy and I, with all the honesty of which we were capable to save the marriage—he by facing his conflict, I by the patience and waiting which were so hard for me. Of the outer details I will not write. It is enough to say that finally, as all joy went out of the house and I watched him suffer, I knew that I must offer him a divorce. This knowledge came suddenly with such an imperative voice that, against the advice even of Toni Sussman, I had to obey. She supported me unreservedly once she realized the depth from which the decision came. My husband, too, then made his decision, taking the responsibility with real conscious suffering. Of the extraordinary experience of those last weeks I have already written.

The
mandala

During this dark time I painted a mandala which has remained to me the most numinous of the many I have drawn. A true mandala is born, so to speak; it emerges and is not consciously thought out. I remember vividly the moment of its conception. It was only a day or two after the decision to part from Timmy, and I was returning late at night from a visit to Willow Robertson, the close friend who had first brought Jung into my life. I stood waiting for a bus in one of the most dreary parts of London imaginable, at Notting Hill Gate. The bus was a long time coming, the streets were empty and silent and I stood on the pavement and watched the periodic change of the traffic lights—green, yellow, red, green, yellow, red. Gradually the rhythm of the lights proclaiming order in the streets became in me the rhythm of the universe, and I was filled for some brief moments with a sense of that pattern of which Dante sang in the *Paradiso*, and in which my personal sorrow and pain took on the joy of meaning. At the same time it was as though I felt my weight on the earth. I can only express it so—some vital link from the core of my body going down through the hard pavement into the earth under the city.

The next day I began to paint the mandala, and, oddly enough, it emerged in various blues and white against a midnight-blue background. Yet all the time I knew that the red, yellow and green of those lights were its genesis. Dr. Meier, my analyst in Zurich, said later that it was almost entirely introverted.

I went then for two weeks to Ascona on the lake of Lugano in Switzerland to face my pain alone. I walked each day in the mountains, spent long hours in the high places, and on one never-to-be-forgotten day I came on a small deserted church and above that, in the woods, I found a deep, clear pool of ice-cold water. I stripped and immersed myself in that water, then lay in the sun, and afterwards I climbed a steep hill through underbrush and emerged onto a high meadow of unbelievably intense green. I drank from a mountain spring and came down by a path to the lakeside and the boat which took me back to my hotel. The experience of that day was like an ancient mystery and had the quality of myth. I was now ready to go home.

At the end of the war we had sold our house in Binfield and moved back to London, buying a house in Hampstead, near the Heath. It was now that a new friend came into my life without whom I do not know how I could have weathered the next years. Saidie Mitchell joined us in Hampstead as housekeeper, bringing with her her daughter, Betty, who was then in her late teens and worked in London.

Mrs. Mitchell was—and is—a big, warm-hearted Irish woman from near Belfast. Her cheerful serenity, her loyalty and love were a bedrock of support through all the agonizing decisions and upheavals of that time. I could not have left the children for six months when I first went to America without the certainty of her love for them, when I knew my mother was dying and would not be there for them. Mrs. Mitchell brought them out to me in Los Angeles and took care of us there until leaving to make a home for herself and Betty, who prospered greatly. We are all separated now but the warmth between us remains, and my sons still remember and love her as a second mother.

I will mention one dream from this time. It was an "initiation" dream, and showed the kind of commitment that lay ahead. In the dream I came to the gateway of an enclosed square space. It was like an Oxford quad, with its intensely green, smooth grass and the surrounding ancient walls, but much smaller. In the gateway lodge was a porter—a guardian of the threshold. He was an old man, and, as I approached to enter, he said to me, "Only sculptors can enter here." I turned sadly away, but his voice stopped me. He called after me, "Unless you are a lover of the art." I turned again with delight and passed under the archway into the square. And there at my feet on the green grass lay a huge stone cross, its foot in one corner, stretching inward towards the center. I went forward and stood on the center of the cross itself. Then I attempted to move away again, but found that my feet were rooted to the spot. However, it seemed that while I was unquestionably held there, I could also move freely about—as though some

An initiation dream

essential "me" was rooted, but I was free to stay with it or go away at will. I went back to the porter and said, "What shall I do? I am rooted on the cross." He replied at once, "Then decorate it!" I must begin to work as a "sculptor" in stone, however inexperienced. I saw the cross now as a Celtic cross waiting for the carvings to be made.

My work with Toni Sussman had brought me into a whole new world. The door of the unconscious had opened; symbol and image had sprung to life. All this evoked in me a deep response to the meaning of Christian symbols and to the rituals of the Anglican church. I was confirmed in September 1947, just before my trip to Ascona. St. Cyprian's Church near Baker Street had all the Catholic rites, and its priest, Father Robson, was an old man whose holiness was a blessing without words. He never moralized or exhorted; he simply communicated love and worship. Thus the "old wise man" and the "old wise woman" supported me through these two and led me to the search for them within.

Jung Institute, Zurich

The divorce went through at the beginning of 1948 and soon afterwards I was able to go to Zurich to study at the newly opened Jung Institute there. My analyst there was Dr. C. A. Meier, then head of the Institute, and my work with him was the perfect counterbalance to the years with Toni Sussman. He it was who led me to the discovery of the tools for the "carving of the stone." The animus was emerging from the spider's web; Logos values were strengthened and I found the beginnings of courage to face criticism and disapproval in those areas of independent thought where I felt most threatened.

I very nearly ran away from this challenge which Zurich brought to me. As I said earlier, it was the second crucial opportunity to emerge from the protection of the "Mother." It was no longer a question of the personal mother, but the drama was essentially the same as in Jerusalem, ten years earlier, when I had nearly given up and came near to dying; in Zurich, had I given up, it would not, I think, have brought physical death but something much worse.

It was at the very first class at the Institute that I met Robert Johnson. We were asked to find a partner so that we could give each other the Word

Association test. Shy and scared, I looked anxiously around that roomful of, to me, most formidable-looking doctors and brilliant people. Then my eyes met his. He was having just the same sensations as I, and we knew at once that we were, so to speak, natural partners. And so indeed it proved. From that Word Association test sprang the long partnership which was to take me to America and was to last until a new era came for us both in 1961.

Robert—he was always called Bob in those days— came from Oregon. He was a musician for whom a life in the collective American culture was agonizingly painful, and, having been through deep waters, he had worked with Dr. Fritz Kunkel in Los Angeles. He then sold everything he had in order to come for a year to Europe, and, after traveling around, he found himself in Zurich. He was sixteen years younger than I, but I was very young for my age and he was in many ways mature far beyond his years.

So began my second deep and lasting friendship with a man. Its quality was very different from that of my marriage. It was based on the point of meeting which was the one thing missing in my relationship with Timmy—our mutual response to the symbolic life of the unconscious. Bob's introversion fed and supported mine, which was constantly threatened by inferior extroverted activity. Dr. Meier once said to me, "You are far more introverted than you appear." Timmy, though respecting this side of me, could not respond to it in any explicit way, whereas with Bob it was nourished in a great richness of exchange.

During my time in Zurich, Jung's daughter read my horoscope for me. I remember how she somewhat apprehensively asked me about my marriage, and, when I said it was over, she was obviously relieved and went on to say that the horoscope showed that I could not find my true creative work unless everything in the "House of Marriage" was sacrificed.

Sacrificing the "House of Marriage"

I ask myself now what the "sacrifice in the House of Marriage" ultimately means. It involved for me at that particular stage of my journey the actual parting with my husband, but the sacrifice itself is surely an experience which sooner or later everyone on the way to wholeness is bound to meet and accept. However, nothing can be sacrificed—made holy, whole—before it has been lived. That is why the hard work of individuation involves above all things the learning of relationship. The kind of love and friendship that I have described—that extraordinary sense of exchange, of ease and trust with another person which brings an intuition of what wholeness may be like—is something that can exist between any two people, not only between man and woman, though true marriage is the symbol that carries its full meaning. There are even some whose fate it may be never fully to know response from another in this world, but who nevertheless must consciously face the sacrifice in the same way.

This particular form of the universal experience—the form of it known in the "House of Marriage"—is a peculiarly feminine way, for the loss of relationship is the greatest loss of all for a woman. For a man, the challenge may come more often through the loss of prestige and approval in his work, his field of accomplishment. For all, it will mean separation from that which is the most precious thing in life, the loss of that which we conceive to be the best in ourselves.

Perhaps such a relationship in its fullness is possible only once in the lifetime of a woman; it may come either early or late and may either precede or follow the long struggle towards consciousness of its meaning and the total acceptance of the inevitable parting. If it comes early, the ego and shadow will long desperately to repeat or to hold on to so powerful and beautiful an experience, but from the moment of accepted separation the inner task will be to enter into the full experience of the loneliness within until perhaps that sense of ease and trust, that love and freedom, may return hidden in the mystery of the whole, of the "Hierosgamos" itself. For most, this moment will not come until after death, but to a rare few it may come in this life, and "exchange" then would no longer be something repeated now and then, but would become a state of being in relation to every person, every thing, every meeting in this world and beyond.

Of that final vision towards which we grope, Charles Williams wrote with piercing beauty in *All Hallows Eve,* not long before his own death. Lester, in the story, had been for some time dead when the ultimate moment of separation came to her. Since her death she had been growing fast in the ways of love and exchange; her husband, Richard, was still alive, but relationship continued and love deepened between them across the barrier of death. Then came the time for her to leave him.

> [She] felt again the awful sense of separation. It was like a sharp pain in a great joy. She gave herself to it; she could no other; she had consented long before—when she married Richard perhaps—or was consenting now—when she was leaving him. Her heart sank; without him, what was immortality or glory worth? and yet only without him could she even be that which she now was. All, all was ending; this, after so many preludes, was certainly death. This was the most exquisite and pure joy of death, in a bearing of bitterness too great to be borne.

She was standing in rain shot through with light and she knew every drop of it as distinct and separate, at the same time as she knew all the raindrops as one with the waters of the great river into which they fell "from some source beyond all clouds."

> [She] no longer thought of herself as bearing or enjoying; the bitterness, the joy and the inscape of those great waters were all she knew, and among them the round hall, with those mortal figures within it. . . . Even Richard's figure there had lost its immediate urgency; something once necessary and still infinitely precious, which had belonged to it, now lay deep, beyond all fathoming deep, in the current below, and could be found again only within the current or within the flashing rain. Of any future union, if any were to be, she could not begin even to think; had she, the sense of separation would have been incomplete, and the deadly keenness of the rain unenjoyed.

I add a "synchronicity" postscript to this. I had just written the above few pages when the Quaker magazine, *Inward Light*, for Fall 1974, reached me, and I read in it accounts by three people, one woman and two men, of their passage through solitude to awareness of the state of being I have attempted to describe. Of the two men, one was a monk and hermit, the other was happily married. Both of them described the transformation of their attitude to work as the crucial turning point. Their experience could be called the sacrifice of achievement through separation of the ego from their activity. The woman's story was precisely mine in its essentials, though differing of course in its outer details. She described the sudden loss of her companion and lover, followed, first, by the consent of the will, then by the long journey into the heart of loneliness which leads to acceptance by the whole individual being.

The horoscope, the choice

To return to Zurich and the horoscope: it also told me that I had a choice—I could either work or be physically ill. It was this choice that now faced me.

I had gone home for Christmas and returned to Zurich in early January. On the journey itself, I felt a pain in my right arm, and by the next morning was horrified to see that it had begun to swell right down to my hand. The pain was horribly reminiscent of the beginnings of the thrombosis in Jerusalem. It is rare indeed, I believe, for such a thing to happen in the arm, but so it proved. There were still at that time no drugs for dissolving clots, and the doctor told me to stay in bed with my arm raised on a pillow and to put frequent cold compresses on it. Quite apart from the discomfort, anyone who has had circulatory troubles knows how extraordinarily depressing they are. Again I was alone with strangers, but the Swiss family with whom I lodged were immensely kind to me, and it was during those weeks that my friendship with Bob really blossomed; for he climbed the steep steps up the hillside to the house almost daily, bringing me juices and fruit, and we would talk about everything under the sun and moon, so that the depression did not swallow me.

I managed to get to my analytical hours with Dr. Meier, however, and at one crucial session I told him that I was frightened and that it looked as though I would not be able to get to the Institute for a long time, so I was trying to decide whether to fly home or not. What a relief it would be to be in my own home! I remember that he said not one word to influence me one way or another, for which I am deeply grateful. The decision was mine to take alone; but nevertheless his strength flowed to me, and I decided I would stick it out, fear or no fear. It was after this that the swelling began to go down and my strength to return. Moreover, I had two never-to-be-forgotten dreams.

I dreamed that I was standing in a row of students who were to be "tested" by a distinguished visitor. A smallish man with a pointed beard, wearing evening dress and carrying an ebony cane passed along the line—I somehow knew he was Mephistopheles. As he came abreast of me he stopped, and, raising his cane, he pressed the tip of it into the flesh of my thigh. It was agonizingly painful as it sank in to a depth of about two inches, but I knew that it was of immense importance for me to stand firm without moving and to make no sound. As the cane was removed I was aware that there was no blood, no wound, but that he had, as it were, branded my thigh, for the end of his cane held a signet that was both a circle and a square. "A squared circle," I said to myself. This mark was now deep inside my thigh.

Two dreams

The second dream had equal power. I was watching in the dream a clot of blood inside my arm. (It was my left arm, not the right arm as in outer fact.) The clot was slowly moving downwards towards my hand and I was in despair. Then I saw the whole bloody mess dropping off the end of my fingers and with it the clot came completely away, leaving a free, strong, fresh-looking arm. Then I felt as though I were shedding a skin; it slipped off me and, underneath, something shone out with the color of a melon. As this happened I heard a voice say, "You have a new name. It is 'Melon.'" But I was crying bitterly now because, although the word had been absolutely clearly "melon," I had transposed the "m" and the "l" and heard "lemon," and had thought, "Alas! I am nothing but a squeezed lemon!" (Those who know me well know how typical this is!)

At the end of my time in Zurich Dr. Meier asked Jung to give me one hour, and I told him this dream. His comment was, "You identify with the husk" (the old skin of the arm), a remark which has helped me innumerable times. He then went on to amplify the meaning of the melon and bring it alive for me.

*Meeting
Jung*

The whole of that hour has remained vivid in my memory. As Marie-Louise von Franz has described, Jung as an old man did not talk about specific problems, even to his old students; he just said to people whatever came into his mind and almost always the person went away with the answer to his or her questions. In my own case the wisdom he gave me applied to things which had not yet happened in my life. We talked a lot about three specific themes and all of them were related to the most important experiences of the coming years, though I had foreseen none of them at that time.

He talked first, to my somewhat annoyed mystification, about the specific problems he had with American patients and the peculiarities of the American psyche. "What in the world has that to do with me?" I thought! Then he launched into a story about a life-long Christian Scientist who not long before his death had begun to work with Jung, and who had in a few brief weeks come through to an extraordinary wholeness. Some months later I was to see this same thing in my mother as she lay dying. The third thing touched me at a more personal level, though again I did not know its relevance.

As I was leaving, Jung came to the door with me and suddenly asked, "Why do you think you can do this work?" For long afterwards, my cheeks burned when I thought of the idiotic way I answered. I couldn't think of what to say, so I muttered incoherently something like, "Well, I do have a degree!" There could not have been anything sillier, but on the whole I am inclined to think that, Jung being who he was, I might have done a lot worse. I could afterwards think up the most beautiful-sounding replies, but it is possible my idiocy told him the truth—i.e., that it was not something I thought I could do; it was just something that was happening to me with the inevitability of fate.

Dr. Meier advised me, when I left Zurich, to approach the Jung organization in London with a view to continuing my training and beginning control analysis—that is, doing work with patients under the control of a training analyst. He suggested I go to see Dr. Barker, one of Jung's early pupils, to whom Dr. Meier wrote a letter recommending me. Dr. Barker welcomed me with great kindness and was very willing to take me on, but I had, of course, to have the official backing of the London Jung Club, of which he was a member. I applied for this and was staggered by the reply. It announced that, if I wished to work with one of their members, I must go back to the beginning and do a personal analysis all over again, since they could not recognize anything I had done either with Mrs. Sussman or in Zurich. I knew, of course, that Mrs. Sussman was persona non grata to them (for reason stemming from the past), but apparently at that time, when the whole matter of how Jungians should be trained was in the melting pot, the mistrust extended even to Zurich.

The work begins

I went to Dr. Barker and, aided by my dreams, we agreed that I should simply return to Toni Sussman, who was ready to start me with patients, and do control analysis with her. She later was recognized as an official training analyst by the Zurich Institute. Dr. Barker remained a friend, and the support and goodwill which he gave me so generously continued in the years after I went to America.

I began at once with two or three analysands. The Guild of Pastoral Psychology (prodded by Toni!) elected me to their council, and it seemed that I was launched onto a career in London. But then came the letter.

It was from Bob Johnson in Los Angeles, who was likewise beginning to practice under the aegis of Dr. Fritz Kunkel. He simply said that he and Dr. Kunkel has been discussing the need for more woman analysts, and Bob added that he wished I could be there. Laughingly I told Toni this at our next meeting. To my stunned astonishment she sat bolt upright in her chair and said with the utmost conviction, "You are going to America." Her tiny figure seemed almost to be sending out sparks! I began of course to protest. "Don't be absurd, Toni. It is an impossibility. Have you forgotten my children and the currency restrictions? It's a wild idea." Yet somewhere down in the pit of my stomach, I knew. The lightning had

"You are going to America."

struck and there was nothing to be done about it. Toni continued, "You are to tell no one at all, but go home and write to Bob *before you go to bed tonight* to ask if you could get an affidavit. Moreover," she added, "meditate on the difference between the important and the essential." I did so with much heart-searching in the days that followed—all the important things were against the move, but the one essential remained. It was the answer to my deepest need, as Toni had seen—a completely new beginning after all that had happened, an opportunity to build a new life without the protection of the mother—that is, without Toni, without even the mother country. I wrote the letter that very night.

Robert has described to me his own sense of shock when he read my letter. His reaction was similar to my own. The outer difficulties loomed large, and he was very conscious of the risks involved, but somehow he knew it was a fateful thing, and he replied saying he would send an affidavit and giving me warm encouragement. It was May 1949. From that moment, the outer difficulties were overcome one by one; my visa was granted and I booked a third class passage on a French liner due to sail on November 10.

The dream of the scholars

I had no idea at this time of my mother's approaching death, though the cancer that killed her must have already been well advanced. Being a most faithful Christian Scientist, and moreover an extraordinarily selfless person, she had said no word of her suffering. The temptation to hold me back when I told her of my plan to go to America must have been very great, but she gave me strong support. In the early summer, however, a dream came to me which, I realized afterwards, foretold the testing time ahead. I was staying for a few days with close friends in Suffolk. Their house was the restored gatehouse of an ancient abbey, and I have rarely felt so strong an atmosphere from the past still alive in a place as I did in that house and its surroundings. The monks' fishpond, remote and quiet, was still there, and the thick walls of my bedroom with its high arched stone ceiling (where the bats sometimes flew) brought the past to numinous life. There were stories of ghosts, but they were not frightening. It was a beneficent place, and I mention it because it is somehow intimately connected in my memory with the power of the dream.

I stood in the dream on the edge of a great fire which burned fiercely like a wall in front of me and high above my head. I was aware that I was one of eight people standing in a line with two or three feet between each person. Three were to my right and four to my left. We were awaiting the inevitable moment when we must voluntarily step forward and enter the fire, two by two. I knew that the first two to enter would be either the two at the center—that is myself and the one on my left—or the two at the outer ends of the line. In the latter event I would be one of the last pair and the dreaded moment, I hoped, would be deferred; but with a stab of fear I knew that the command had come for the central pair to step first into the fire. I did not hesitate, and I found myself walking in the agonizing heat of those flames which burned but did not consume, and I saw that around me others were walking in the fire, particularly one whom I recognized—the young country girl, Kathy, of Binfield, whose courage and simplicity I have mentioned earlier. She walked erect in the midst of the fire, bareheaded and wearing a scholar's gown, with a look of mature joy and strength on her face. She had in fact left school at sixteen, but she was, it seemed to me, a "scholar" of the spirit and of the earth. As I saw her, I began to stumble with the pain of the burning, and I feared that I would lose consciousness and fall in the fire, but a hope came to me that Kathy, or others like her, would perhaps find me, lift me up, and restore me.

I woke in the big bed under the arches of stone, and my blood was pulsing all over my body. I felt literally on fire. I have told of this experience in full because it has held such profound meaning for me. It is an example of the truth of Jung's saying that if one dreams of a great suffering it will not be long before it is experienced consciously.

It was September when my mother collapsed and went into a Christian Science nursing home. As soon as I realized how ill she was, I told her that I would of course not leave her and would defer my passage. It was then that she showed her full maturity and inner freedom. With a calm authority and certainty that left me no choice at all, she said that, no matter how ill she was or might be when the time came, she wanted me to be on that boat. She said she knew that I must not fail to leave on the chosen date, and that if I did not go it would do a far worse thing to her than physical death. She added, "I have always wanted a true career for you and this is the crucial moment for you which you must not miss. It will make me very happy."

Separation and death

And so it came about that in those last weeks I watched her slowly sinking, but she remained always calm and cheerful with me. It was an agony, but somehow shot through with joy. She had set me free, and I had let her go. We met, and endured parting, as two adult friends, and the cul-

mination came on my last day in England. I said goodbye to her in the afternoon, and, agony as it was to leave her so close to death, when I came out onto Hampstead Heath I was flooded with a sense of gratitude for the freedom she had given me. The sun had just set and a new moon was in the sky. At eleven o'clock that night I had a telephone call from the nursing home. My mother had gone to sleep and just quietly died.

It is impossible to write adequately of the extraordinary beauty and wonder of that moment of sorrow and joy. There could not have been more perfect timing, and this is always the mark of the operation of the Self in human life. It was as though my mother had chosen the one perfect moment to go, with her constant care of easing my way. There was time the next morning for necessary business; her close friends were at hand to see to her funeral. We had parted cleanly and consciously, and I did not have to face any of the aftermath of death, the outer social contacts and sympathy, the display of a funeral. That morning I saw Father Robson and Toni, both of whom exclaimed at the "terrible" beauty of her death. I sailed in the afternoon and for the next five days I was to all intents and purposes alone—which is for an introvert the one way to confront any profound experience.

I will add here one dream, which came to me some nine months later. It was both a dream and more than a dream, and I am certain of the objective reality it contains. It brings to an end the story of the personal relationship between my mother and myself. I dreamed that I was moving with her in a kind of dance around a center. Without ever touching, we moved in slow rhythmical steps, now one step towards, now one away from this center, and our eyes were always upon it, not on each other. Then my mother spoke. "I was with you all the time during the first two days after I died," she said, "and I have not been far away since. But now it is time for me to move on, and you must go back into the world and take up your work." As she spoke I heard the distinctive bell sound which in Los Angeles at that time announced the presence of the milk delivery van, and I knew that this was my job, to deliver milk, and I turned and walked towards it with a sense of deep but quiet grief at the final parting and acceptance of what was to come.

CHAPTER EIGHT

THE FIFTIES—LOS ANGELES

I AM THANKFUL that I was born before the air age and therefore have so many and such varied memories of travel by sea and train. How I loved the great express trains of Europe! The excitement of crossing a frontier comes back to me—the fascination of the sudden change of atmosphere and the sound of a new language in my ears. Even such prosaic people as customs officers were romantic at these moments! Then there was the joy of watching the changing aspects of the countryside, the plains, the mountains, the glimpses of rivers or of little hill towns, and finally the slow approach to the great cities through dreary suburbs to the vital center—Rome, Florence, Paris and the heart-lifting return to London, the City in my unconscious. So also sailing in ships, between the excitement of leaving port and the still greater one of arriving, there lay all the changing moods of the sea in calm or storm.

Nowadays in the air we get a bird's eye view of some of these things, and there are, of course, other thrills, but there is no leisure in travel; one is picked up and dumped down again, and in between there has been no time for the imagination, no time for the soul's journey from one part of the earth to the next. Train and ship are already far from foot or horse or sail, but they do not divorce one from the feeling of contact with earth and sea. Strangely enough, I find car travel much more "mechanized" in its effect. I feel closer to the car engine than to the country, especially on the freeways and surrounded by traffic. Also in a car one is beset by the need for decisions about speed, where to stop and so on. In ship or train one has simply to get on board and relax, free from all interruptions and from responsibility for the journey. Even meetings with fellow travelers are fraught with no obligations past or future, no involvement beyond the possibly intense meaning of the present moment.

Of all my journeys, the crossing of the Atlantic in that November of 1949 is, of course, charged with the most powerful mana, for it was the symbol of the end of an era and the beginning of a new life. I remember the day on which we were to pass the halfway point between England and America. I went and stood in the stern of the ship and watched the seething white wake streaming out behind us and dissolving again in the distance into the undisturbed blue-green of the sea which now cut me off from the past. Then as we came nearer and nearer to the new world I looked out over the bows as they thrust forward to the unknown in front of me. The tremendous depth and majesty of the sea somehow entered into me on that voyage, and my personal concerns, the receding past, the hidden future were not deprived of meaning but lifted into that strange impersonal-personal significance which comes with a glimpse of the whole.

Here I pause on my journey to reflect on the extraordinarily clear-cut division between the first and second halves of my life. I had been, as it were, ruthlessly stripped of the past. I had lost husband, home, and mother; I had left children, teachers, friends, and country. The childhood dream of the dark road on which I must walk alone into the unknown comes back to me. Actually, I suppose that the second half of my life began, in psychological fact, six years earlier at the moment of my discovery of Jung and my dream of death and rebirth. From that time the stripping process began; but the outer dividing line was drawn with the utmost precision as the great ocean liner sailed down Southampton water and out onto the open sea.

The beautiful skyline of New York moved me as it has moved innumerable others traveling to a new life in a new world. The friend of an English friend had come to meet me, and I was immediately plunged into the infuriating experience of the customs inspection at the Port of New York, something about which the less said the better, as all who have known it will agree! I was then carried off in a taxi, at what seemed to me enormous speed, to the apartment of this friend, where I was to spend the night.

I have over the years been several times to New York again and have fallen under the spell of that unique and fascinating city, but those first days left me figuratively gasping for breath. I felt as though I had landed on the back of a huge monster rushing along at a terrible rate and with ear-splitting noise. I could not sleep for anticipating the next banshee wailing of the sirens, the like of which I had never heard except in the fearsome sounds of the air raid warnings at home in the war. The memory of the details of my journey by train across the continent is vague. The sense of strangeness, which lasted for many weeks, surprised me by its intensity, especially as the open friendliness of people everywhere was so heartwarming. After all, there was no language barrier, yet never had I felt so alien, not in any European country, not even in the Middle East with the Bedouin in the desert, with scarcely a word of each other's language. The fissure between the old world and the new runs so deep that, although the strangeness of course wears off, it takes at least a generation fully to bridge it, I believe.

Los Angeles

On the day before Thanksgiving I arrived in Los Angeles, and my memory of that is very clear indeed. There stood Bob as I emerged from the arrival platform, solid and comforting, and he drove me to the very pleasant area where he lived. The trees and gardens and Spanish-type houses were a surprise and a delight to me. He had rented an old house on Hoover Street, where he both lived and worked. There was plenty of room in it, he said, for me to have an office too (for the as yet hypothetical patients!), and he had taken a minute apartment for me in a house almost opposite his. My first two shocks over American domestic living came when I realized there was no door between my bed-sitting room and the kitchen, and when I saw that there were no hedges or fences between one house and the next. How in the world can people bear to live in such an exposed way, I thought!

On Thanksgiving Day Bob had the rare, unconventional tact to go to his own friends for the celebration and to leave me to myself for the whole day. I don't know anyone else who would not have even asked me to decide whether I would prefer to be with him. I might have evaded my need to be alone if he had. I explored the surrounding streets, ate my first meal at a drugstore counter, and began to orientate myself.

The story of the next six months may be briefly told. With the help of Dr. Kunkel and of several of his other students, we managed to get started with a few analysands. I had been allowed to bring six hundred dollars of my English money, and, with the little Bob had, we just kept up with our expenses. I had the great good fortune to be recommended to a rising gynecologist who sent me one after another of his neurotic patients—plus two of his nurses. In those days one simply went to the city hall and took out a license to practice, and we always sent people to a medical doctor for examination and referral before accepting them. The Jungians, notably Dr. Kirsch, were friendly to us personally but could not help us professionally, "unqualified" as we were. Dr. Kirsch invited me without charge to some of his seminars, which was generous indeed, and I learned much from them.

Jung wrote of his early days of analyzing people, saying how little he knew at that time, but that he did his best and Heaven prospered him. How much deeper was our ignorance, and we had indeed great cause for gratitude to Heaven! A young woman came to me in those early days who was both crippled physically and, I realized, on the edge of psychosis, but held together by a strong thread. She had been to several other psychologists but never stuck with one for long. I was at that stage of enthusiasm and confidence in the possibility of curing almost anyone which is an occupational danger. After I had seen this girl, I dreamed that she came and stood before me, holding out her two hands. Upon each of them a top was spinning steadily, and she said to me with great seriousness, "Don't ever, ever try to put these two together. If they should once touch each other both would fly apart." Indeed I felt the protection of Heaven when I woke. I obeyed the dream, and through all the years in Los Angeles she continued to visit me. She weathered many ups and downs, gradually gaining psychic strength. My dream was an enduring message to me not to interfere with life, however good the intention.

Six months was the time I had allowed for discovering whether I could make a living for myself and my children in America. I would not have left them for longer. I had taken a two-way ticket when I left England so as to ensure the possibility of return should I be unable to earn enough, and now the time came for decision. It was a considerable risk to bring them out to me with so little behind me, but Mrs. Mitchell and Betty wanted to come too, and they would each be able to bring an allowance of currency, which I could supply them, and the boys were allowed three hundred dollars each. So I rented a small house for us all and took the plunge.

I have not yet written of the heart-searching and the pain I went through over the decision to leave the children for those months. I doubt

if I could have done it had I not thought my mother would be there. Nick was ten years old and Robert eight. Two and a half years earlier Nick especially had been greatly disturbed by the divorce, being just at the age when he needed his father, not young enough to accept and not old enough to understand. It had been agonizing to watch him suffer, and it left a wound in him which took long to heal, so that it was particularly difficult for me to leave him. But the need for me to build a new life was, I knew, paramount for their sakes, ultimately, as much as for my own. In the event, the years in Los Angeles brought to them the inestimable gift of a close relationship with a man; for Bob was endlessly good to them—a father in the deepest sense, and has so remained in their hearts.

So we settled down in the little house with the Mitchells (Betty got a good job at once), where we stayed until, after five years, I was allowed to bring money out from England; having sold the house in Hampstead, we bought our own home in Los Angeles. It was a most charming one-story rambling old house with a small patio behind high walls. The Mitchells moved at that time to their own home.

So the years passed, and both Bob and I had enough work to keep us as busy as we wished to be—but before going on to the next turning point and the approach to what I think of as my third life, I must pay tribute to St. Matthias Church and to the greatness of its most remarkable rector, Father James McLane, for both the man and the church were of great importance in my life during those years.

I found St. Matthias after only a week in Los Angeles. It was a small, undistinguished building in a poor district, but inside were things of great beauty, reflecting Father McLane's impeccable taste. (He was a real connoisseur and owned many original paintings by Chagall, Braque, and others.) The church was "higher," more Catholic even, than St. Cyprian's in London, yet unmistakably Anglican nonetheless. The Anglo-Catholic church, I always felt, embodied either the worst or the best of the two great values of Catholic and Protestant. At its worst it was imitation Catholicism and emasculated Protestantism; at its best it touched a real union between those two great opposites. At St. Matthias during those years, the best could be experienced. The small congregation came from all parts of the huge city and consisted of the few for whom the church meant worship and the interior life, and who had no use for the social activities with which the vast majority of churches are concerned. It was that exceedingly rare thing—a church without groups or clubs. (Such activities are admirable of course, but they are not "religion"—a word whose true definition is the human state of awe and worship in face of the divinity.) A small branch house of the Sisters of the Holy Nativity in Fond du Lac, Wisconsin, was attached to St. Matthias and did much to help Father McLane in parish and church. It was a place of quiet and recollection, and for me, shaken as I was at first by the noise and extroverted busyness of the surrounding culture, it was indeed a sanctuary.

A real
priest

Father McLane was a real priest. A *minister* is an agent, one who "ministers" to others or carries out some purpose. A *priest* is one who has been ordained to perform the "mysteries," to be the guardian of the sacramental or symbolic life. A good minister will perform his task—whether as servant of state or church, using all the abilities of his conscious decision-making ego—but a priest, as priest, makes no decisions. His job is to empty himself so that he becomes a channel for the mystery, and the abilities or the behavior of his ego are in the final analysis quite irrelevant. Naturally someone who is ego-centered can never succeed in carrying the priesthood without identifying with it—and this clear distinction between the ego and the function is the absolute essential for a true priest. There was never any doubt at all about it in Father McLane. As a man, he was full of fire and often outrageous! As a priest, he brought the fire of the spirit to life. One who is identified with his priesthood says the Mass in a *personal* way which is most disturbing. One who is clearly conscious of the distinction will say it in a *unique* way, which is an entirely different thing. Such a one always has a very strong personality and a dark shadow of which he and others are fully aware, but it never intrudes upon the mystery; the rites are then celebrated with power.

In his sermons Father McLane never exhorted or moralized. He expressed his own adoration of the mysteries and evoked response in his hearers, whether they understood his words or not—and very few did. I wish they had been preserved. He had come late to the priesthood, having taught English, I believe, at Harvard. His friendship was a great strength to me. He died in 1960 and was spared the pain of seeing the demythologizing of the church in full spate. St. Matthias itself, symbolically enough, fell to the bulldozers some years later when the road was widened.

I went back to England for a visit in 1952, using my return ticket. In part I went because I sensed that it would be very difficult for me to put down roots without returning home once in order to confirm, so to speak, my decision to remain in America. I also knew that all was not well with me physically and, if an operation were necessary, I preferred to have it in England. My English doctor confirmed the need for a hysterectomy, and I was admitted to a small and cheerful hospital run by Anglican nuns. This hospital was in the old building in which Dr. Pusey founded the first Anglican sisterhood in London in the nineteenth century and still contained their chapel with its extraordinarily beautiful dark oak carved choir stall by Grinling Gibbons.

Visit to England and a dream

This experience brought a dream a few days before the surgery, which I remember as another "initiation." The loss of my physical womb meant the end of any possible motherhood in the ordinary sense, and the dream, as such deep dreams always do, brought to me the certainty that all my outer losses could, if consciously accepted, be transformed into a "womb" on another level.

I dreamed that I lay on a low couch with others in similar positions to right and left of me. We were waiting for something which was to happen before surgery. Then I saw a bishop in cope and mitre slowly approaching the line of patients with his attendants. When he reached my couch he made the sign of the cross over the place of my womb, then bending low he breathed on it, making a cross in the four directions with his breath, exactly as in the most ancient of all Christian rituals, the blessing of the font on Easter Saturday. He then put his arm under my shoulders and, lifting me into a half-sitting position, he kissed me on the brow, and I awoke.

As I write I see now for the first time that this dream was reminiscent of that other dream of Mephistopheles which came to me in Zurich. This time there was a line of patients, instead of a line of students, awaiting some visit of immense importance. In the first dream Lucifer came, in the second the Bishop, who is a symbolic figure of Christ. So both the dark and the light sons of God had sealed me, as it were, the one with the wound in the thigh, the other with his blessing of the womb.

Such dreams come at the vital moments of life to guide and to warn. Let it not be supposed that I have not always been subject to all the ups and downs of the lesser dreams from the level of the personal unconscious and the usual goings on of shadow and animus. Indeed, no. It is thus that the ego is kept firmly on the earth and saved from the danger of identifying with the great dreams, whose meaning goes far beyond the merits and demerits of the little "I." The right attitude of the ego to a great dream is surely similar to the attitude of a true priest when he says the Mass. One is filled with awe before the mystery.

During the weeks of convalescence in London, I was strengthened by renewed contact with the love and support of many old friends, and of Timmy in particular; and when I sailed again for America I felt, paradoxically, a greatly increased freedom from the past. But I did not really get into deep contact with the soil of this country until some years later when Bob and I decided to buy a little house on the hillside above Malibu Lake. We had of course driven often through the beautiful mountains near Los Angeles and spent holidays in Sequoia and beside the ocean with the boys in the happiest way, but it is only when I have had a home in a place for some time and spent hours walking alone in the country around that I begin to feel deeply connected. It is as though roots begin to sprout through the soles of my feet.

The retreat

We had two conscious purposes in mind when we bought the cottage. Already we had a few analysands who had become students and friends— among them was Else Hope, who had been working with me for some time—and we thought that a house like this could be used by them as well as by us for times of quiet away from the city, and this could perhaps become the nucleus of a small group of like-minded people. I see now that it was the first stirring in the unconscious of that which was to come to fruition six or so years later in Three Rivers. Actually it turned out that

Else was the only one of the possibles who proved truly of like mind and who used the house. She and I had a long way round to go before we came together again and our partnership at Apple Farm began—but the seed first sprouted on the hills of Malibu.

The second reason for acquiring the house was, we thought, to ensure to Bob in particular a retreat in which he could find nourishment for his deep introversion. It is ironic that in the end it was I who used the retreat constantly, while Bob discovered that it was not what he wanted at all. It is obvious now that his danger was too much introversion; he needed to gain strength in the outer world; whereas for me a time was approaching when I would feel an imperative need for a period of withdrawal from outer activities as complete as I could make it.

Von Franz, in one of her studies of fairy tales which I read years later, has spoken of this need which comes to many women who seek individuation—a complete inward-turning, during which some major change takes place in the unconscious. I gradually realized that my energy was retreating from work with people and from social contacts of all kinds; only with Bob and my two boys did I feel a sense of fruitful and "right" activity. I knew it was a dangerous thing and, moreover, something that was certain to be misunderstood. And so it proved with almost everyone. I could certainly never have done it without the unwavering support which Bob gave me both practically and inwardly, convinced as he was by my dreams that I was obeying the genuine inner voice. I was at that time going through menopause—though, owing to the hysterectomy, the physical symptoms were of course relatively few—and I was intensely aware of the transformation of energy that may come for a woman at this time. I am convinced that, though the necessity for such an extreme withdrawal as I undertook is probably rare, yet a degree of retreat is for most women desirable at this important time. Otherwise the meaning of the transformation is apt to be lost in a compulsive increase of busyness, and I was acutely aware of this danger myself. The transformation was, it seems to me, most beautifully expressed in the imagery of my dream before the hysterectomy.

I spent long days alone in the Malibu hills, walking with Kimbo, Bob's dog, a much-loved Irish water spaniel, and much time at St. Matthias in recollection, or with the Sisters of the Holy Nativity at their daily offices, which gave form and content to the solitariness of my days. This and my normal contacts with the family kept me from the dangers of loneliness

and from floating off the earth. It was during these months that I first wrote down any of my thoughts on inner matters. Much later these notes were made up into a small book of meditations.

It was enormously hard for me to face the misunderstandings and, in some cases, the violently expressed hostility of many of my most valued friends. Once more I felt driven onto the lonely road of my dream. Even Father McLane disapproved, while respecting my decision; and only after the time of retreat was over did he tell me that he could now recognize how right it had been. It is hard to recapture the absolute urgency I felt at the time. I see now that the unconscious was pushing me towards the change which made possible my "third era."

The period of retreat lasted just about nine months. At the end of that time I began to be restless. Some new change was needed, I knew. The boys were growing up and needed me less; I began to think in terms of working again with people, but hoped I could do it in conjunction perhaps with the sisters' Retreat House at Santa Barbara, and so continue a semi-hermitlike life.

"I hate all tracts, period."

It was now that the dream came which ended that particular misinterpretation, though at first I entirely failed to grasp its meaning. I dreamed that I was driving a friend to a Roman Catholic church. She was in actuality a member of St. Matthias, and later actually did become a Roman Catholic. As we came to a stop at the entrance, someone stuck his head in at the window and offered us some religious tracts. My friend said, "I hate Protestant tracts," and I replied, "I hate *all* tracts, period." She then got out of the car. I was about to drive on when I felt the car, out of control, begin to slip backwards and then to roll over and over down a steep hill. I closed my eyes and relaxed completely, thinking it might mean death and accepting it. The next thing I knew was that I was standing at a place that reminded me of the spot at Malibu where the ocean meets with a small estuary and marsh and also with the beginnings of human dwellings. I had spent wonderful hours on this marsh watching the many birds. I stood alone in my dream some yards from the first houses on the sea front, and I wondered where was the car, which, I thought, must have crashed and ejected me there. Then it came to me that I was dead, and I began to search around for my body. But an inner voice said to me, "You won't find it because it has turned into bread and is being cut up and given to people to eat." This seemed to me a perfectly natural explanation, and feeling greatly relieved, I woke up.

The meaning of this dream became abundantly clear later on, but I missed entirely the point that it was the refusal of *all* "religious" tracts which brought about the transformation of my life. Taken in conjunction with another dream I had around this time, it is with hindsight doubly convincing. In this other dream I was forbidden to enter the church itself but found that my job was to stand in the porch and give loaves of whole wheat bread to those who asked for them as they emerged. It has proved so indeed; the vocation of these later years has led to the feeding of people for whom the church has lost its meaning, turning, as it lamentably has, more and more to the "tract" attitude and away from the symbolic life.

Blindly, however, I continued to think in terms of possibly going to live as much at the Santa Barbara house as possible. But I thank God that, since the dream had failed to awaken me, the unconscious proceeded to sterner measures! What now happened is the clearest possible instance of Jung's statement that if we refuse to listen to an important dream it will put itself over outwardly in often disastrous fashion.

I set out one day to drive to Santa Barbara in order to discuss my deluded plans. I had a feeling of exhaustion as I set out, but thought I'd get the drive over and be able to rest. On a long straight stretch of the

A stronger hint

divided highway I went to sleep at the wheel. The car went off the road onto the center strip, turned over two and a half times, I was told by an eyewitness, and ended on its side pointing back to Los Angeles. Being asleep I was completely relaxed and, waking in the middle of the somersault, had much the same feeling of acceptance as in the dream. People from other cars helped me out through the window, and one woman exclaimed, "The Lord must love you—I thought you would surely be dead!" I knew at once, as I stood shaken and bruised on the road, that the dream had been clearly declaring the hermit time in the church to be over, and that I must go back to work at the meeting place of man with the unconscious (that is, where the human dwellings meet the sea at the river's mouth).

The car was wrecked. An immensely kind Highway Patrol man rescued me, and Bob came out to drive me home. I had a cracked rib and spectacular bruises, but nothing worse. I again took up my work, and people immediately materialized who wanted to work with me. All seemed as before the retreat time, except that I knew that I worked from a new center. Then from the outside came an indication of the first step on a new way. It came through Else Hope.

Else is Jewish and came to this country from Hitler's Germany with her mother and two sisters. She grew up in a predominantly Catholic part of Germany and had always felt a kinship with Catholic ritual. Soon after she began working with me, she was baptized at St. Matthias Church, and during my withdrawal time, while she was working with Bob, she had decided to join the Sisterhood of the Holy Nativity, whose motherhouse, as I wrote earlier, was in Fond du Lac, Wisconsin. The novice mistress at the convent, Sister Martha, confided to Else her difficulties with some of the novices and also talked of her own personal problems; so Else suggested that Sister Martha might consult with me. Over the next year or two she came to visit me in Los Angeles and sent two badly disturbed novices to spend a year working with me.

Meanwhile my son Nicholas had left to study in England and two years later Robert decided to follow him. Father McLane died at the end of 1960, and it was plain to Bob and me that our work in Los Angeles was drawing to a natural close, and that it was time for us both to move on to something new. His interest as well as mine was centered at this time on the possibility of working in cooperation with the monastic orders in the church, and thus it was that in 1961 I moved to an apartment in Fond du Lac, where Sister Martha and the superior of the convent there welcomed my help with those of the sisters who were emotionally disturbed. A little later Bob joined St. Gregory's Priory at Three Rivers, Michigan, in order to work psychologically with monks and guests. St. Gregory's is the only Benedictine foundation in the Anglican Communion in America and was at that time still a branch of Nashdom Abbey in England. So began what I have called the third era of my adult life.

CHAPTER NINE

THE BIRTH OF APPLE FARM

I AM STRUCK with the thought that since the time of my illness in Jerusalem, which was in truth for me the threshold of adulthood, the three ensuing periods of my life have each lasted for twelve years. It is likewise a pleasing thought that in 1937 I was thirty-three years old (the age at which hobbits became officially adult!). Twelve years later, in 1949, I left for America, and twelve years after that in 1961 I began the new life in Fond du Lac which was to lead, after prolonged and very difficult labor pains, to the emergence of Apple Farm. Now, as I write, another twelve-year period draws to its close, for Apple Farm has entered its twelfth year and changes are pending, which mean perhaps as big a revolution in my inner attitude and function here as took place in the previous outer changes.

The number twelve

Perhaps all these twelve-year cycles were, it suddenly dawns on me, symbolically hinted at in the twelve small circles of the blue and white mandala I painted in the forties, around which the lines of the three interweaving squares move in a continuous pattern. This winding movement cannot be seen in the wooden carving of the mandala, only in the painting itself. Twelve is the number of the Zodiac—of the complete circle of time in the heavens. It is moreover a multiple of three and four, a union of active and receptive, of the trinity and the quarternity. I realize now with greater force than before why that mandala has been for me so powerful a *yantra*. (I wrote much earlier of its birth at the darkest time of my life.)

In Fond du Lac the nine months beginning in mid-1961 were perhaps the most lonely and difficult period in many ways of any that I can remember. The whole move could appear as superficially disastrous, but it was in fact one of those creative "mistakes" without which there is rarely any stirring of new life. Those months in Fond du Lac and the following year in Three Rivers were an interlude between the end of the twelve years in Los Angeles and the beginning of Apple Farm, and during that time both Bob and I believed that it was possible for us to work within the old forms of the religious life. We hoped that if we brought to those for whom the symbols of the church were losing meaning the possibility of making contact as individuals with the great images in the unconscious, they might find again in the ancient rituals the nourishment they so deeply craved. This hope and belief was shared by those within the orders, such as Sister Martha and the Father Prior at St. Gregory's, who realized the great need for breaking out of the old rigidities of interpretation and for the finding of a new language for the ancient truths. All of us reckoned without the immense pressures from the collective unconscious of the time, pressures which were indeed preparing a crack-up of the old order, but in the opposite direction. The church was on the threshold of changes which led her not into a deeper symbolic life, but into more and more social action, extroversion, and outer changes in ritual and language which drained the poetry from the rites and so opened the doors to personal emotionalism. All these things tended to weaken the mysteries and to increase the desperate hunger of the individual for myth and symbol, without which there is no meaning in human life.

In 1939 Jung, speaking to the Guild of Pastoral Psychology in London, said that the Catholic and Anglican communions were still true churches wherein the great images nourished the unconscious of men, and that as long as a person could find that nourishment within the protection of the church it was always right for that person to stay there. He spoke of the many people who had, through work with him, found their way back to their particular church as the collective imagery it carried leapt to life within them. But also, he said, there were others, like himself, who found they could no longer stay inside that protective circle. These people were then forced to take up the individual Quest; they had "to go through the solitude of a land that is not created" with only their dreams for guide. For such a one the need becomes imperative to find an individual symbolic life—his or her own myth.

In 1939, as Jung spoke of these things, the number of those forced to the Quest was comparatively small; twenty-five years later, enormous numbers were bemusedly searching to reestablish the lost meaning in their church by "reforms" which destroyed the very thing they sought. Charismatic movements, encounter groups, and so forth then arose, seeking to bring back the inner fire of the spirit, but, alas, only too often the result was an emotional and dangerous mass-produced stirring up of the unconscious.

Nevertheless, in the midst of all this, an ever-increasing number of individuals were finding the courage to take the way that Jung described— the lonely descent into the depths to the finding of the *mysterium tremendum* within, a journey on which no short-cuts are allowed. However sad the loss of the old beauties of the church traditions may be to one who knew them, and however tragic the rationalism which has replaced them, yet there can be no doubt that the deep purposes of the Self are being served. The loss of the collective symbolic life is forcing its rebirth in individuals.

The years 1961 and 1962 were the eve of the landslide to come. I believe that my dream of the "tracts" and the somersaulting car and my subsequent death had prophetic meaning on a collective level. It foretold that the Catholic as well as the Protestant church institutions might lose the power to nourish, and that the new bread would come through individuals who were seeking the wholeness which involves the death of the ego as center. The outer accident, of course, only revealed the dream's meaning to me in a very limited way—it ensured the next step I must take. But it was not until years later that I realized to what extent I would be forced from within to recognize the necessity of emerging from the formal church. I had first to make the "mistake" of thinking that I could work in close cooperation with it—and indeed the mystery was still alive for me therein. From that "mistake" sprang the friendships and the marvelous support of many individuals that made possible the new way onto which, I believe, we were led by the Self through the rejections and misunderstandings of the "authorities."

Just before I went to Fond du Lac, there was an election at the convent of a new mother superior. Else and I and all the younger and more conscious sisters had confidently expected that Sister Martha would be elected and that she would introduce the kind of new life we believed possible. On the night before the election I had the following dream. In the first part of it I dreamed that Martha had been elected and that she lay sick and in great distress on a couch calling to me for help; in the second part of the dream the election had gone the other way. The older conservative candidate was elected, and she stood at one end of a big room with most of the sisters gathered around her. Feeling very bad, I nevertheless went up to her and congratulated her courteously, and then went over to join Sister Martha, who stood apart at the other end of the room with a few others. I knew she was suffering much, but she was not in a state of miserable collapse as she had been when elected. She stood erect with quiet dignity.

The dream of the election

This dream did much to give me courage when in fact Martha was not elected, and it did reflect an objective truth about her life, I believe. But I see now also its personal significance in my own unconscious. If my work had met with acceptance and approval in the church, I would probably have poured out my vital energy in an attempt to oppose the rising flood of collective extroverted change which was upon us. As it was, I was finally forced out onto another path, parallel but very different, just as Martha found in the end that she must leave the religious life in the old sense.

The new mother superior seemed at first to welcome my psychological help with some of the sisters. But she could not understand it at all, and felt threatened when it happened, as was inevitable, that some of them discovered through their work that they did not belong in the convent. Dom Francis, the very wise priest from St. Gregory's who was chaplain to the sisters, had supported me strongly when I made it clear that if they sent someone to me my loyalty must be to the individual way of that person, no matter what emerged. He likewise supported Sister Martha in her decision to leave. All this aroused great resentment among the older sisters who could not conceive of the forces at work in the unconscious and began to attribute all their troubles to my presence. I could not leave at once, largely because Martha and others were going through so terrible a time in seeking release and were in real need of my presence nearby. So I stuck it out for some months, without the support even of Dom Francis, who had resigned from the chaplaincy owing to the incompatibility of his attitude with the prevailing atmosphere at the convent.

Meanwhile Bob was doing well at St. Gregory's and was fully accepted by the Father Prior, who also supported me from a distance and helped me through this very painful time. So it was with renewed faith in our way within the church that I left Fond du Lac and went to live in Three Rivers, welcomed by the Prior, since more and more people came as guests to the Priory who were in need of psychological help. Another year was to pass before it was finally brought home to us that the close cooperation we had hoped for was impossible. The blow fell through the Abbot of Nashdom Abbey who came on a visit to the Priory. He listened to Bob and me and to the Father Prior and other friends in the monastery, and he seemed at first to be encouraging us in his response. He then listened to the others—to those who, as at Fond du Lac, feared and resented our work. We had not suspected the strength of this opposition. Then one day he sent for us both and said he had decided no monk could be allowed to work with either of us again. The Father Prior remained a friend and indeed was to give us great support as Apple Farm took shape, but all cooperation was at an end, except for Bob's work with the guests.

Later a dream summed up the situation. I had been summoned in this dream to a solemn meeting of church authorities and had been closely questioned. Finally the presiding churchman announced, "You must either give up your proposed individual way or suffer excommunication." I stood up and replied, "Even if I am damned to eternity I have to follow this way." Then I turned and left.

The withdrawal in fact was gradual but I knew now that I must take the lonely road. The "hard-faced woman" of my dream had spoken again. I have remained, I trust, faithful to those great dogmas of Christianity which Jung said were the deepest possible expression of the truth of the psyche and of man's relationship with God, but from that time I knew that I must refuse all "tracts." I have often thought of Simone Weil in this context, if I may be bold to make the comparison. She said there were people whose vocation lay on the threshold of the church, and who were in fact forbidden by the voice of the Spirit within to belong to the outer organization. (Of the company of such people, she was the greatest.)

I must return now to Fond du Lac and tell of the seeds of friendship which began there and led to the building of Apple Farm.

Among the novices was one Sister Janet (Jane Bishop), a deeply introverted intuitive who had grown close to Else and had heard of me from her. She told me long afterwards that while listening to Else's words she had the strangest feeling that she and Else and I had work to do together in the future. She almost wrote to me about it, she said, so strong was her intuition. Jane was already unhappy at the convent and left soon after beginning work with me, but she found a job nearby in order to continue analysis. Else was at this time away from Fond du Lac in one of the branch houses of the sisterhood, but kept in touch with me by letter and telephone. Thus the links between the three of us were being forged and, during the uncertainties and false starts of the next year or two, the links held firm. Jane made a brief attempt to find the way of life she sought in another convent. With Martha and others she entered a contemplative order in England but soon returned to the United States and arrived unannounced in Three Rivers one happy day, to my joy. Else meanwhile had decided to finish her two-year vows period and then leave the convent, so she did not finally join us until early in 1963.

The fourth "companion" of our fellowship came also from the convent.

Nancy Hector was another young novice, who was greatly disturbed by the atmosphere. After leaving the convent, she went to Denver and got a job, but, when she knew I was settled in Three Rivers, she decided to come and live there too in order to continue analysis. She was in fact the first to join me there.

My three companions had among them great complementary strengths. Else is the practical one with deep insight into the unconscious as well. Her strength and great wisdom keep us all firmly rooted on the earth. Jane is, as I have said, the intuitive, often pointing out unerringly the danger signals and the potentials of a situation, and her warm feelings are felt by all who come. She is also the "farmer" among us. Nancy has that inestimable quality of simplicity and warmth of heart, and her loyalty to the Quest led her, after a time, out into the world to work, but it has now brought her and her strength back to the Farm itself.

It must be understood that during these months we all still held the mistaken belief that a new contemplative community could be founded by Martha, Else, Jane and Nancy within the church. Martha and Jane had in fact gone to England in the hope of being trained to that end. The Abbot's attitude brought a rude awakening, and we realized the fact that the rejection in Fond du Lac was not just a localized conservative reaction but a settled attitude of church authority, though now, as I write, things are changing again. There could be no true acceptance of the individual way as we understood it within the collective religious institutional life at that time. It seems odd to me now that I believed it possible for so long, but nevertheless the attempt bore much fruit, because, and only because, we were able to let go of the old way without bitterness when the time came. As always, because of this letting go, which was not a rejection, the great value which we had all found in the old traditions was not lost but transformed into a new way of life in the community that did finally emerge.

It came about in this manner. People were hearing of the presence of a "Jungian" in Three Rivers and began coming at intervals for talks. There was nowhere for them to stay. Else, Jane, and Nancy were now living at a farm belonging to the Priory that they had rented for three months.

(Martha did not leave the religious life until later, and she then trained as a psychologist. She now lives nearby and works at a Family Center.) At first the household at the Priory Farm had been seen as a move towards a formal community; then, after our awakening, as a stepping stone to another kind of fellowship. Else had a job as a nurse, Jane was teaching in a grade school, while Nancy kept house. They already had animals—a cow, horse, dog, cat, and chickens. At the end of the three months they had to move, and the idea of a "community" without rules or formal structure, run by the four of us for guests seeking counseling and times for introversion, was taking shape. With support from friends, we took a risk and bought our present house and land. It would be, we hoped, a center for people of like mind with us, where a contemplative attitude to life could be nourished, without any interference with ordinary living, through the approach to the unconscious made

possible by Jung. The best summing up of the quality we sought is in A. M. Hadfield's *Introduction to Charles Williams,* where, writing of the "company" of people who gathered around Williams, she said, "There was no pledge or initiation, no standard asked by others. . . . In all matters the compulsion is interior . . . it is a spirit which will work within everything we do and will reject nothing of our ordinary life. . . . It is the birth and life of love, of Christ, here and now. . . ." Williams's concept of "exchange" was the guiding thread of his company. Jung's way of individuation is ours.

Bob by this time had also left the monastery and started a similar house, run by men, nearby. But he was never really at home in Michigan and soon moved St. John's House to California, near San Diego, where he now lives and works and is happily settled.

Some of our old friends from California and their families joined us as time passed, along with several more who had been in convent or monastery. The Rev. Morton Kelsey, who had studied in Zurich, sent us some very fine people of our kind, many of whom now live nearby and give marvelous support and much time and energy to the Farm. We made no appeals for money, but we had enough for each need as it arose through

the generosity of those who joined us. A barn was built, an old school house was moved to the property and reconstructed by degrees into a guest house, and later a little house was built for me. All this belongs to the history of Apple Farm and I will not write more of it here except to say that, after twelve years, we have about forty "members," men and women, living and working in the area and as many more who come at intervals. Else and Jane now do most of the counseling and others are beginning to help in this. From the beginning I have had study groups at which we discuss the great images in myth and story, and it is some years now since I began to write of these things in the Apple Farm papers. I say "thank you" here to Father Benedict Reid, the Father Prior of St. Gregory's, now Abbot, who first urged me to write, and published my first effort in the monastery paper, *Benedicite*.

There is no more I want to say about my outer life, which has been quite uneventful for the past twelve years. But there is an inner story with plenty of events.

CHAPTER TEN

THE INNER JOURNEY—
1963–1975

**THROUGH
PSYCHOLOGY
TO "STORY"**

IN 1974 I HAD A DREAM in which I was walking with a new "guide" from the Beyond. I knew that when in her company I had had profound experiences of "the Beyond." Someone asked me, "Is she another psychologist?" and I answered, "No, she is a storyteller."

What does it mean, this change from psychology to story? C. S. Lewis, in his essay "On Stories," points out how very little critical attention has been paid in our civilization to pure Story. There have been, he says, three notable exceptions—Aristotle in *The Poetics,* Boccaccio writing in the Middle Ages, and, in our own day, Jung, with his theory of archetypes. Almost all other critics assume that Story should exist in adult literature only as a means to something else—for example, for the sake of the characters or of social or psychological analysis, or, I might add, for the sake of allegory. When on the other hand characters and thoughts exist to give the story life, such books are apt to be despised as "only fit for children."

The truth is, of course, that any story written especially for children is not Story at all, in the real sense of the word. Lewis, Tolkien, and Richard

Adams all agree on this. The true Story springs out of the archetypal patterns underlying all human life, the perennial battle between good and evil. The joy and wisdom which can come to adults or, in their degree, to children, from the pure traditional story lies precisely in the fact that the characters illuminate the story, the pattern, not the other way round. We sense that at once in the very few great modern stories, such as *The Lord of the Rings* by Tolkien, and *Watership Down* by Richard Adams. In the work of such great conscious storytellers the characters are true and unique individuals, as they are not in the folktale, but this in no way alters the primacy of the story itself. It remains central—as it did in Homer, in the Greek tragedies, and supremely in Dante's *Commedia*.

In the later plays of Shakespeare, tremendous as the characterization is, the emphasis is not on personal psychology as in *Hamlet*. In *King Lear*, in *Othello*, we are swept into the overwhelming terror of archetypal forces as they seize upon human beings and transform them, dragging them either into Hell, or, with individual choice, through Hell to Heaven. Even in the simplest and most primitive of traditional fairy stories, it is human choice that decides the issue. Without that, there is no story, only natural events. At the last, in *The Tempest*, which is steeped in the atmosphere of Faerie, Shakespeare says, "We are such stuff as dreams are made on." Here I would quote the beautiful comment of H. C. Goddard, which indeed was the origin of the title I have given to these memories. "There is one little word here that makes all the difference," he writes, noting that most commentators assure us that Shakespeare meant "made *of*."

> Whether we are such stuff as dreams are made of is at best a matter of opinion or conviction, even though Shakespeare's authority is supposed to support the assertion. But that we are such stuff as dreams are made on is a matter of fact. It is indeed the one datum of consciousness. . . . Perhaps the final secret and definition of matter will turn out to be not some mathematical formula but simply this: matter is that stuff on which dreams can be imprinted, that substance in other words on

which creative energy can be projected. How else could things as frail as dreams have survived the tempest and chaos of material evolution?

So it has seemed to me that to trace the pattern of any person's "big" dreams from childhood to old age, together with the events that accompanied them, can be to tell a Story, not in order to illuminate the intricacies of that person's psychological states or character by the dreams, but through the story to show the shapes of the dreams projecting themselves upon a human life. Laurens van der Post tells us that the Bushmen ask, "Do we dream dreams, or do they dream us?" Perhaps the answer is that both these statements are true in that mystery of "Exchange" and of Incarnation, in which the two worlds are eternally one and distinct.

It seems to me that the changes of these latter years of my life can be expressed in terms of the slow discovery of the meaning of life as Story, in the sense I have tried to define it. The whole focus of attention is altered, with the ego fighting a rearguard action as it realizes the sacrifice that is implicit in this change.

Out of the great number of dreams, fantasies and active imagination which have emerged in these years, I shall therefore seek to remember here a few that seem to me to show clearly some threads of the story which has been and still is being woven into the pattern of my life.

I was astonished to find that the "storyteller" appeared for the first time as long ago as 1967 in some active imagination following a dream. I was told in the dream to go from a great house with rich furnishings, which I had inherited, into an old building on the seashore where people, it was said, lived in squalor and misery. Here the dream ended. I imagined myself entering this place and at once the unconscious moved in response. This is "active imagination." I found first an empty stable and beyond that a room with a window opening onto the sea. In it there was no squalor, but stark cleanliness and signs of extreme poverty borne with dignity. An old man sat by the window and I knew that he was blind. Hearing me, he called me to him and said that he sensed I was in trouble. He bade me sit

The "storyteller" emerges

beside him and held my hand. Then he spoke as follows: "Perhaps you need not speak of your trouble even, for I have no words of sage advice to resolve it for you. Yet I can tell you many things—tales of the sea, of her moods, her anger and her gentleness, of storms and calm, of tides and currents—tales of the life she nourishes, of the whale and the killer shark, of the wise dolphin and the playful seal, of the tiny crabs of the rock pools; and last but not least I will tell you of the men who sail over the sea in their ships, seeking food, or knowledge, or riches, men who strive with her, pitting their puny strength against her mighty power, and win if they love her in their heart of hearts, but lose if they hate or despise her and so are swallowed up forever. I spent my life on the sea and beside it. I was born near here in a fisherman's hut and the sea has nourished and taught and disciplined me as child and man, and given me such wisdom as I have. So now I am content to sit here and listen to her voice as she sometimes whispers and sometimes shouts and roars under my window—and I have no need to see with my eyes." There was a long silence between us—only the sound of the gently breaking waves filled the room. Then in my vision the old man's granddaughter arrived, a woman tall and austere. She softened when he spoke to her, said a fisherman had given her fish, and asked me to eat with them.

I told them how I had inherited the big house but would not live there, for others would take care of it. Many, I said, would perhaps stay there from time to time, and those who had ears to hear would come to listen to his tales and so find courage and wisdom. I myself would build a little house close to his on the seashore and live alone there, and I would come often to hear a tale when sorrowful and confused.

This last paragraph contains my conscious thought about this vision, and it refers obviously to the Farm. It is valid because it was just at this time that I had begun in earnest the slow withdrawal from the regular counseling work here for which Jane and Else were now ready to take responsibility. At the same time I had started writing for the groups, and the Apple Farm Papers were initiated. With the exception of *Three Tales,* none of them is a story, though almost all are inspired by stories. I believe indeed that they all came from the "storyteller" in the unconscious, who was extremely prolific in my active imagination at this time. I am no originator of stories or anything else; but I do have, it seems, a gift of response to the core of true story and almost all my writing springs out of that response and its interpretations. Incidentally, my tale, "The Hunter and the Hunted," also ends with the old woman becoming a storyteller.

A dream came on the night after I had discussed with Else and Jane the possibility of my writing for the groups. I dreamed there were lines drawn in black on white in squares—it was, I knew, a kind of writing that could be read and studied. These drawings were distributed to many (at one point I saw someone making a "recording" of them—many copies). But I knew that there was one drawing which was not the same as these; it consisted of squares, as did the others, but they were of solid gold. This was a single unique drawing that could not be duplicated. Only a very few people would see it and these had no need of the other drawings or of busy studying.

I dreamed this in April of 1967. In August came the decision to "retire" *Retirement* from the bulk of analytical work and in September the dream of the blind storyteller and the house by the sea, which I have told above. Blithely, I thought then that the change would be, though painful, a relatively easy matter, but not until 1974, seven years later, did the unconscious inform me, in the dream with which this chapter begins, that the storyteller guide in the Beyond had finally taken over from the "analyst," though I had often spent time with her along the way.

Outwardly it was obviously impossible that the retirement could be sudden. It did not and still does not mean that I have ceased to work with those who counsel other people. There are more of them now than just Jane and Else, and through the seven years there were, besides the counselors, many others whom it seemed essential I should see. Gradually the numbers of these latter declined; I see one now and then for an hour, when requested by the counselors. Later I have been blessed by many true meetings with unique men and women—either a visit or a telephone call in which a friendship has begun, to remain unbroken by time or distance. At the Farm I have become perhaps a "consultant" rather than a practitioner. All these changes took place in due time and gradually, without too much difficulty, in spite of a continual falling back into unnecessary busyness.

The inner change of attitude, however, was not so simple. It seemed easy when first propounded; I had no premonition of the profundity of its implications, of the purging of my life-long dependency on other people which lay ahead. The "sacrifice in the House of Marriage," begun so long ago when I was forty-two (6×7) has been a continuous process until now when I am seventy (10×7), and still deepens, I trust, towards its fulfillment.

Closely related to this experience is that deepest of all my instinctual ties, the mother-daughter identification within me. The dependence of the daughter on the "mothering" of friends, the clinging of the mother to her daughter, projected onto those I have taught along the way—both these things have come under the surgeon's knife over and over again. At last, I believe, the pain is no longer in the region of invasive emotional affect; it has passed to another place. Such affect as comes is usually soon detached— but who knows! If it returns, it is to be accepted too.

The last and perhaps most difficult of all the separations is this con-summation of the transition from psychology to that which I have called "story." Anything can be turned into a mother, and the role of psychologist is particularly dangerous to women in this respect. The peril comes not only from the temptation to identify with the "great mother," but also from the tendency to turn the psychological attitude itself into both mother and father within—the source of comforting reassurance and of authority which can prolong the fruitless efforts of the ego to improve itself far past the appropriate time, and so pull one back from the simple delight in the Story of life, and its Creator. The Crucifixion is the death of the best, not the worst, and that alone can release us into the state where best and worst are equal in the joy of the Story.

The Road

Related to the images of the "Storyteller" during these years is the recurring image of the "Road." This is a symbol of the journey of man from childhood to old age, outward to the moon and beyond, inward through Hell and Purgatory to Paradise and to that which is beyond all three. At the last this Road ceases to be a straight or winding line from one point to another and begins to be known as a circle.

As Frodo recounted in *The Lord of the Rings*, Bilbo "used often to say there was only one Road; that it was like a great river: its springs were at every doorstep, and every path was its tributary. 'It's a dangerous business, Frodo, going out of your door,' he used to say. 'You step into the Road, and if you don't keep your feet there is no knowing where you might be swept off to. . . .'"

Yes, indeed; once started on that Road there is no escape except into catastrophe, but what of the moment when "many paths and errands meet"? That will be death and the unknown Beyond, but yet there is in this life a coming back of the Road to the place where it began.

> *We shall not cease from exploration*
> *And the end of all our exploring*
> *Will be to arrive where we started*
> *And know the place for the first time . . .*
>
> *A condition of complete simplicity*
> *(Costing not less than everything).*

> T. S. ELIOT
> "Little Gidding"

The Road for me began as a "conscious" image in childhood with the dream of the milestone and the woman driving me out onto the dark, lonely road. I say "conscious" because, though of course I was totally unaware of its meaning through so many years, the image remained alive in my memory from the moment of its appearance until it blazed into significance at my first awareness, through Jung, of the unconscious. I have written above of the long journey to separation and sacrifice, and the link is obvious with the image of the woman driving me out and with my first dreamed experience of sacrifice, when I saw my mother burning at the stake as I stood alone on the road.

I have had, as we all do, numerous dreams of the road, of journeys, of travel to south, east, west, and north—dreams trivial and profound in which we move toward a desired goal. The years between the beginning of the move towards "retirement" from ordinary psychological work in 1967 and the spring of 1972 had been for me very productive. Most of the shorter Apple Farm papers were in being by 1970, and in that year I began to enter deeply into Dante's long inner journey, to write of its meaning to me, and to share these things with the Apple Farm groups. It was for me a very real personal experience as I moved in imagination with the poet on the tremendously exciting road from the dark wood at the beginning to the white rose of the end, where Dante saw the great river of light flowing at last in a circle instead of in a straight line.

"Will you each write about the Road?"

I finished the study in April 1972 and there came to me two dreams at this time—one a few weeks before I had completed the writing, and one not long after. Both concern the image of the Road. In the first, von Franz had come to the Farm to teach "writing." Her work on fairy stories has been to me a deep well of wisdom. She is herself a true storyteller. As we sat, in the dream, with pen and paper—each of us separate, not ranged as in a classroom, she went away into an inner room and lay down on a couch. For fifteen minutes there was stillness, and I knew she was waiting for the subject of our "writing" to come to her. She then rose and came out to us saying, "Will you each write about the Road?" I was scared, my mind running around at first trying to think of impressive and interesting things to say about the "archetype" and so on and on. Then suddenly I pulled myself together and said to myself, "Stop that—just write down the things that fascinate and excite you about the Road." And immediately all worry about an "assignment," about making a good impression, left me entirely and I had that wonderful feeling of one thought giving birth to the next, that sense of unfolding and recognition which is the mark of creation. In other words, I ceased for that moment to strive along the road towards a goal—the road became the circle whose "center is everywhere."

The second dream brought the central image of a whole series which both preceded and followed it through the years—the image of the Great

Stone. I tell it here because it speaks of the end of the Road, of the place where "all paths and errands meet."

I was standing in the dream on a path, looking back over the way I had come. The road stretched away in an absolutely straight line until it disappeared on the horizon. It sloped gently down from where I stood on a hillside and up again in the distance. It was as though I saw for the first *The image of the Great Stone* time with great clarity the road that I had traveled and was astonished both at the distance and at its straightness. I was waiting for someone to come to whom I wished to show the road. But now I moved a little and there was no longer a road under my feet. Looking up into the sky I saw a great many-faceted crystal stone moving towards me. It was to my sight about twelve feet in diameter. The sky was grey and the stone was both dark and light against it. Glowing light shone out from the lines defining the darkened facets of the stone, and the darkness of it was itself somehow luminous. It gave the impression of substance and weight, but floated in the sky as though weightless. I saw also that behind it there was a small luminous cloud which seemed to be pushing the stone towards me, and I wondered in a puzzled way whether this cloud con-

cealed a man, perhaps a pilot in an aeroplane. I began to worry as the vision approached lest it might obscure the sight of the road or even obliterate it altogether, if the vision descended, as seemed likely, to earth; and because of this concern I did not fully respond to the extraordinary beauty of the stone, until, as I woke, the splendor of it burst into consciousness. I thought at first that the idea of a man guiding this great image towards me was somewhat shameful, but then I remembered Jung's words about the woman who dreamed she was teaching a dove to walk up and down stairs. He said that human consciousness does have to "teach," so to speak, the Holy Spirit how to live in this world.

The particular aspect of this dream I want to stress here, however, is its affirmation that I must soon come to the end of the "road," to the end of following a goal, to the end of showing people the way. This was my major concern in the dream. If the road was obliterated, how could I share my vision of it?

In the feminine psyche the compulsion to share can be a last bastion of the possessive mother. A woman may also of course suffer from the opposite of this, a secretive hoarding of the precious thing, but this is a refusal of her femininity. The natural instinct of woman is surely to share herself and all her gifts with those she loves, for through this she seeks to establish relationships. In its purity this instinct is a thing of beauty, but it can so easily become contaminated with the possessive pride of the ego or, more subtly, with the fear of that aloneness in which no one is going to reassure her anymore that she is right, no one is going to tell her she is needed, and there will no longer be a path visible to others on which she may safely walk.

The cat and bird, and the glowing stone dreams

I remember two other dreams foreshadowing this. The first, in the early stages of analysis, brought a glimpse of the union of opposites in the image of a cat and a bird in friendly contact with each other. My (extremely British) reaction was a delighted thought of how I would like to write a letter to the *Times* about so strange a phenomenon!

The second was, like the 1972 dream, about the Stone, and it came during the early days in Three Rivers. I was alone in an empty barnlike place with high wooden rafters. My friends had all taken refuge in the cellar, since we expected some kind of bombing attack. I had remained above because of an imperative feeling that whatever the danger I must meet it in the open, above ground. There came a great crash and down through the roof fell a huge cube of glowing stone the color of a cantaloupe melon. It missed me by inches but I felt no fear, for I somehow knew that wherever I had been standing it would have fallen just beside me. As it hit the ground a shower of blazing sparks of light broke from it, which were, I knew, at the same time solid chips of the stone. The great cube itself was in no way diminished or damaged by this "breaking." Several of the chips had fallen, I knew, upon me and entered into me, though I felt nothing physically, but was filled with an ecstatic joy at the glory of the stone. Then I thought of my friends below and of what they were missing and I ran to the head of the stairs calling down to one of them to come at once and see this beauty. As I cried out to her, the stone left the ground and, floating up to the rafters, disappeared. As it rose, it ceased to be a perfect cube, becoming oblong before it was lost to sight.

There are things one may, indeed must, share, and things which every person must experience alone and which are immediately diminished when communicated by any act of conscious will. It is the same message, I see, as that conveyed in the dream of the black and white squares which were symbolic of shared words and the golden squares which were seen only by those who saw them without words.

This warning was again repeated in an image that was a sequel to the early dream in which I was told to "decorate" the stone cross. It came at the beginning of the work on Dante. In a dream I saw two people, one of whom was chipping out a human form hidden in a great block of stone. I knew that, although the other was watching the process, when the vision hidden in the stone actually emerged the sculptor would not share it and the watcher would not see it because there are certain things that cannot be communicated, that must be discovered and experienced alone.

In the cat and bird dream I was too unconscious to recognize the hint of the union of the opposites as more than a unique phenomenon to be shared with the generality. The desire to share the melon-stone cube vision came from generosity but was still compulsive, for I could not yet accept loneliness of heart. But in the dream of the crystal of darkness and light, I stood on the verge of this loneliness. No one was in fact there to whom I could point out the road, let alone the stone. Moreover, the approach of the stone was not halted by my fear of the obliteration of the goal-oriented struggle. The stone was indeed propelled by a symbol, as I believe, of the individuated human spirit, as yet hidden from me in the luminous cloud. It is nearly three years, as I write, since this dream. It may be many more before it finally touches the earth—perhaps at death, perhaps after.

I want now to gather together a few more of the images from dream and active imagination which have remained with me as vital experiences—parts (in H. C. Goddard's words) of the "pattern that was being slowly woven."

CHAPTER ELEVEN

THE SYMBOLIC LIFE

THERE IS much publicity these days sur-
rounding the Chinese *Book of Changes*, which Richard Wilhelm,

with Jung, first rescued from its obscurity here in the West. The present
collective longing for the restoration of meaning to life is drawing large
numbers of people to use this ancient text, often as a kind of magic to
replace the lost mysteries of true religion. Like all great religious books of
wisdom, the *I Ching* is as dangerous as it is profound; its use can quickly
degenerate into superstition as soon as it becomes popular, and it can be
quoted, like the Bible, to prove whatever the devotee wants to prove. Again
like the Bible, if interpreted on the outer level only it may lead to possession by the unconscious. (I have myself known one woman who, as she
herself told me later, was precipitated by its indiscriminate use into a psy-
chotic episode lasting several years.)

The *I Ching* itself issues a warning. It says of itself that it does not
speak at all to the "inferior man." The translation "superior man" and "inferior man" means in our language "the conscious objective person" and "the
unconscious ego-centered person." The book, for all its practical wisdom
and applicability to objective situations, speaks a highly symbolic language,
and, just as we can rarely interpret accurately our own dreams, so we must
beware of our interpretations of the *I Ching*. If we use it as an "oracle," it

is extremely important that we check our interpretations with a "superior man" who is aware of both our conscious and unconscious selves. Otherwise the inferior man within us, blinded by the shadow, will almost certainly mislead us, and possibly bring disaster.

With this said, we may turn to the contemplation of the riches of wisdom which using the *I Ching* may bring when one has glimpsed the Tao and is willing to accept in humility the guidance it may yield. I was introduced to it in Zurich immediately after the Baynes translation of Richard Wilhelm's German version was published in England, with Jung's introduction, and I asked my first question with much trepidation. There are two ways one may consult the oracle: first, by simply asking for "wisdom for the moment"; and second, by framing a very precise question, such as Jung describes in his introduction.

Sign 26, "Taming Power of the Great"

On that first occasion I asked simply for wisdom. I was in the midst of a great crisis, at a major turning point of my life, and the answer was Sign 26, the "Taming Power of the Great," with four changing lines. I do not remember which lines they were, and therefore I do not know what the prognosis sign was, but the aptness of the answer in Sign 26 to my situation leaps to the eye. I quote here from the Judgment and the Image: "Not eating at home brings good fortune. It furthers one to cross the great water" and "the superior man acquaints himself with many sayings of antiquity/And many deeds of the past, /In order to strengthen his character thereby."

The crisis then facing me was the decision, described earlier, either to stay in Zurich and study, or to go home because of my illness. To stay surely meant a vital "crossing of the water" within me, a transition on which my whole future depended, and the image states quite clearly the necessity for studying the "sayings of antiquity." Moreover, in symbolic language the study of the past means the exploration of the unconscious. This answer became even more impressively apt when a year later I crossed the great water of the Atlantic, and ate a very long way from home! Dr. Meier questioned me somewhat skeptically at the time about my throwing of the coins, because, he said, four changing lines was unlikely. They indicate a major change—and a major change it was, but still evidently not so great a revolution as came to me during those months of retirement and introversion years later in Los Angeles.

When I was going through the doubts and hesitations preceding that extremely difficult decision, I asked the *I Ching* for judgment upon it. This time I had the quite astonishing and rare experience of throwing six changing lines. This said, in effect, that the decision would bring a total reversal of the direction and quality of my life, as indeed it did. The sign given was number 41, "Decrease."

Sign 41,
"Decrease"

> *Decrease, combined with sincerity*
> *Brings about supreme good fortune*
> *Without blame.*
> *One may be persevering in this.*
> *It furthers one to undertake something.*
> *How is this to be carried out?*
> *One may use two small bowls for the sacrifice.*

And the Image:

> *At the foot of the mountain, the lake: the image of Decrease.*
> *Thus the superior man controls his anger*
> *And restrains his instincts.*

The meaning in brief is that the higher values in the personality are enriched by a decrease in the unconscious instinctual drives (as the growing things on the mountainside are watered by evaporation from the lake). This is to be achieved through great simplicity and sincerity and by discipline in small things. The lines contain advice about achieving this decrease with consideration for others but without any compromise where it is a matter of one's own basic inner need.

The wisdom of this guidance for my particular situation is obvious; it was a great support through those months. The new situation which might

Sign 31,
"Influence"

follow was also most beautifully described. The six changing lines brought the Sign 31, "Influence"—a lake on the mountain. The peak of the mountain is sunken and holds the lake. "The superior man encourages people to approach him/By his readiness to receive them." The stillness of the mountain holds the lake and people are influenced through the unconscious and not any more by conscious and willed effort.

These are two examples of the wisdom of the *I Ching* in crucial situations. There is another way, however, in which the *I Ching* has been to me a constant support. In the midst of the busyness of life and the whisperings of the negative animus, all too easily we feel cut off from the deeper voices of the unconscious; active imagination dries up and the dreams are chaotic. To question the *I Ching* then, as one would a wise teacher, has meant for me almost invariably a reconnection with meaning, an exorcism of the trivial values that so easily invade us. If you become importunate, the book itself tells you so in no uncertain terms! This use of the book is entirely safe *only* if the questioner is in no way looking for magical solutions and has come to intuitive awareness of that which Jung called synchronicity and Charles Williams called co-inherence—the intersection of time with the timeless beyond all chance or accident.

One dream about the *I Ching* came to me in the summer of 1968 and belongs, interestingly enough, in the storyteller series. I dreamed that on my outstretched hands there lay a page of old yellowed parchment on which was drawn in large lines, filling the whole page, the sign "Decrease." As I looked, the page turned over from right to left and lay now on my left hand, the same lines showing black on the yellow as though they were not written on the parchment but were a part of the texture of it. I was dimly aware that on my right hand lay the next page of the *I Ching* bearing the sign for "Increase," but this was dark, and I knew rather than saw that it was there. As I held my attention on the sign "Decrease," a voice spoke clearly, and with authority, from I knew not where, saying, "She will tell a story."

The association to this dream was, of course, the vital significance of this sign at that watershed of my life in Los Angeles. Returning now in

1968, the dream seemed to say that attention to the wisdom of Decrease would bring me to the verge of a time of Increase—a time when the creative spirit becomes active—and that this would come through telling a story. As I look through my papers I see that 1968 and 1969 produced the *Three Tales* and many other "stories" from the unconscious and led on to the beginning of the Dante study in 1970.

These few examples may serve to illustrate how this ancient wisdom may enrich an ordinary life today.

SYMBOLS OF THE
NATURAL LIFE

I had a dream once about some dogs that gives me more sheer delight than any other dream I can remember. There is no active imagination in this—it is pure dream. Here is the text.

I am watching a pack of dogs—a leader and four smaller dogs. The leader is also the mother of them all, steady and wise. The oldest of the smaller dogs is Shari, my own dog. The mother's coat is pale gold color, with a sort of numinous quality. Like Shari, she is perhaps a mixture of shepherd, collie and golden retriever. They move swiftly and with the utmost grace over all sorts of terrain, including city streets full of traffic. I am fearful for them on the streets, but see how surely and safely the leader takes them through the traffic. I have a glimpse of them out in sandy country and see the leader pause at a hole and reach down into it, seeking perhaps a fox. She is teaching the others to hunt now. When she senses the younger ones are tired, she seeks out a safe spot and they all sit down and rest before going on their way again. Now they are near the ocean, and I see to my distress that the youngest and smallest has fallen into a pool and the leader has not noticed. I run and lift her out and think desperately she should have artificial respiration and I have not the skill, and I start running, calling for a man who has an "artificial respiration clinic." Meanwhile I press on the dog's ribs. A little water comes out; she gives a cough and starts to breathe naturally. The artificial-respiration man hints that, after half-drowning, a *painful* treatment in his "parlor" is essential. I wonder if I should give the dog to his ministrations but am sure that nature has done all the healing necessary. I put her down and she happily joins the others who are waiting for her. The leader serenely takes them to a spot off the road beside a house, so that the little one may rest and recover. A few people are watching. Some seem to have known the leader for a long time. A man says to me, "She has new younger dogs with her since I last saw her." I tell him how old Shari is and that the others must be from subsequent litters. I am worrying again—will they get home safely through all the traffic, and should I take Shari with me now? Then I remember the extraordinary poise and awareness of the mother-leader and know it would be all wrong to take Shari away from this, her natural place. She must take whatever risks there might be. Friends drive up at this point and I join them in a car, looking back as we move off, because I am reluctant to leave the extraordinary beauty of the resting animals. They have an aloofness, a feeling of fulfilling their natural instincts, guided by the quiet maturity of the older dog, and of going their way utterly undeterred by all the modern mechanical noise or the fussings of humanity.

I don't know if I have conveyed at all the moving quality of this dream—its peace, and the sense it carried of the purity of the instincts in themselves. Anyone who has a true and objective love of animals experiences this purity and does not need a dream to help them, but the particular quality of this dream comes, I think, from the images of the "dog" within us fulfilling its nature in the very heart of man's mechanized world. The dream seems to be stating that constant vigilance is needed, not to protect the dogs from the bustle of the modern world but in case "the little one" should wander and fall into the unconscious. In this case conscious human intervention is essential—but assuredly not intervention from a censorious animus, coping with a lapse through artificial restoration of life, and trying to insist that a fall through instinctual weakness must be paid for with a complicated and painful treatment (probably a reference to the pangs of *false* guilt). Since, in the dream, I was aware at once of the fall, all that was needed was a simple squeeze and life was restored.

We are confronted in our time with an open clash between the immensely strong puritanical tradition in our heritage and its opposite, the demand for untrammeled instinctual indulgence. There are signs that in a great many individuals the true Christian reverence for the holiness of the flesh is being reawakened—an awareness that can only come when, through discipline without repression, we have emerged from the danger of possession by instinct, from the temptation to use it for the satisfaction of hidden ego-demands. The dream expressed most beautifully for me the *freedom* of the dog-instinct, controlled, so to speak, by its now-mature wisdom, which can be realized only so long as the ego is separate and aware, knowing when and how to cooperate.

I have mentioned earlier the dogs in my life. Here I want to pay tribute to a noble dog who was mine for only a year or so. He was given to me by Nancy Hector in those early days in Three Rivers, when she and I were the only two of the future "company." He was one of a litter of Walker Foxhounds, about four months old. He had, superlatively, the quality of aristocracy that one meets in a few dogs—and I do not mean simply that he was pure-bred, since most highly bred dogs do not have it at all. Later, we came to know his mother, an old hound, the mother of many; her name was Miss Ginger Pickett, but she should surely have been called "Lady," not Miss! Most of her sons were just ordinary hounds who ran with the pack, but my dog, who had come straight to us when Nancy and I looked at the puppies, had inherited from her that indefinable aristocratic quality. I say "my" dog, but the word is not accurate. He was, I repeat, a noble dog and I called him Taliesin after the Welsh seer and King's poet. No one who had a feeling for dogs, meeting him in that brief year, has forgotten him, I think. Affectionate, yet aloof and self-contained, he lived with me for a while, and then one day, when we were visiting at the Priory Farm, where Nancy, Else, and Jane were then living, he disappeared. He was found two days later in the Priory woods lying dead without a mark on him. We never knew what had happened. It was not long before we were to move into Apple Farm, and it was as if he were instinctively aware that, with his hunting instinct and his need to run (he would follow the car at thirty mph for three or four miles with his long, swift, graceful stride without so much as panting), he would become too great a responsibility for

Taliesin

us in the difficult days of our beginnings here. However that may be, he was buried there in the woods by Robert Johnson and a young man staying at the Priory, who had found him. This young man wrote a touching little poem saying no less than the truth—that Tali had meant something indefinable to all those who knew him. Later we chose the name Taliesin for the guest house at Apple Farm.

The beauty and healing power of man's relationship to animals in a love untouched by sentimentality has been much before the public of late. The enormous popularity of the English veterinarian James Herriot's books, *All Creatures Great and Small* and *All Things Bright and Beautiful,* bears witness to the response in the human heart to a story of man's relatedness to the animal creation. Moreover, all the really great naturalists have had this kind of love which transmutes their work into poetry. The integrity of their devotion to what Blake calls the "minute particular" in nature is the very stuff of the imaginative life. From Gilbert White in the eighteenth century to Loren Eiseley today, they not only add to scientific knowledge but also produce works of the feeling imagination.

In my experience, women dream much more frequently of animals than do men, probably because the feminine psyche is closer to nature. Symbolically, the animal is both subhuman and superhuman and is thus the image either of that which is not yet conscious or of that which has regained the primal innocence. Hence gods and goddesses all have animal symbols associated with them. Sometimes animals are transformed into humans in dream or fairy story, but they also speak to the hero out of their own natural wisdom without which the Logos dries up into mere intellect. As von Franz has pointed out, in the world of fairy story there is only one universally essential attitude for the hero: he *must* attend to the animals he meets on his way. To reject them is disaster.

There are many kinds of animal dreams and stories—images of the healing or destroying bite of the animal, of the transforming sacrifice and so on. Here I will tell two more animal dreams, one about horses, one about birds and cats; both emphasize the interdependence of human consciousness and the animal world, as hinted at in the above dream of the dogs.

While the dog is the intuitive instinct, standing also for loyalty and friendliness, and in woman is often the instinctive feminine intuition or the "animus-hound" sniffing around, the horse is the basic libido which serves and carries man when he is in good relationship with it. When the psyche is sick or badly disturbed, the horse may appear wild with panic or crashing to disaster—and this may also mean physical illness or death. The cat is the remote and half-tamed instinct. She may be the familiar of the witch, or the independent beauty and mystery of instinct when it is accepted and fed by man. In Kipling's "Just So" story, the  dog is man's First Friend, the horse is the First Servant, but the cat walks alone, even when welcomed to the human cave, and says, "I am the cat that walks by himself and all creatures are alike to me." Birds are those intuitive thoughts that come from the unconscious and connect us with the mystery; they are the messengers of the air, of the spirit, that breathe life into the imagination.

I dreamed that several of us at Apple Farm were on a journey, and we came to a village at dusk. The horses were being stabled some distance away by those in charge, and someone came to tell me that one of my two horses had died (or had been killed by "the enemy"). Of those two horses, one had been tired and spiritless and the other full of vigor. I was very anxious, fearing it was the latter that was dead. I turned back to go to the stables and on the way I saw that my friends were just finishing burying the dead horse and that the grave was in a cleft, a narrow ravine which divided the village in two. They now were shoveling or pushing big quantities of earth into it, so that the cleft would be filled. The burying of this old horse had filled the whole ravine, and the village was no longer split.

I fearfully approached the stables to discover which horse remained. I came to the stall and to my great relief I saw my spirited horse. He was a

The dream of horses

dark chestnut color and he was lying down. He got up as I approached and suddenly I saw him for a moment as a great grey-white horse of archetypal majesty and power. I took a step towards him, but his front legs kicked out in warning and I stood still. Now I had my elbows close to my sides and my forearms pointing towards him and I knew that his terrific strength was being infused into me through my fingers, hands, and arms—not in order that I might possess it, but because I must *guard* it during the next dangerous stage of the journey. He would attract the enemy if he were to appear in his divine aspect. He was now my ordinary horse again and that other form must be hidden, protected by me, and I must be constantly aware of it, as a trust. Of horses I shall have more to say later.

The last of the dreams I tell here of the natural world was the first in time. It came to me long ago in the early days in Zurich, and I remember how astounded I was that the unconscious had produced a complete fairy story. (Dr. Meier said, "Where else do you suppose fairy stories come from?") It told how all joy and health went out of a village when the birds deserted it. This exodus happened because no one in the village listened anymore to the birds' song; at the same time, all the cats were badly neglected and ran wild. These two things, the story made clear, were interdependent, and the final images showed the return of the birds to the field and life to the village, when a child, a little girl, came to live there with her grandmother—a child who could speak the language of the cats and knew how to listen with the whole of herself to the song of the birds.

SYMBOLS OF
THE WAY   The inner journey has been known by many names—the Hero's Quest, the Search for God, the Way of Salvation, the Eight-fold Path, the Spiral Way, and, in our time, the Way of Individuation. I have written above of the image of this road which is both winding and straight, forever spiraling around the center, but also straight in the sense that it is a one-way movement towards a goal that brooks no deviation once it is entered upon.

The Chinese, however, have another word for the Way. They call it the

Tao, which conveys the truth that only when we arrive at that state of consciousness in which "all strivings cease" does the realization dawn that all stages of the road are incarnate in the present moment. This is also of course what is essential in any true story—for it remains merely a narrative of successive incidents unless, when we come to the end of it, we recognize the wholeness of it and experience the end implicit in the beginning, the beginning still alive in the end. So, like Dante, we have to live each part of the story, both down in the pit and striving up the mountain; we must question everything, move from experience to experience on the way, if we are ever to come to that point from which we may begin to see the whole journey present in every moment. The incidents of the journey are recognizably the same in all the records that have been made of it in all ages past and present, however greatly the language or the interpretations may differ. Yet this sameness does not alter the fact that every person experiences these things in his or her own unique manner.

To those stories already told of how some of these universal experiences came to me in dream and active imagination, pointing the Way for my life, I will here add a few more.

I think it was Esther Harding who said that the mark of true active imagination is that it has an intensity of life for the one to whom it comes which remains so vivid through the years that its content may feel more real than one's memory of outer factual events. This is certainly true of those stories I shall remember here.

In this context it is important to recall again the danger that is never absent when one relates a powerful dream or tells an inner story—the danger of identifying with the images, and so of ego inflation. The truth is that such dreams are archetypal and therefore beyond cause and effect. The ego is not the center even when the dreamer plays an active part in the dream, even when the dreamer feels that he or she receives a clear message from it. Patricia Berry, in an article called "An Approach to the Dream" in *Spring*, 1974, writes that "the way we treat narrative is the way we treat our own psyches. To hear the dream story as a moral allegory with a message for right and wrong behavior (progressive, regressive) is to sit in judgment upon our souls. When we view the tale as archetypal, however, the characters all become valuable subjective entities, both lesser (only a piece of, not an identity) and greater (with more archetypal resonance) than any of our particular narrow and ego-concerned viewpoints." I meant the same thing when I said earlier that in Story the characters exist for the story, not the other way round.

The Place of the Roots

"The Place of the Roots" is the name I give to a story, springing from a dream, which contains images of a deep confrontation with the shadow. The personal shadow is, of course, included in this, but it goes far beyond that to the horror of the collective feminine darkness. In the dream—the story—I was walking alone along a path and I saw ahead of me a small man, seated cross-legged on the ground. I approached in considerable curiosity at his strange appearance. He was an Oriental—either Chinese or Japanese—and he stood up and bowed to me. His straight black hair was cut in a pudding-basin style and he wore a tunic, belted at the waist, which flared out into a kind of short skirt, and under it three-quarter length tight-fitting cotton trousers. He was slightly shorter than I. He did not speak but stood back and pointed to a circular hole in the ground about six feet in diameter, and I stepped to the edge. An iron ladder ran down at one side of the hole and disappeared into the darkness. The small man looked at me, a question in his grave eyes and began to climb down into the hole. An urgency seized me and, as his head disappeared below, I followed almost in a daze onto the ladder and began the descent.

The circle of daylight above my head had dwindled to less than half its size when I realized that the little man was standing beside me on a kind of wooden platform through which the ladder passed. I stepped off it and stood beside him. As I did so he struck a match and lit a small oil lantern, which he must have found down there, and I saw that the shaft had about doubled its diameter. For some reason, the circular floor of wooden planks reminded me of the lid of an old butter churn. Over in one corner there was a small sack and my companion pointed at it. I went over and looked inside. I was mystified, and indeed considerably disappointed to discover nothing but a bag of dog kibble. I looked questioningly at my companion, who smiled and nodded; he then stepped again onto the ladder which continued downwards through the platform, and began to descend. As his head reached the level of the floor he held the lantern high so that I might see the rungs, and after a brief glance upwards at the faint daylight above, I followed him, my heart beating faster now.

This descent was about as long as the first one had been. Again we reached the same kind of wooden platform; again the shaft had widened and was now the size of a large room; but this time there were two sacks against the wall. "If it is more kibble, I shall begin to feel somewhat annoyed," I thought. "Whatever is it all about?" I looked into the first sack—sunflower seeds for the birds, which I had plenty of at home. In the second sack was peat moss mixed with fine dark soil. I plunged my hand into it feeling the acute pleasure its texture always gives me, with its strange and powerful promise of rich growth, and my annoyance was stilled. The little man was beside me, and now he sat down and handed me the lantern, pointing to the shadows at the opposite end of the chamber. For the first time he spoke—one word only. "Choose!" he said. Wonderingly I crossed the room and understood. Here there was a rough staircase cut into rock, going down, still further down, and if I chose I could go that way—but this time I would be alone. I stood hesitating for a long minute. I could go back up the ladder without blame, taking with me food for the dogs, food for the soil, food for the birds, and my life would be rich in warm friendships, in the beauty of growth, in the swift coming of winged thoughts—or I could go down alone to the unknown darkness below. I found now that, even as I formulated the choice and my heart yearned for the ladder and the daylight, my feet had moved onto the staircase and were taking the first step downwards. I had chosen, it seemed, without conscious thought, and clinging to the lantern as though to a lifeline, I went down and down and down into the silent dark.

I came at last into a great cavern and stood still, peering into the dark beyond the small circle of light from the lantern, and listening. At first I heard only the beating of my own heart, but then a sound reached me which froze my blood and almost sent me running up the staircase again.

It was a kind of growling moan conveying so much hate and fear and misery that I began to shiver as though at the impact of a bitter wind. For minutes I was incapable of moving either back or forward—I simply stood listening in an agony of cold and fear. But now it seemed to me that the misery in the sound became the dominant note—that somehow through all the hatred there sounded a cry for help. Slowly I began to move towards the voice, and as I did so it fell silent, as though the creature had seen the approaching light of my lantern—and the silence was more threatening even than the voice. But I was committed now and moved steadily on. I heard a movement to my left and a horrible gibbering sound, and raising my lantern high I saw her only a few feet away. Her face was a woman's— white and horribly distorted by naked fear and hate. Lusterless fair hair that could once have been golden fell straggling and matted to her shoulders, and her eyes seemed to gaze on vacancy, on the horror of meaninglessness. Then I saw her body. A huge and bloated belly was supported not by legs, but by an immensely powerful-looking scaly tail like that of a crocodile, and, most gruesome of all, in place of arms there were four short jointed limbs, two level with the top and two with the bottom of the belly, and these had long black gnarled hands, the fingers ending in sharp-looking curved claws which reflected the light like shining steel. I shrank back in terrified revulsion against the wall of the cavern. "I must run, I must run from this horror," I thought incoherently, "back—back," but my feet would not obey and my eyes were held to the creature in a terrible fascination, and I knew that if indeed I should run, I would be haunted by her image all my life.

She was making a clutching movement now in my direction with those dreadful claws, but I began to think more clearly and realized with a rush of pity that her appalling frustration and misery came in part from the fact that she could not reach her prey unless it came unwarily too near her in the dark. She could not walk, nor use her tail while upright, and if she were to lie flat like a crocodile and use her four limbs as feet and free the tail, then she could not clutch. Setting the lantern in a cleft high up in the rock wall, I braced myself and spoke. "You were a woman once," I said.

"Will you not speak to me from your human heart?—for I would serve you if I could." For the first time she was still and silent for an instant and I saw recognition come to those vacant eyes. She knew me for a woman instead of as potential food for that great belly, and I believe that in that brief flash she remembered herself. Then with a wailing cry which echoed on and on through the huge cavern, a cry which seemed to come from the depths of humanity fallen and lost, her claws flashed out from all four of those powerful grisly hands and she plunged them into her own belly. I too cried out in horror and started forward but I was flung violently back against the wall by a jet of thick foul-smelling liquid, which spouted in fountains from the jagged tears of the bloated belly, covering me with filth, so that I retched and vomited and cowered back with my face to the wall, and so stayed, dazed and conscious of nothing for a while but of physical misery and revulsion. When I began again to be aware, I realized to my surprise that, though the stream of liquid was still pouring onto my back, the smell had quite gone, the ground at my feet was washed clean and, indeed, pure water was now flowing over me. As I realized these things, the jet of water stopped altogether and it seemed that almost at once I felt dry and fresh and renewed. I turned round and nothing remained of the crocodile woman but a long shriveled skin such as a snake sheds as it grows and at one end the woman's hair, golden again now and shining.

I stood gazing at it with a feeling akin to reverence and, picking it up, I found that it was dry and pleasant to the touch. "I will take it with me," I thought, "and if I find my way to the upper air I will bury it with honor." I wound it round my waist and the hair was like a golden tassel. Then, fetching the lantern again, I looked for a path, knowing with certainty that I could not return by the way I had come.

A tunnel led out of the cavern downwards, still further down, I saw with a sinking heart. Nevertheless I entered it boldly and pressed on, following the winding path with my small circle of light. After a long time the tunnel widened and I thought I heard the sound of water. There were shadows to right and left which looked like great limbs of trees all leaning forward and inward until they were lost in the darkness ahead of me.

Then suddenly I stopped. The path was blocked by one of these huge tree-like growths. Slowly I edged my way around it and peered ahead. I sensed that on all sides now there was water—only a narrow path led over it like a bridge. I leaned against the tree, if it was a tree, my arm around it clinging to it for safety. And now without warning my lantern flickered and went out and I clung to the limb in terror. Then a voice spoke out of the darkness ahead—a woman's voice, so calm and deep and strong that at the sound of it my fear receded and turned to awe. "You are come, daughter, to the roots of the Tree," it said, and at the words there came a faint glow of light and I realized that the shapes around me were enormous gnarled roots plunging down into the waters below, and it seemed to me, with my head pressed against one of them, that I could hear the water rushing upward to nourish the great tree above. The light grew and faintly I could now make out a shrouded figure sitting at the base of the great taproot of the Tree, and in front of her lay coiled an enormous snake, its head slightly raised at the center of the coil. The voice came again from the motionless woman, whose face remained shadowed, and I sensed a being ancient beyond thought. "Do not fear," she said; "move straight forward and stand beside the serpent and then be still. It is time for you to return to the world above and you will be taken there if you have the courage to make no move." Courage and faith poured into me at the indescribable sound of that voice. I moved steadily on the path over the waters and my feet touched the coiled serpent.

Once more the voice spoke. "Close your eyes now and be still." I obeyed and then I heard the hiss of the serpent as it uncoiled and I felt it wind itself around me and lift me swiftly off my feet—and still, such was the power of the voice, I did not fear. Up and up the snake carried me to the limit of his great strength, and then I felt myself seized by strong arms— they were hairy, like the arms of great apes. I was passed unresisting from one to another in the darkness, from root to root, and presently I fell into a kind of sleep, aware at first of movement and of the strength of the supporting arms and then of nothing.

I awoke in bright sunshine, lying on the grass under a tree so immense that looking up through the huge branches I could not see the top. "The Tree," I thought. In my mind's eye I saw again the great roots and the water thrusting up to the tiniest leaf on the topmost branches. I lay still for a long time, watching the many colored birds and the rustling leaves. When I finally sat up I was not surprised to see the friendly figure of the little man sitting nearby. He rose and bowed with his quiet courtesy and pointed to the three bags he had brought from the first stages of our journey. "Food for dogs, birds, and soil," he said, "and this for you." He took from his pocket an old parchment scroll, rolled and tied with a leather thong and handed it to me. Then he bowed again and moved unhurriedly away without looking back. I looked curiously at the scroll in my hand. "I will open it at home," I thought, "but first I will bury the skin of the crocodile woman and her beautiful hair, here under the Tree!" The soil was loose near the base of the trunk and it was not hard to make a hole with my hands. I laid the skin and hair in the ground and covered it, adding a sprinkling of peat moss from the bag—knowing somehow that the grass would grow thick and green on that simple grave, and that someday, perhaps, from the golden hair would spring golden flowers.

The next story, which I call "The Diamond Dentist," is a dream of the animus, the working-out of which has gone on for twenty-five years. I have chosen it among the hundreds in which that potent spirit in woman has appeared in both negative and positive form because in this dream he is exercising both sides of his role as mediator between the ego and the unconscious, both exploring and digging out the personal darkness, and bringing up the "great treasure" into consciousness. It came to me towards the end of my analysis in London, before I left for America. *The Diamond Dentist*

I dreamed that I had been to a dentist for many sessions and that he had now cleaned out all the decay hidden in my teeth, and each one awaited filling. The dentist told me that he was about to fill them with diamonds, but that this would take a very long time and would be exceedingly painful. I must tell him when I wished to begin. I was frightened of the pain and hoped I could wait a day or two, but I knew it couldn't be long delayed.

This dream is a wonderfully concise statement of the true function of the animus. First he probes with the sharp tools of discrimination, uncovering hidden motives and decayed attitudes, emptying the woman of her second-hand opinions and plots. Then he begins the long, painful work of cutting grooves into the "teeth," into her natural life, so that the new life of the Spirit may be firmly anchored within it. The diamond is a symbol of the indestructible thing, of the Self, of wholeness. The "teeth" are that part of us with which we bite into life, chew our experiences so that we may "digest," so to speak, every fact that we encounter. Thus we release and become aware both of the meaning and of the mystery as we "ruminate" (which means also to chew the cud) and all life becomes sacramental.

This dream is to me a fascinating image of the work *contra naturam* of individuation, of the coming to consciousness of man and woman. It is a work against nature, but not a separation from nature; the diamond is to be united to, embedded in, the natural tooth and will not be seen from outside; it will render digestible any food, any fact, however hard, and break down all our resistances to whatever life may bring us for our nourishment. The dream expresses the moment in the *Commedia* when, having passed through Hell, Dante is on the threshold of the mountain of Purgation.

It is not easy to return day by day to the diamond dentist and the pain of his work upon us. Often one is lured away by that legion of animus dentists who fill our teeth quickly and painlessly with base metal. Then there is the return and the temporary filling must be dug out again by the animus who both probes and creates within us.

A dream
of Jung

To the archetypes of the Way that have already appeared in the dreams I have quoted, I will here add one more of the Wise Old Man and one of the Wise Woman, both of which contain a hint of the way as Tao. The first is an example of the teaching of the masculine Logos from the unconscious, the second of feminine, instinctive wisdom.

To all of us who owe so much to his work, Jung himself is indeed a symbol of the archetypal sage. In this dream I knew that some terrible events had taken place in the world, and I saw all the people around me hurrying to the scenes of disaster. I was ashamed that I did not even know the details or what should be done. I thought I must listen to the radio and find out about it. Then Jung was there standing quietly beside me in old clothes, puffing his pipe, and I wondered why he had not gone with the rest. I said to him, "I ought to know all about it but I don't." He replied, "You have only to stay where you are and 'recollect' yourself over and over again. Your thoughts and feelings and trivial dreams move outward continually—just *let them go* and come back to that central place where your subtle body is fixed. Remember this every time you move out, as you inevitably and rightly must, and then your center will not go with the movement."

The strange phrase, rather alien to my conscious imagery, "where your subtle body is fixed," brings a strong association with that early "initiation" dream in which I found myself "rooted on the stone cross," though at the same time I could move away. I did not then call the rooted part of me "the subtle body," but so it truly was.* In the unconscious these images do not die, however fickle the conscious attention, and they are brought back to our awareness by the grace of God when we are in greatest need.

The Wise Woman dream

The Wise Woman dream came in 1972, when I dreamed that I had been with someone who had been a great help to me, but now I was in a large public building attending to some business or other. As I was about to leave, an acquaintance said to me, speaking of the person who had been so helpful, "She will always be there at need." I emerged from the building at the top of a long flight of stone steps and saw "her" sitting in the raised driving seat of a horse-drawn wagon, holding whip and rein and waiting for me on the road. Just then a policeman went up to her and told her to move on. She called a greeting to me merrily, saying, "That's life—moving on," and with a shake of the reins she drove off. I was puzzled about it all, wondering why she had waited for me, since I surely had no need of her then, and wondering why she hadn't seemed in the least concerned about leaving me behind. Then suddenly I remembered that my child was playing outside the building and I had temporarily forgotten that

---

* The word subtle comes from the Latin *subtile*, "thin, fine," and has the now obsolete meaning "rarefied, tenuous, unsubstantial."

she, being so young, might have been in trouble without someone to keep an eye on her. Then in the dream a feeling of great happiness and freedom came over me. Yes, life moves on—but in the Tao it is a movement of the utmost precision and beauty as in a dance: the Child, the Law, the "business" of this world to which the ego attends, the Horse, the four-wheeled chariot which is so often a symbol of the incarnation, and the Wise Woman holding the reins, here or not here, fulfilling the pattern of the dance in the present moment.

WATER AND
STONE

In his book called *C. G. Jung and Herman Hesse,* Miguel Serrano has told of a dream that came to him in October 1961, about three months after the death of Jung. In the dream he was walking with Jung, who was in the dream a very old man. Jung spoke and said, "I have now lived my life and the time has come for me to die." The dreamer turned to him and asked, "What is death?" And he answered, "Death is Li and Tata," which he translated as "Water and Stone," and went on, "I have spent eighty years trying to discover what was behind water, and all that time I was in it. I have now passed through it, and in the end I have come out to the place where the horses run."

I do not know when I have been more deeply moved than on reading this dream. With astounded disbelief I went on to read that Serrano himself felt great desolation after it and wrote, "I was afraid that Jung had returned from death to tell me that he had discovered nothing, and that there was nothing." I do not know of course what Serrano's associations were with horses, but a dream of that nature goes far beyond the personal unconscious, and whoever hears it may be awakened by its images in his or her own depths. Serrano himself says that, when he later visited Jung's house in Kusnacht, his experience was such that he thought perhaps he had misinterpreted the dream.

The place where the horses run

"The place where the horses run." What is it about a running horse that is so exciting? The image does not speak to me of wild horses; rather, I see that marvelous image in *The Lord of the Rings* of the great grey horse

Shadowfax, running with glorious swiftness over the plains to meet Gandalf, knowing that he has been called, that he is needed, running to carry the man who is his friend wherever that friend may choose to go. For, as Gandalf affirmed, no man could tame Shadowfax or order him to this or that like a slave. He was a willing servant to the man who loved and respected him, a man who spoke the language of the beasts like Solomon the wise.

Shadowfax would accept no bit or bridle. He responded to the word and to the heart of Gandalf the wizard, the wise man who had passed through the deepest places of the unconscious, through the waters of death, and had come to the heart of stone (the opposite of the stony heart). He had emerged reborn from the darkness of Moria and had come to the place where the horses run, and there he had found Shadowfax, "the horse of the White Rider."

> Even as the old wizard spoke, the great horse came striding up the slope towards them; his coat was glistening and his mane flowing in the wind of his speed. As soon as Shadowfax saw Gandalf, he checked his pace and whinnied loudly; then trotting gently forward he stooped his proud head and nuzzled his great nostrils against the old man's neck.
>
> Gandalf caressed him. "It is a long way from Rivendell, my friend," he said; "but you are wise and swift and come at need. Far let us ride now together, and part not in this world again!"
>
> J. R. R. TOLKIEN
> *The Two Towers*, p. 108

The bond between a man and his horse is a moving thing in any context, but in the inner world it is the most powerful and beautiful symbol imaginable of the union of the conscious spirit of man with the natural wisdom of the instincts. The man who has passed through the death of water and stone is still carried by the wisdom of the senses, with which he is now in perfect harmony.

To me, what Jung tells us in Serrano's dream is that the death of the body does not mean a transmutation into a purely spiritual existence. He is saying the same thing as was affirmed in such different language by the church in the dogma of the Assumption of the body of Our Lady, who is the archetype of matter, of all humanity: that is, that the "body" lives beyond death. Thus the flesh and the animal world are also redeemed, brought into wholeness through the coming to consciousness of the human individual soul. Shadowfax sailed with Gandalf from the Grey Havens into the Beyond. This may seem a far cry from the language of the dogma, but the imagery speaks to many of us today the same truth.

"The land of the running horses," said Sophocles, writing of Athens in *Oedipus at Colonus.* "Last and grandest praise I sing to Athens, nurse of men. . . . Land from which fine horses spring, land where foals are beautiful! Land of the sea and seafarer. . . ." Athens—symbol to us of so great a leap in consciousness from the darkness of the ancient world that it carries more than a hint of that greater leap which may come to an individual at his death. To that land, to a stone in a holy place, Oedipus came to die after his long, innocent suffering, beloved of the gods because he had carried individually the guilt of man's real sin, which is the refusal of consciousness. Antigone, his daughter, said to him, "Rest on this rough stone. It was a long road for an old man to travel." And the Chorus sang:

> *The land of running horses, fair*
> *Colonus takes a guest;*
> *He shall not seek another home,*
> *For this, in all the earth and air,*
> *Is most secure and loveliest.*
>
> *The crocus like a little sun*
> *Blooms with its yellow ray;*
> *The river's fountains are awake . . .*
> *And here the choiring Muses come,*
> *And the divinity of love*
> *With gold reins in her hand.*

Here, Oedipus, who had come to the land of running horses, died. No man but the King knew how or what became of his body—and his blessing on the land remained forever.

Jung's own last dream before his death was that he saw a huge spherical stone and at the foot of the stone were engraved the words, "And this shall be a sign unto you of Wholeness and Oneness." His life was complete and he passed through the water to that which is beyond.

In alchemy, the *lapis,* the stone, and "our water," the *aqua permanens,* are closely related and sometimes even synonymous. The lapis emerges from the water and yet is also the water itself. Jung quotes from the *Turba Philosophorum* (*Psychology and Alchemy,* p. 223 of the London edition, note 7): "The permanent water out of which water our precious stone is generated," and again, "That stone is water of a living fountain." The water and the stone are both referred to as the beginning and the goal. The absolute hardness of stone and the absolute fluidity of water are one thing—unconsciously, in the chaos of the beginning; fully known in the harmony of the end. The Stone which "the builders rejected" and the aqua permanens which is "sold publicly for a very small price," since it is unrecognized by the "merchants" (*Turba Philosophorum*)—both are obviously symbols of the Christ within. (Jung devoted a whole chapter to the lapis-Christus parallel in *Psychology and Alchemy*).

The imagery of Water and Stone in my own life has been, as must be obvious from what I have written, of paramount importance. Particularly I have quoted many dreams of the Stone—from the milestone of my childhood to the great crystal of dark and light. Moreover, as far back as I can remember I have felt a kind of ecstasy whenever I have looked into very clear water. I have been more deeply moved by it than by any other kind of natural beauty. Creation began with water, both externally with the ocean, the origin of all living things, and interiorly, as in the Biblical myth, with God brooding over the darkness "upon the face of the deep" and saying "Let there be light." How ludicrous it was for our forebears to see science and religion as mutually exclusive! They are one truth, the long process in time towards the evolution of conscious beings, and the identical inner journey of the individual soul from the infancy of *identity* with nature to the full consciousness of *unity* with nature; and, greatest mystery of all, the coming of God to consciousness of Himself through his Creation, culminating in the Incarnation and the *Hierosgamos*.

During his long search for that which was behind and beyond the water of the unconscious, "all the time I was in it," said Jung of himself in Serrano's dream. While we are still here in the dimension of time we must always be "in it." Nevertheless there may come to us by Grace an image of the essential nature of the water of death through which we must finally pass. It came to me first in a dream many years ago in Los Angeles, and again in a dream-vision not long before (I believe) my reading of Serrano's book. In both dreams the water was surrounded by stone, by great bare rocks, and the essential quality I spoke of was its unearthly clarity—a clearness far beyond that of the purest water we know with our physical eyes. It is not strange that this dream had a particular power which seemed to reach forward and backward over my life.

The dream of the hills of Moab

I stood in the dream by the roadside high in the hills of Moab and looked out northward over the valley to the bare, rolling country beyond. That view is surely one of the most lovely in the world. Down in the valley is the line of green, the oleanders along the bed of the brook, Jabbok, the place where Jacob wrestled with the angel under the stars until the dawn broke. In the dream I looked beyond the stream and then I saw something that wiped everything else from my mind. I saw—it was many miles away and yet distinct to my eyes as though it were immediately before me—a circle of rocks rising out of a sand-colored desert, and enclosed within this circle was a small lake of water so incredibly clear, so completely transparent that I wondered how I knew that it was water at all. Yet I did know it without any question. Every stone, every grain of sand under the deep water was distinct and clear to my eyes. Such vision is not possible, I thought, even in this country where the light is so clear that twenty miles can seem like one. Yet it was so, and the image did not fade. There was no vegetation at all in the lake, no sign of any life—only water and stone; the white and golden sand seemed to give out light to meet the sunlight. My whole being was gathered into an intense ecstatic awareness of the purity of that invisible water. A great longing seized me and I knew that I must set out and journey to that water however long and difficult the way. I moved to descend a narrow path into the valley but at that moment I heard a movement behind me. An Arab boy stood there and with him was a small hill donkey, surefooted, sturdy. "You cannot go alone," the boy said; "the donkey knows the way." I thanked him, paid for the donkey and without another word, with my hand on the animal's back, set off down the path. The pool was out of sight now. I must pass the rocks before I would see it again.

This dream came in Los Angeles twenty years after I left the Middle East, but that road beyond Jordan, that view, is associated strongly with the time of my emergence from the shadow of death in Jerusalem, when Timmy and I spent three wonderful months in Amman across the Jordan during my convalescence. That is what I mean by the dream reaching backward into my past because I see the place of it so vividly and feel its relevance to that crucial time, so that it takes a slight effort of consciousness to place it in the fifties, around the time of the car accident, when I was emerging from another brush with death.

Recently von Franz, answering a question when at Notre Dame, said that our fear of death comes from our separation from our instincts, from the animal, and that many people approaching death with conscious acceptance dream that an animal—a dog or horse—is leading them through a door into the unknown. Death dreams, she said, do not speak of an end, of oblivion, but always seem to assume continued life in harmony with the instincts. My dream donkey was surely a hint of this.

In Palestine in 1937 I had been unconscious of the inner implications of my experience. In Los Angeles I was indeed aware of the meaning of the inner journey towards death, and then in 1967 the dream reached forward and brought to me another image of that indescribable water which is clearly the water of death, water that springs up into eternal life, and just as certainly the aqua permanens of the alchemists. "It is repeatedly stressed in the literature that the much-sought-after aqua permanens would be revealed in a dream." (Jung, *Psychology and Alchemy*, p. 252.)

> *When I have gazed into a tidal pool*
> *And seen the texture exquisite of stone,*
> *Of life and plant, deep in the lucid cool,*
> *It seemed no greater wonder could be known.*
> *Yet there's a cleanness I have known in dreams –*
> *In those rare dreams that are like blessed wine—*
> *A pure transparency wherein it seems*
> *Is traced the form of the Creator's line.*
> *Distinct and clear appears each man and thing,*
> *And every grain of sand, as though I see*
> *Through unseen water; and the angels sing*
> *An unheard tone from Heaven's melody.*
>
> *So wonder grows to crystal-cut lucidity*
> *Defining the great pattern of eternity.*

My father, Kenneth Reinold, died in 1905 at the age of twenty-nine. I was eight months old.

My mother was a person of such integrity and courage that her suffering forged in her the real self-lessness of mature love . . .

*. . . and
therefore,
when I had
finally
broken the
crippling
unconscious
identification
and was in
search of
my own
identity, I
was able to
recognize
that her gift
of love to me
had been an
inestimable
strength.*

I could never have risen to a first-class degree at Oxford, for which original thought is a necessity, though I easily achieved a good second.

California, 1950s

The first months passed in Jerusalem with the sense of the rising of new life . . .

*I began to
read
everything
of Jung's
that I
could lay
hands on.
I read and
read far
into the
nights,
absorbed
as I had
rarely
been since
I read ad-
venture
stories in
childhood.
. . . it was
as though
my whole
being
recognized
and
responded
to his
words.*

I have written a real letter to Laurens van der Post with special gratitude for The Heart of the Hunter.

Yesterday came a real "shock" in the form of a letter from the President of St. Mary's College, asking me to deliver the Commencement address to the class of 1981 in May, and offering me an honorary degree, no less!

Father Bede Griffiths stayed overnight with us and gave with great generosity of his time and energy . . . I am sure that none of those who heard him will forget the impact of his spirit and his message to us.

PART TWO

THE JOURNALS
1976–1994

EDITOR'S NOTE

WHEN HELEN LUKE ASKED ME whether, after her death, I would be willing to read through her journals, selecting for publication anything I found of possible interest or help to others, I of course said I'd be glad to. "There may well be nothing there of interest," she said. Never having seen Helen writing in her journals, knowing how very full her life was, how much energy and time went into her published writings, her correspondence, and her therapeutic hours—and knowing as well that she was in her seventies when she began her journal writing—I envisioned a small collection of journals, a dozen or so, perhaps, containing the occasional paragraph I might mark for possible publication. Instead, what I found after she died was a set of fifty-four volumes—more than ten thousand pages of tiny script, much of it written in the dead of night, and most of it of considerable interest. Deciphering, selecting, typing, and editing the culled material has been a significant part of my life since Helen's death—and the fact that Helen asked me on three separate occasions whether I would undertake this task, each time listening carefully for my answer, makes me think that she knew exactly what she was asking. What she could not have anticipated, of course, was the immense pleasure the work has afforded me.

It is hard to overstate the seriousness with which Helen approached her work in her journals. The entries can be described as conversations with herself in which she explored her dreams, reflected on images and events in her inner and outer worlds, and worked out thoughts that made their way later into essays and books. When each journal was filled, Helen carefully annotated it, marking in the margins each dream, each "story," each "reflection"; she then indexed the volume. The journal entries make clear that she used the indexes extensively for locating, for example, dreams from years earlier that seemed to her linked to a more recent dream or that she now, years later, understood more fully. Every journal is thus annotated and indexed, including the final fifty-fourth volume, which takes her through her eighty-ninth year.

The outer events of Helen's later years, the twenty-three years covered by her "Diary of Vowels," have remarkably little impact on her Diary. There are mentions of letters from publishers; there are early attempts to work out ideas that appear in polished form in published essays; there are glancing references to trips to England or to Stratford, Ontario; and there is an account of her amazement at receiving a letter from the president of St. Mary's College asking her to accept an honorary doctorate from the college. But the pressures and demands of her final twenty-three years—the publication, for example, of seven books (*Woman: Earth and Spirit,* 1981; *The Inner Story,* 1982; *Old Age,* 1987; *The Voice Within,* 1988; *Dark Wood to White Rose,* illustrated edition, 1989; *Kaleidoscope,* 1992; and *The Way of Woman,* 1995, published posthumously); daily therapeutic hours; an unceasing flow of correspondence, interviews, audio- and video-taping—these are scarcely mentioned in the Diary. References to the hazards of the aging process—failing eyesight, painful teeth and gums, side effects of blood-pressure medications—are recurrent, but only as these difficulties affect the inner work.

Charles Taylor's insightful introduction to this volume provides the needed context for the work Helen pursued in the Diary. I will here add only that my principle of selection was to try to follow Helen's lead: that is, in selecting dreams and images, I chose those that she herself returned to for further thought and expansion. The patterns that she discovered in her inner life usually began with a dream, continued with her work over a period of days or weeks with that dream, then sometimes picked up years later as that dream came back into her consciousness in connection with a later dream or image. I looked with careful attention at each paragraph she herself marked as a "reflection." I omitted, with regret, most of her "story-work," her development of images in active imagination. This work is so extensive and so individual that, on the one hand, it defies condensation and, on the other, it is of less general interest than the dream work. A few of the images from her active imagination—Simon the Praise-singer, for example—so filled her inner life that they also appear in her reflections on dreams and in her general thinking about her own individuation—but most of her dream-work can be understood apart from the story-work. I also omitted her more extensive encounters with the *I Ching,* fascinating to those familiar with this Chinese *Book of Changes,* but too technical for general interest.

I would like here to thank those who have been especially supportive during the selection and editing of the Diary entries: Alison Day, Penny Gill, Patricia Finley, and Charles Taylor; the entire Apple Farm Community, especially Don Raiche, Dee Jochen, and the late Charlotte Smith; and, above all, Jane Bishop, who has been by my side throughout the process.

BARBARA A. MOWAT

A DIARY OF VOWELS

IN AUGUST 1976 I had a dream in which I was told by a voice that it was time for me to become a diarist of vowels. This puzzled me until I realized that the vowels of language are the sounds that are not interrupted by consonants. They are the pure sounds of the breath—"the central sound of a syllable," as the *American Heritage Dictionary* defines *vowel*. The word is derived from the Latin "vox"—the voice itself. The consonants are the sounds that accompany, "sound with," the vowels. Therefore I knew that my diary should contain the "central sounds" of life—the meanings, the unblocked sounds from the unconscious as they came to me day by day. The dream involved my being given a new "seat" or place.

I began this diary on September 8, 1976. It is perhaps significant that I had finished the story of my life up to age seventy, begun in 1974, not long before beginning the diary, and that ever since then that story has been more and more an inner one, a matter of vowels with fewer consonants.*

* *Editor's note:* Helen wrote this short "Prelude" on January 23, 1986.

1976

SEPTEMBER 8

It is the birthday of "Our Lady"—a seldom-heard title nowadays, but how beautiful a title it is: the "lady," the "kneader of dough" in the old English derivation of the word. I am reminded of the Bread Kneader of my dream some years ago, in whose service I was, and I am greatly heartened to think that this, my new venture, is beginning on this day of the birth of Mary, the incarnation of Sophia, the woman who is also "lady," kneading the bread of earth until it is united with the bread of heaven.

I remember the lesson from the Mass of this day, which is always so exciting to me:

> I was set up from eternity, and of old, before the earth was made—when he prepared the heavens I was there—when he balanced the foundations of the earth, I was with him, playing before him at all times, playing in the world, and my delight is to be with the sons of men. Blessed is the man that heareth me and that watcheth daily at my gates and waiteth at the posts of my doors. He that shall find me shall find life.

Could there be a more lovely dedication for a diary?—especially a woman's diary: To watch daily at her gates, the gates of the woman who plays from all eternity and is also—perhaps precisely because of this—the kneader of the bread that feeds us all.

In putting down personal thoughts, feelings, sensations, intuitions, I hope to discriminate, to see and feel objectively the daily story in my life. It is this objectivity, this impersonal relationship to the personal that constitutes individuation, "that ruthlessly important task," as Jung said towards the end of his life. "Objective cognition lies hidden behind the attraction of emotional relationship. It seems to be the central secret. Only through objective cognition is real *coniunctio* possible." (*Memories, Dreams, Reflections*)

Mary, the Lady, is blessed in the depths of every individual man or woman—and we are blessed by every crumb of the bread of our lives as if she had kneaded it—the bread of *facts*, evil as well as good, that nourish our living and our dying.

The thought of writing things that I shall not share gives a great freedom—though I realize, even now as I write, how always I have a care to a hypothetical reader. This persistent eye to an audience is initially troubling; but on deeper looking I am as sure as it is possible to be that this is not just a vanity of the ego—that of course one must write for "the other." Life is a drama and no drama is complete without the participation of an audience. To write without a sense of a listener, a reader, would be sterile indeed, even if the listener is "the companion" in oneself. This is quite a different thing from the hubris of writing for the edification of others, which can kill all delight, all play. I see this diary as a means to awareness of the "ruthless task" of individuation in the patterns of my privacy.

I have recently been more aware, I believe, of the life in things, not only in things of beauty but in the ordinary tools of everyday. Jung used to greet his very saucepans in the mornings at Bollingen! I begin to understand this. In my life-long impatience, how much I have missed. Last night, washing the dishes, I really looked at my iron frying pan in the dishwater. The light made visible for a moment a tiny rainbow—a light through water revealing all the colors of life. It is so easy to miss the tiny symbols. Finding them is something quite different from the business of trying to hatch up big symbolic experiences. It is *recognition*, not *pursuit*, of meaning—recognition of the sacramental, of the intersection of the two worlds, breaking through unsought because one is *attending*.

∾

SEPTEMBER II

What is the "vowel" for this day? I woke tired, reluctant. An "hour" of counseling in the morning, another in the afternoon. Both talks alive and real, but the busyness of the world, of so many fine people doing so many fine, good things sounded a frightening note. Both are women who seek feminine values but drown them in "good works," "conferences," "workshops," projects of all kinds—so excellent each one, but producing sheer exhaustion.

1976

Simone Weil said that real education is the awakening and training of the faculty of *attention,* ultimately so that we may attend to the voice of the living God. So many words, so much and always more to be packed into each week, and the attention is fragmented so that nothing can be heard but the "consonants." Even here in our quiet life, that noisy emptiness invades—and I then affirm things with talk and with arbitrary opinions springing from the demand for prestige. Well, the truth, however humiliating, must be welcomed.

Then a reference to *Hamlet* at sherry-time brought the vowel of the day. I came home and refreshed my memory of the whole passage which had sprung into my mind. Hamlet says to Horatio:

> *for thou hast been*
> *As one in suffering all that suffers nothing—*
> *A man that Fortune's buffets and rewards*
> *Hast ta'en with equal thanks: and blest are those*
> *Whose blood and judgment are so well commingled*
> *That they are not a pipe for Fortune's finger*
> *To sound what stop she please. Give me that man*
> *That is not passion's slave and I will wear him*
> *In my heart's core—ay, in my heart of heart*
> *As I do thee.*

Thus Hamlet in the very center of his tragedy. At the end, his words are again to Horatio, the man who dwelt in his heart of hearts: "tell my story." The man who was not passion's slave, alive in Shakespeare, told it, and one of the greatest stories of the world was born of Hamlet's defeat. The commingling of blood and judgment, the final acceptance of "Fortune's buffets and rewards," is brought nearer to countless individuals who *attend* to his story.

Colin Fletcher, in *The Man Who Walked Through Time*, has written about "vowels and consonants" as I perceive their symbolism. The consonants in his life were the hard physical facts of his solitary journey through the Grand Canyon, the body's struggle with the immediate reality; the vowels were those moments of breakthrough to the meaning, to the "sound," the rhythm, of life and time—his individual pattern at one with the pattern of the whole. At first these breakthroughs were single moments coming at the unexpected sight of some simple thing: "The world has crystallized into vivid focus. And you respond. You hold your breath or fall into a reverie or spring to your feet, according to the day or the mood. . . . [S]tanding there on the red rock terrace, still watching the lizard, I was knife-edge alive. It did not last of course. They cannot last, these climax moments . . . you sink back from your peak of awareness. . . ." But he goes on to say that he remained more aware of "the simple things that the trivia had been smothering." He describes how from these magic moments, strung out at first as on a chain, there came at last after long solitude and silence, and for the time being, a continuous sense of being one with the rhythm of all life and all time, of being inside as well as outside the life of everything he saw—animals, insects, the living rocks, the wind, the river; and finally, most difficult of all, he could feel even the craziness of modern man as part of the unbroken pattern of eternity.

I remember always with wonder and gratitude that my three most intense moments of such awareness all came upon me in places which one would imagine to be the very last to inspire such a thing. The first was at midnight in one of the dreariest parts of London watching the flashing of traffic lights in the empty street as I waited for a bus. I was going through a time in my life of great personal suffering. The second was in Los Angeles in a large supermarket; the third only a few weeks ago, also in a market, triggered by a smile from a stranger. The last was the most human, so to speak, of the three. I walked around the market feeling "inside" the lives of every person I looked at—a sense of the absolute rightness of each in

1976

the pattern. One cannot really describe these things—only hint. The first time in Notting Hill brought a sense of indissoluble rootedness in the earth itself and its rhythms. How strange, with the pavement under my feet and the ugly buildings around. In L.A. it was more an ecstasy of joy in every smallest object. The last was a more explicit experience of "co-inherence," of man the microcosm.

SEPTEMBER 29   ∽

From Margot Fonteyn's autobiography (medicine for my recent regressions!): "The one important thing is the difference between taking one's work seriously and taking oneself seriously. The first is imperative, the second disastrous." She means the ego, of course. That is indeed a "vowel" for today.

She says another delightful thing. She is writing of her first dancing teacher and remarks that "Miss B." had "the ideal personality for teaching infants, always cheerful and encouraging and completely absorbed in what we were doing. Her degree of concentration held ours, so she rarely had inattentive pupils." This is a marvelous description, not only of the essential for a teacher of infants, but for teachers of all kinds of pupils of any age. It was said of Charles Williams that, when he lectured, his objective concentration and love of his subject directed the eyes of all his listeners, not towards himself, but onto the object of his concentration. From teachers in kindergarten to the most learned professors, this quality alone compels *attention*.

OCTOBER 14   ∽

The Jung letters we at the Farm have been reading make very clear the function of groups as a place for learning human community and exchange, *not* an alchemistic crucible, for consciousness is always lower in a group. The social experience is an essential on the Way, but is not the *means* of transformation.

∞

It has become plain that I must lower my eyes to the very small and to remember that the whole is never reached by overlooking anything. I feel frightened. A lifetime of habitual reactions stands like a dark block in my way, or like invisible hands holding me. Always I have wanted to get the unpleasant or so-called "unimportant" things over in order to arrive at a goal.

I am certain of one truth: as long as an individual is alive, he or she *works*. There can be no letting up until death comes, if the personality is not to be fragmented but brought at last to the whole circle of the individual life. I have had dreams recently of a *small* work horse replacing a race horse—of *minute* white doves with brown wings on an old woman's arm—of my small son's clear-eyed vision.

∞

I dreamed this morning of pressure on me to concern myself with Sirius, the great shining dog star. When I refused this, there came the joy of a new vision of the Pleiades—not only the six visible "daughters of Atlas" but also the countless individual stars in the constellation not seen with the outer eye. Perhaps my concern passes from Orion and his hound to the women he pursued and who were rescued by the god Zeus and transformed into stars. Sirius and the Pleiades were the most numinous stars to me in my early childhood. I remember them vividly from that time, whereas many others remained just names my grandmother told me. Aldebaran, Arcturus, Vega, Capella—and Sirius, most lovely of all. Now, from Orion the hunter and his shining dog star to the Pleiades, the pursued and hounded feminine.

This dream came after a talk with Else and Jane about changes. The dream suggests that I am to be no longer in the forefront, the shining "star" of Apple Farm. Retirement means eclipse of the easily seen light, but at the same time the dawning of the vision of "suns" so remote that they are not seen and admired by the many. Sirius is so bright not because he is in himself bigger and brighter than all the others but because he is so much nearer to us than they.

Later, on the day I wrote the above, came the letter from Richard Payne of Paulist Press. He suggested that I write a book giving examples of my experience of women—their conflicts, their choices, the way to the discovery of the inner life for them, their latent creativity of the Spirit. I asked the *I Ching,* "Is this for me?" and the answer was Sign 46, "Pushing Upward"—the hexagram of the direct rise from the roots, associated with effort. "Pushing upward has supreme success. One must see the great man. Fear not. Departure toward the south / Brings good fortune" (south = work). "The superior man / Heaps up *small things* / In order to achieve something high and great" (emphasis mine). "Wood grows up from the earth without haste and without rest, bending around obstacles." The fifth line changes: "Pushing upward by steps . . . skip no stages . . . calm steadiness, overleaping nothing."

The hexagram changes to 48, "The Well." "The town may be changed / But the well cannot be changed. . . . They come and go and draw from the well." "If . . . the rope does not go all the way or the jug breaks, misfortune." "The inexhaustible wellspring of the divine in man's nature." Image: "The superior man encourages the people at their work."

I am giving up much work; that now belongs with Else and Jane at the Farm. The outside work that comes to me independently is my business, but always springs from and returns to that which nourishes and is nourished by the Farm.

The insistence of the *I Ching* on "the small" fits with the Pleiades dream, and also, it occurs to me, with that dream some months ago of seeds not falling near my house, as expected, but being shot out over the pasture to grow and bear fruit unseen at a distance.

Suddenly an intuition of what it is to live one's fate consciously, with karma seen as a simultaneous living of the opposites—the self-disgust and torment to be welcomed as the right and joyful payment for the ego's hubris, and with the only release coming through sacrifice—the sacrifice of attachment to results. As Jung said in a letter, "if the vision on the road to Damascus had not been given to Paul he would have had to go on persecuting the Christians." If we cannot stop persecuting—beating ourselves for what we conceive to be sins within us—then we must go on in complete acceptance of our powerlessness. Sooner or later the moment of sacrifice may come.

These are new and nebulous thoughts for "the book." It is extraordinary how different I feel whenever all the nonsense about merit, usefulness, etc. is swept away, and the agonizing effort and joy of doing my best to express these nebulous things takes over.

Persecution is nine times out of ten a horribly evil projection—but the tenth time, because of *who* does it, it can be the way to the "vision." Of course it is no less evil, but because of the individual's relationship to that evil in himself, it is a kind of devotion to his present vision of Truth. So the things that I "persecute" in myself and try so hard to eradicate are often the elements that through hating I may come to value and, once accepted, they are purged and become salvation. Through the attempt to eliminate something, one gets very close to it. One who hates God is often nearer to enlightenment than the so-called lover of God, who so easily forgets him. Thus say the Indian sages; and Charles Williams: "Unless devotion is given to that which must prove false in the end, that which is true in the end cannot enter." The necessary proviso, of course, is that one always have the fundamental humility to accept the falseness when it is seen. It is the basic humility that redeems in the final test.

✑

NOVEMBER 19

A dream last night confirms the revolution, the big change in my life, the dream ending with an image of my holding a shining copper bowl and within it a precious liquid—as if a wine had matured through the years, and I must carry it as an offering with care, attention and humility. This was my task and none other.

∞

A dream of a newly born child—naming her, caring for her—no longer involved in war.

1976

∞

On the night of the 21st I dreamed of an old man who died of a "broken" heart—and I saw his heart literally break open into four crescents, as though it were a melon or a pomegranate, the segments still joined at the bottom. His wisdom and compassion had become so great that they literally "blew" his heart (see *Antony and Cleopatra*) and broke it open so that the seeds could fall out onto the ground. There was a prologue and an epilogue to this dream. It began with a very poor family—father, mother, and children. They were not peasants, but intelligent, cultivated. There was no furniture in their room except for a large mattress on which the whole family slept. It was very clean and the food was meager vegetables. There was a sense of exchange of services between me and them—giving each other short "lifts" (American "rides") along the way. When I wrote above of the old man, it was this man, who was the father, whom I then saw in his old age.

Finally, in a kind of epilogue, I was listening to someone many years, perhaps centuries, after the old man's death, who was telling me how, whenever he was in conflict or lost heart, he loved to read the story of that old man's life and death. Then, as I woke, I heard the words, "There is no more beautiful, rewarding thing than the study of 'suburban' lives and their relatedness as they press towards the Center (of the city)." *Suburban* here would mean the periphery of the city—and also the image of the most humdrum, banal collective life.

This image reminds me of the dream many years ago about Willa and her life story, of her misery and her sense of failure, and of the quarter turn in the dream which revealed the beauty, the mandala with mother and child. This time the four quarters release the white seeds of the melon, the black seeds of the pomegranate. How unimportant the "messes," the failures, always provided that in the heart lies the intensity of devotion, pressing towards the Center.

On the day after this dream, the writing began to flow. It is the most agonizing thing to start. After that, though it may end up quite changed, one has hold of a thread and can follow it.

1977

JANUARY 1

OUR FOURTEENTH YEAR AT THE FARM

The new writing is sparking inside, though the bringing to birth is another matter. I began the "spirit" chapter again. *Mysterium Coniunctionis* is a big help.

JANUARY 6

Yesterday after much rewriting and doubt I gave Charlotte the first five pages to type. Last night I was almost sure I'd have to give up on it—too difficult for me altogether. Then I woke at 3:00 A.M. with ideas popping. With all the recent dreams I cannot doubt that it is right to persevere. As long as I don't think about *publication,* I won't be discouraged. Many of my questions have nothing to do with the *work*—only with publication, which will or will not come—*no matter!* "Passing disturbance, no soul!" Jung heard that marvelous heart-lifting phrase when in Ceylon two vehicles collided and the owners bowed to each other and said it—instead of the familiar Western cursing. Often there can be the same nuance in our inelegant "so what?" when it is spoken from the heart.

FEBRUARY 2

I came on the following in *Answer to Job* this morning: "All opposites are of God, therefore man must bend to this burden; and in so doing he finds that God in his 'oppositeness' has taken possession of him, incarnated himself in him. He becomes a vessel filled with divine conflict."

I somehow *recognize this*—begin to feel it. Perhaps that is why my ups and downs seem no longer a matter of exultation and depression, but something much more powerful. Even when my personal emotions are involved, a part of me remains detached (in dreams as well as waking). To be a vessel filled with the divine conflict of opposites—what a tremendous thought

1977

that is, lifting one out of petty rights and wrongs, and challenging one to add that grain of salt, the tiny individual effort towards awareness.

FEBRUARY 3

"The continuing incarnation"—the coming of the Holy Spirit to everyone who can receive him—is only possible after the departure of Christ who was the unique personal incarnation of God in history, conceived as a symbol of the perfect and the sinless. "It is expedient for you that I go away." Without that departure, the spirit could not come and the ordinary sinful man or woman could not "conceive" and in due time give birth to the holy child within. This is the "second coming." When "Mary" is taken in the flesh into Heaven, ordinary human beings may become the "bride" in the holy marriage—not just the "sinless" Mary image and the collective church. What an extraordinarily exciting thing! The Paraclete is the spirit of truth. It is that which forces the individual to discriminate his or her unique meaning—the truth of his or her whole life, good and bad, regardless of any "opinion" and at any cost.

MARCH 7

I have been sick and feeling miserable but I have had a powerful dream which remains with me. I dreamed that at last the two opposites—male and female—had been separated so that they could freely unite, because I had finally been able to uncover and remove the creature that had been constantly undermining the process. It was the skeleton of a large crab-like creature, its bones picked clean. At first I cast it aside, thinking it was finished with, but a voice spoke to me saying, "That is dangerous. It could easily start to regain strength and creep back unseen." I knew somehow that the name of the creature was "Thersites." (Thersites is the crude, crabby man of the ranks who, in the *Iliad,* is continually jeering at and undermining the actions of the heroes Agamemnon and Achilles. There is in fact truth in his accusations against them and they might have done well to listen to him, but instead they wholly reject him, and Achilles finally kills him in a rage.)

In my dream I at once picked up the crab-like skeleton with my left hand—it seemed more like an enormous crab shell now—and I felt one of the huge claws move, groping for my hand, but I held it by the claw and thought I must bury it. But the ground, I knew, was too hard and I thought I would take it far off from my home into the pasture and leave it; but I was not satisfied, thinking it could still regain strength and crawl back. The thought came that I must get a large stone to put on top of it, hold it down, crush it. How to find one big enough, then how to lift it without help?

The dream continued with a fire ritual and an offering. Half waking, there was some active imagination merging again into dream in which the crab shell was finally crushed with the help of a man who lifted the large stone in my garden. The dream ended in a surge of relief as I stood and addressed the crab creature: "You are bone meal," I said, bone meal to nourish the bulbs hidden in the earth beside the stone.

✍

MARCH 9

The dream of March 7 was an intense experience of the opposites: Achilles and Thersites, the hero attitude and the crabbiness, superior and inferior, ego power and ego-denial, generosity and meanness.

I have been forced recently to face the apologetic shadow which reveals my hidden arrogance. The dream shows the possibility of standing the tension—keeping the crab in sight, turning it to nourishment of the quiet growth of new life from the earth—with the help of the man who was in the dream an "accountant," the keeper of the balance sheet, who can lift the stone when I appeal to him and give me the opportunity to let go of the hidden negative mother feelings and offer them to the grinding action of the lapis, transforming them to nourishing "meal."

It is time to get back to work. I am thrown again by lack of faith in the value of what I am writing. What do I know about these things? So again I must return to simple awareness that this is not of any importance. It is my struggle with the "crab" thing, my search for the reconciling symbol—the stone. Suddenly the link with my childhood dream of the milestone on which I sat and the cold negative mother figure at the window hits me. The milestone was the first of so many stones. Always the complete objectivity of the stone has supported and led me. In this dream once more it alone can transform the cold, rejecting, undermining Cancer mother-thing into nourishment.

MAY 5

&

Yesterday I read an article about meditation techniques, Eastern and Western, and, as usual, I fell into guilt about my own "exercises." A dream last night that I am waiting in line. Each person is receiving a small piece of bread onto which a man like R. J. (with whom I associate meditation techniques singularly unconnected with his life) is putting a dab of mustard for each recipient. All very solemn! Then the mustard, not being properly mixed, begins to run over onto the table. I burst out into friendly laughter and step out of the line saying, "Don't worry, I'll mop it up for you with the bread and eat it!" Then he laughs too, as do the others—all the pompous solemnity gone!

This is the sort of response from the unconscious that is apt to come when I beat myself for not adopting this or that technique for arriving at enlightenment. . . . That way is not for me, but Jung's way of daily attention to images.

1978

JANUARY 21

I have been reading John Dunne's *Reasons of the Heart,* of which he has sent me a proof copy. He is a rare spirit and the growing impact of his "way" shows a hunger for the inner wisdom of the heart.

I have come to the part about being loved and understood by God. Most talk of God's love for us leaves me cold—even slightly repelled—because of the way the words are used to express a concept of a god resembling an all-powerful man and the sentimentality that has gathered around this image. John restores the words to their real meaning. It is only when we come to total and unconditional "love" of our own darkness that

we can know God incarnate in us, loving and understanding us in our totality. He quotes Pascal's saying that no man can love God without knowing
his own misery.

I dreamed of a personified "bone of contention" blocking my way. Then,
confronting this, there came a moment when I saw beyond it to a reality
of "worship," of vision, so new and whole that all questions were answered,
all "bones of contention" were taken up into the very bones of love. Half
awake, I strove to know it clearly; fully awake, only a memory remains to
assure me of that which is beyond the contentions of my thoughts and little dreams.

Surely my great danger is still the need to bolster up my ego by seeking reassurances. Dunne speaks of the danger to the solitary man of return
to dependence on the opinions or love and understanding of other people.
He quotes Jung on the discovery of that which supports when all other
support is gone, and says this is what is meant in truth by God's love for
us. Dunne does indeed go to the heart of the matter when he speaks of
the woman's need to be needed. Over and over again this need creeps back
and must be sacrificed.

Later: I dreamed of the *I Ching.* I was trying to fit the upper trigram
"Wind" to a lower trigram not clearly seen, always failing because I tried
to make line three, top line of the lower trigram, a yang line. Then suddenly I knew it must be a yin line, and immediately I saw the whole
hexagram clearly and it was "Inner Truth" (the guiding hexagram of my
life). I had been refusing the feminine, the emptiness, the dark at that place
of transition from unconscious to conscious ego.

We have had a great blizzard and have been snowed in. We had a gor-
geous and hilarious time yesterday evening. Nancy and Jane came on
snowshoes and dragged me up to the house on a piece of plastic. I was
soaked to the skin—and very happy to be with them again.

I thought that if I were entirely honest I would admit that everything that I had ever done, said, thought, or felt in my life had sprung out of the need to "feel good," to be a success. Even actions, choices, that had brought great suffering had been tinged with the need to applaud myself, to feel noble. Even the long attempt to know and accept the shadow, integrate the animus, has been a ruse to make sure that I am able to become a fine, wise, "individuated" person.

The hope of improving, purging the ego of this urge, is nil. There is only one cure. I have known it for a long time in my head, but return ever and again to the purging efforts and the resultant sense of failure. The ego, of its nature, forever strives to be the center of life. Whether it is being "selfish" or "unselfish," there is exactly the same hidden drive. Its power is dissolved only when it is known objectively as the servant of the Self. All this is nothing new. I have talked endlessly about it in my fine words. I have been sincere according to my degree of vision, but perhaps I have come now to a new point of tension, a new possibility of letting go. Many dreams have pointed to this in the last months.

Not long ago I asked the *I Ching* about the still-lingering, deep-seated, and hidden anxiety that I am so often aware of, however much decreased its power may be. I said, "What am I afraid of?" and the answer came: 18—the top line, "He does not serve kings or princes—sets himself higher goals." I don't know what I expected—some kind of reference to dark and evil things, I suppose. But the *I Ching* is quite right of course. It is the fear of God—like fear of that which is in no way a wise, just, ruling authority, directing, lawmaking, resolving doubts—the goal, the center in which the ego's desires are not improved but wholly dissolved. And I am horribly afraid of that crossing of the threshold (*Vishuddha*). Maybe I won't come to it in this life—but lesser images of a threshold which intuit the great one are surely with me now and then.

Perhaps the new thought—which was in fact a newly experienced vision of the ego's inflated goings-on—came to me in the guise of a little flying bird, showing me the way over the next threshold by descending to

the earth and walking under the skin wall (somehow inside the body)—
showing me that I must get down on my knees and crawl into the "tied-up
sack" (*I Ching* Hexagram 2) under the heart in which the new vision of
the glory is hidden.

⟋⟍

I am frightened. Warning dreams: Something in me could so easily curl
up in a womb and turn my back on life. The *I Ching* once again gives me
18—"Work on that which has been spoiled"—with line two, "Setting right
what has been spoiled by the mother. One must not be too persevering."
The promise is of supreme success and the prognosis the serenity of
"Keeping Still." But of course only if I do the work. I feel my "spark" has
gone forever. I can only tell myself again and again that it is of no importance if the "spark" has now burned out and passed elsewhere. I have known
clearly since the great white stallion dream (recorded in my autobiography)
that it was never mine to possess. To accept this is perhaps the death before
death—the middle way in which one seeks neither this nor that, content
simply to do whatever work is given to me to do as best I can even if my
"powers" inevitably weaken. As long as one is alive one must work . . . work
to attend (as I so urgently said in the Apple Farm groups). Objective attention is everything, but oh, the power of the longing to simply quit writing
gets stronger. I ask if there is any point in going on with work on "stories"
and so forth—and the answer from the ancient wisdom is "The Taming
Power of the Small" turning again to "Inner Truth." The line to change is
the third, where man and woman fight and so the spokes fall out of the
wheel! In me the need to achieve fights with the longing to give up. When
that fight is replaced by the true feminine—the positive "no," the acceptance of ups and downs with detachment, then may come the balance, the
serenity of Inner Truth.

⟋⟍

I am reading von Franz's *Individuation in Fairy Tales* and something she
says may be very timely. She writes that at quite a late stage the dreams

may suddenly become full of conflicts without any obvious reason and that this may mean that the unconscious is pushing the dreamer to break out of too narrow a situation whether outwardly or inwardly. It feels, she says, as though everything is breaking up and one is right back at the beginning.

The recent dream comes back in which I had lost my spectacles, and first Jane offered to lend me a pair of hers but I could see nothing through them. Then Else offered hers and, though I could have seen enough to read through them, they were otherwise no use to me. Then I realized that I had my own glasses all the time but had been looking through them upside down. As soon as I turned them the right way up, I could see perfectly well.

At the time of the dream, I had been having trouble in my hours with Else and Jane, looking for reassurance instead of trusting my own vision. The dream suggests I don't have to take on their vision, having lost my own. I haven't actually lost it; I was looking at it upside down. That would mean looking at details—the small things at hand—with distance focus and at the far-off view with the close-up focus. This seems to me to hit the nail on the head completely.

&

I have been thinking how easy it is to dissolve into fragments among the ten thousand things—how only *work* can hold one together—work outer, work inner—work that is the incarnation of one's own inner truth—a building of something, within and without, and ultimately of the diamond body itself. To spend all the energy one has, but not to fritter it, and to accept the price. This is the way till death. A team horse (line 4 of "Inner Truth") works with all his strength as a member of a team, but to a conscious individual comes the moment when his horse, his energy, must separate itself from all "teams" and go forward alone without looking to right or left towards the inner truth that "links together" (line 5) all life—from the "pig and the fish" to the "great man."

My way, it has been shown to me, is via the (highly conscious) innocent spontaneity of the inner child. But that child must be protected with the utmost vigilance via *work*. It must also be allowed to move freely in the world; it cannot be protected by never being exposed or allowed out.

AUGUST 25

✧

I have been reading a small book of essays about Thomas Merton by monks and others who knew him (*Thomas Merton, Monk*). It makes me want to read some of his later works especially. The quotations about solitude are extraordinarily beautiful. A lovely phrase also about an experience that comes to me very rarely but is familiar to him: "Thank God, thank God I am like other men! . . . It is the function of solitude to make one realize such things." Merton is in a Louisville shopping center and experiences the feeling that "there is no way of telling people that they are all walking around shining like the sun."

AUGUST 27

✧

The Thomas Merton book is moving me deeply. It takes me back to the St. Matthias days and my time of "retreat," and renews my increasing longing for solitude. His reiterated words about there being no necessity to be a hermit in order to be a solitary are with me. But hours on end quite alone are essential to anyone who seeks himself in the Self. To find is merely to experience what already is—and finding one's own identity so is to find unity with all.

Nothing new, but every time it is re-expressed by someone who has lived his own truth with utter devotion and intensity, it reawakens in those who hear it *their* truth. "I have a good goblet. I will share it with you." Some form of *expression* is vital. Merton said that if he did not write he would soon be in a lunatic asylum. Mine is in the analytical hours with people and also in writing.

1978

IN STRATFORD, ONTARIO

We have seen *The Winter's Tale* and *Macbeth*, both beautifully done, and Maggie Smith's Lady Macbeth long to be remembered. Also it is a very happy time with Else and Jane, particularly so.

The beautiful thing that Maggie Smith brought out in Lady Macbeth was her *love* for Macbeth. It somehow moved me deeply to more than pity. Shakespeare's genius is something so all-encompassing as to plunge one again and again into a love of life, a wonder, a sense of glory that is indescribable—also into a sense of shame at the superficial littleness and blindness into which I fall. Yet all that too, as he reminds us, is part of the glory when "looked at" in the drama of life.

AT HOME AGAIN

Driving on the last lap to the Farm I began to yearn forwards to being here instead of staying with the moment, and I realized the constant attention necessary if one is to be the "Wanderer" who has no home, and yet whose home is everywhere.

How horridly persistent the demand—the most foolish demand—to *arrive* is! In the psyche it is far worse than the impatience to arrive home that I mention above. It is just the same refusal to stay with the moment and therefore a rejection of *death*. For to stay wholly with each moment is the death of the ego, who lives always in either past or future.

"On whatsoever sphere of being the mind is fixed at the time of death—and the time of death is every moment—this and this only can fructify in the minds of others" (T. S. Eliot, quoted from memory). I have thought often of late that the meaning of the big change of this year is that it is time to prepare much more consciously for death. It occurs to me that, as ever, I am anxiously trying to jump ahead to the final readiness—whereas the only way to grow into it is to set about "dying daily." The "dying daily" of St. Paul is precisely this acceptance of exactly what is, what I am at each moment.

I have been remembering lately that very powerful dream in Los Angeles years ago in which I was told by the Voice, "When you die you will simply be here one moment and there the next," and Bob's comment, "I believe it will be so."

A sudden death of some kind through accident or such like? Not necessarily. But the thought enforces the need to be "ready." "The readiness is all" for anything, any minute—which state will never be realized by the constant anxiety about hurrying up to arrive there!

"I am"—"Thou art"—so each day I breathe in and out, out and in. "Thou art that, yet in this not Thou." "I am" only when "Thou art" flows in to the empty place left by the letting go of "I am."

∞

SEPTEMBER 15

I dreamed I was on a train on the way to France. I found myself standing looking down on what at first I thought was a large, unclothed baby doll. I stood very still, simply looking, and I thought for a moment that I saw its eyelids flicker, but said to myself "impossible." I think it was at this point that I realized it was not a doll but a dead baby. I continued to look but now with intensity and compassion. It seemed to me that the eyes opened and looked into mine—dark and trusting. I'm not clear whether I actually touched the child now, but there was a moment of intense "communication" when I knew that her life depended on my continuing to "look." Suddenly her whole face and body came alive. She lay there healthy, kicking, making small, happy noises. In wonder I turned to the youngish parents who were lying on a wide berth a few feet away, asleep or eyes shut in grief. I roused the mother and said, "Your child needs you." She leapt up and ran to the child, calling to her husband that the baby was alive. The man sat up looking utterly stunned and said, "It can't be. It's a miracle!" At that I quickly left. (At some point I knew that the child had been dead for some time and that the parents were taking her to the coast to be buried near their family home.) My one idea now was to go home. I could not go on travelling after what had happened. I knew I had done nothing, asked for nothing as I looked at the child, but I also knew that life had flowed back into her dead body through me, and I was frightened, excited too, and had a strong urge to share the experience with Else and Jane, to ask for their wisdom in understanding what had happened, which I felt somehow both as a threat (presumably of ego-inflation) and as an awesome responsibility.

1978

SEPTEMBER 16

Yesterday, along with the dream of the resurrection of the child, there came again, after so long, that marvelous feeling of thoughts bursting one from another like a growing plant and giving life to the meaning of "Advent" for me at this time. Indeed, she is a girl child this time! It is a matter of advent in everyday living—not theological abstractions.

I wonder if there was a severe warning in the dream—if, after returning home across the water, after returning to psychological work this week, I start travelling back into the past, trying to be like Barbara Hannah and von Franz, to measure up psychologically, I am in danger of burying the new vision, indeed the child—the "advent" of the self. It is not irrelevant that the child looks like the pictures of my granddaughter, the father in the dream being the animus who leads to the Self in the individual. I note that the child would have remained above ground until the coast had been reached—i.e., until I actually began to "cross the water" eastward, back into the concerns of years past. But a continued regression would finish it.

SEPTEMBER 26

I read last night the strange chapter in *Descent into Hell*, "The Opening of Graves," with its terrible imagery of Gomorrah and Lilith. Now I have woken from a dream of power in which I heard again that "sound" of the universe—the indescribable hum as of a million bees—and with it there was a visual image—the octagonal stone, crystal stone, diamond stone seen through a luminous mist but clear in its shape—and perhaps also a great honeycomb whence came all the "ineffable sweetness" of the experience of the One. But in the dream I also knew that the hearing of that sound and the ego's longing for that honey could be the line leading straight to the horror of "Gomorrah." I stood in the dream and looked for an instant in the fear of God at the awful dignity of man's power of individual conscious choice. Either way one heard the same sound, saw the same "stone"—and either came to oneself in the conscious simplicity of the present moment, or knew it as darkness, fragmentation, dissolution, the prison of desire.

All this, of course, is a repetition, a summing up of Williams's meaning, but in the dream I experienced the meaning briefly through sight and hearing. As I came back to waking consciousness, I was remembering the fact, so unforgettably brought home to us in Charles Williams's book, that the choices may seem externally very small, even trivial, but inwardly they may be the choice between the experience of Heaven or Hell.

SEPTEMBER 28

I need to remember more steadily the "paramount importance of individuation," in Jung's words, towards the end of his life—its absolute priority over every other work. I am re-reading *Memories, Dreams, Reflections,* and was struck by Jung's attitude to Yoga exercises. He says that he only did them when his mind was in a turmoil, and as soon as he quieted down he stopped in order to return to the images. The usual purpose of the exercises is of course to eliminate images; for Jung they were simply a means to clear the way to the images. So it has been for me instinctively.

I have been realizing lately just how much I owe to the dream telling me to keep "a diary of vowels." Without this daily focussing I am pretty sure I would by now have been dissolving into senility! I verily believe that for most old ones—and especially perhaps for women with their diffuseness—this concentration on definition by the word is vital. An image comes of the slow building up of the crystal in the center so that the fragmentation of the shells of memories or of collective attitudes and supports can break up and fall away from that central rock instead of gathering in heaps around it until all sight and sound of it is lost. How quickly I become unfocussed if two days pass without writing, however admirable or harmless my outer activities may seem. I was horrified this morning to realize that I could not immediately bring back the details of the crystal dream after only two days. I had even forgotten the hearing of the "sound."

I think of the inevitable going back into memory that comes with old age and how only by *consciously* gathering those memories around the crystal stone that slowly is built up in the center by devotion to the present moment can the onset of "senility" be transformed into the garnered wisdom of the Senex and of his Sister.

SEPTEMBER 30

My Chinese boatman Chung Li ("Inner Truth") has put his finger fairly and squarely on the worst delusion I am subject to—the root of all the anxious restlessness. I again dreamed of wanting to remarry Timmy, and I went to Chung inwardly and asked him what in the world that recurrent theme meant. He was very vehement for him. "Woman," he said, "it means exactly what it says—that at seventy-four you still have, thank God, the normal feminine instincts and are yearning for the one you loved with all your heart. Your trouble is that you immediately think you *should* not have this longing and *ought* to have grown out of it. Dreams are not reminders that you *ought* to be different—*not ever.* They are simply indications that you are not *conscious* enough of that which they symbolize. Be aware, be *aware* of your own truth, of all the infinite variety of your inner life, dark or light, and, both beyond and within your personal myth, the myths, the truth, of all mankind. *You don't have to change anything*—only know and accept and live the next thing with devotion. Then the changes take place like a dance."

All of which of course I have known for a long time but so rarely *realize*.

NOVEMBER 11

Today is the anniversary of Armistice Day, 1918. I remember it very vividly. Eleven o'clock in the morning, the sudden release from the classroom, everyone rushing out into the grounds and myself running with others down to the gate and back, with an extraordinary sense of lightness, of release from the dark weight that had lain upon us all for what seemed an eternity at that age. I was just fourteen; I had been nine years old when "the lights went out."

On Monday morning there was a "hypnagogic" flash of vision. I saw the books beside my bed—Bible, dictionary, two volumes of *I Ching*—and between each of them there was a flame. I was facing them, it seemed, as though crouching where my bedside table stands—and as I woke, I was seized as with a deep grief. My ultimate supports, three benisons of my life, givers of wisdom and of meaning were burning up and would soon be nothing but a heap of ashes. I saw the row of flames (they were orderly, so to speak, burning straight up like flames of candles) burn higher and wider becoming one huge flame and enclosing all four books. To the right there remained only my diaries—pitiful outpourings of the ego—all that was left to me. I wept as though bereaved—as indeed I felt.

The *I Ching* gave me, earlier in the night, *Huan,* "The Dissolution," with the line: "He dissolves his self." It is a great paradox. One's own truth is found only when the ego is totally accepted as it *is,* not as a copy of any other's way, however holy—and can therefore be dissolved and integrated into the Self, the Truth. Big words again. I feel utterly trivial, bereft.

To continue about the "dissolution." I wonder if the feeling of being right back at the beginning—rudderless, anxious, fragmented—may be part of this stage. It would be very dangerous if one were to be submerged by it, but if objectivity remains and I can, so to speak, look at it clear-eyed and endure to the end it will be seen as an essential experience, provided I do not try to solidify again "the old man." I go from this state to one of happiness—a quiet kind (not a "high") such as I have not known before in my life. It is not a matter of moods, but—can it be true?—of a new kind of response.

Later: I have been reflecting on the mysterious essence of each individual of which one is aware beyond all the "accidents" of behavior, neuroses,

SUCH STUFF AS DREAMS ARE MADE ON

1978

words, acts, blindnesses, depressions, inflections, etc. It is like a nucleus around which all those constantly changing patterns revolve, and *may* be known not as chaotic but as a dance, if only the ego is differentiated from the Self, in oneself and in others. I am struggling ineptly to express an old thing in a new way to fit an awareness that came this morning, but I slip again into theory. Try again. It began this morning with a thought of how greedy one can get about dreams—how I will feel abandoned to trivialities and anxieties about my "state" if I am without a significant and nourishing dream for even a week! It came to me that as in old age the memory of my life becomes more and more circular, so to speak, and time begins at a deep level to lose its linear character, it becomes an absurdity to feel abandoned by the unconscious when the profound dreams of years past are as much here and now as anything that appears or will appear in linear time. Why be always asking for more when there is such a rich mine of images still to be explored in greater and greater depth—dark things, light things—seeing them as the whole sphere of one's life, as distilled out of that "essence," given from the beginning. Linear time is the necessity for the gradual discovery and growth, through incarnation, of the individual consciousness of the sphere. We must discover it in each "minute particular," not in the radiant sphere of the unconscious child. Nothing new here except in the sudden sense of delight in the thought of "Possession in Great Measure" (as in the *I Ching*)—so many images from the beyond to be looked at, and suddenly no need to demand any more. The immediate dream that is here with me now is that of the three bowls—twelve-sided bowls—within which I feed the Indian "guru," myself, and the Self—the latter food being tasteless, colorless.

This illuminates so much of my recent experiences—the clinging onto longing for rich soup or fizzy Coke!

There was a dream in which I was kneeling beside Nancy in some collective place of worship. Nancy handed me quietly a poem she had just been writing, and I thought that she had been truly praying that way, and that I too needed to find a way to pray, since I could not find meaning in the collective way. The poem was remarkable, I thought. Ought I to try again to make poetry?

This reflects my worrying about not having a disciplined "technique" of prayer or meditation.

At the moment I feel confused and incapable of any effort. Every time I try to meditate I go to sleep. "So what?" Dom John Chapman would say. God is as present in sleep as in waking. I suspect my trouble is that I will not stay with the images that came yesterday. The *next* thing—which is to write them—and as usual I am anxious about what after *that!*

I begin to see that the only way for me to pray, to meditate, is this my own way of regular reflection in writing, either here in my diary, in the "stories," if they come, and perhaps in the letters to the few. When people of prayer write to me, that is when I feel that I must be a fraud because I do not pray or meditate the way they do. But the minute I set pen to paper to reply, I forget all that and simply write what comes—and it's clear that, whatever my ego's follies may be, something true and real reaches them, perhaps because of my lifelong wrestling with the angel in disguise. It takes only the change from "I dare not (cannot) let you go" to "I will not let you go until you bless me."

I was once again on the verge of falling into the old guilt about not praying properly. How enormously powerful that kind of guilt is! . . . I truly know and trust that my prayer springs from this journal and the stories—

1979

my discipline not a striving for mystical experiences but the utmost fidelity to the way of attention to the inner images and the present moment, the "nothing but" of the Fool. I have the beginnings of an urge to write something coherent about this. I believe that very many people have this same problem in our day. The honesty, the discrimination, the real introversion (not introspection) that is needed to write a true "diary of vowels" is for me a safer way than the techniques of Eastern origin or induced charismatic experience that are so popular.

Perhaps one may "teach without words and work without doing," in the words of Lao Tzu.

FEBRUARY 8,
3 A.M.

I have had a multiplicity of dreams since Monday, but at the moment only the image with which I have just woken remains. A huge room, perhaps a supermarket stripped of all its goods, except for a large pile of honeydew melons on a central table. I think this table was of metal. The color of this kind of melon is very numinous to me. It reminds me always of that luminous pale green of the sky before dawn above the mountains of Moab. It is indescribable—a pure pale green which is infused with light (not white or cream-color or yellow, but pure shining light). As I think of it, I think that the flesh of a cantaloupe is also infused with light, and in both cases to say one is light green, the other peach color, doesn't convey the quality of the color at all. It suddenly hits me that when in that dream in Zurich I was given the name of Melon, the meaning of the name Helen was included intrinsically in the new one, for "Helen" means "light."

"Honeydew." What a lovely name for the "melon sweetness" of my dream—the dew from heaven that has the natural sweetness of honey.

An association with the dream is the photograph I saw recently of an English produce market wholly empty of food because of the strikes. In the center of this emptiness in the dream was the great pile of spherical honeydew melons. Perhaps this is a reference to the fact, told to me by Jung himself, that for some sects in the very early days the melon was the communion meal, and therefore symbolically the wholly nourishing food of Heaven and Earth when all other nourishment is forgone. It is the kind of communion food that a woman might offer, a symbolic womb in which many seeds lie dormant waiting to be scattered abroad to "die" into the waiting earth and burst forth into new life.

I was watching "The Long Search" on television on Tuesday night, and there was an old Buddhist monk who said two things—not new to me either of them, but awakening me again to contemplation of them. One was that it is simply impossible to love anyone or anything at all unless one begins by loving oneself. Love for others and for the world can grow only from that center. (I remember here the words of Toni: "Love is neither a thought *nor a feeling*.") The way the monk expressed the above—his humor and his serenity—was what went home.

The second thing he said was "When you are walking, *know* that you are walking; when you are sweeping, *know* that you are sweeping." In short, whatever you are doing be wholly aware of the moment. This reminds me of the Zen monk who revealed his lack of enlightenment by the fact that he could not say where he had put down his umbrella when he came into the house. How remote and rare such a state of awareness is!

My mind goes back to that marvelous saying of the *Cloud of Unknowing* monk: "Not *what* I am but *that* I am, not *what* God is but *that* he is." This is real awareness, consciousness of the living moment, whereby one is immediately freed from the ego. Fourteenth-century Christian and twentieth-century Buddhist are speaking the eternal contemplative truth. The ego, of course, is always occupied with *what* it is, what it was, what it wants to be or to happen. While going somewhere, preoccupied with arrival, while working, preoccupied with results, and so on.

I am a little child in this, taking first tentative steps and falling, but if I fall like a child, cry when I cry, laugh when I laugh, and look on all with wonder and trust, then perhaps . . . ?

MARCH 21

I have been reading bits of Thomas Merton's *Asian Journal* this morning. Maureen lent it to me yesterday. Some lovely things. A man on the edge of enlightenment—as indeed he knew of himself—and yet so entirely on this earth, vulnerable on other levels, but invulnerable on the one that matters. He writes that "Compassion is proportionate to detachment; otherwise we use others for our own ends under the pretext of 'love.' Actually we are dominated by illusion. Love that perpetuates the illusion does no good to others or to ourselves." This is a summary of Buddhist thought.

The "infinite number of unexpected possibilities" of which Merton writes, which transcend our capacity to think or imagine, are opened to us with incredible richness when we attend to our dreams. But then comes "the hardest work in the world," through which we discriminate which possibilities are to be sacrificed in this world and recognize those to which we must open ourselves in total obedience.

There are gems in Merton's journal I want to live with: "Compassion is proportionate to detachment." "To live selfishly is to bear life as an intolerable burden"; when we are selfless, we "live in joy, realizing by experience that life itself is love and gift."

Spring is here. Yesterday I uncovered the roses—all still green, and sprouting; bulbs coming up everywhere amongst the still remaining patches of snow. I planted peas. What a joy!

I woke with an image of two glasses of water, side by side, about four inches apart, and someone was trying to balance a small carved elephant on them—front feet on the rim of one glass, back feet on the rim of the other. There was also a vague impression of a small stick of light-colored wood sticking up from the elephant's back and the person was holding this, perhaps thinking to achieve the balance by shifting it to find the center of the elephant—but I *think* it was wobbly!

My thought immediately was that the image of the two glasses came from my reading about Thomas Merton in Asia and symbolized the two ways (Christian and Buddhist) and the elephant the foolish attempt to unite the two containers. The water is already One—the containers are and should remain separate while recognized as each containing the indivisible truth. I had been reading of Merton's visit to a Tibetan monk who warned against pursuing several ways at once. (Someone had proposed a community where all the disciplines would be taught!) But why the elephant? Here I think the personal meaning for me is involved. When I read of all the differing "ways," I am always aware of guilt because I am not following *any* of the inner disciplines—though as a matter of fact I have, however weakly, followed the discipline of the individuation process through images and the "alchemical" process essential to the Western psyche. The elephant has become a particularly numinous symbol to me.

APRIL 17

The stone which Jung found at Bollingen in 1950 was a cube, and he made it into a kind of memorial stone. Reading again the descriptions of the things he carved on its sides, the power of my own image of the stone, especially the cube, is moving in me.

The first thing Jung carved on one side was a verse from alchemist Arnaldus de Villanova (died 1313). And the final thing, under the Arnaldus quotation: "In remembrance of his 75th birthday C. G. Jung made and placed this here as a thank-offering, in the year 1950."

Well, my own seventy-fifth year is here. I too owe a thank-offering. What form? Jung wrote later, "I am no artist. I only try to get these things into stone of which I think it is important that they appear in hard matter and stay on for a reasonably long time. Or I try to give form to something that seems to be in the stone and makes me restless. It is nothing for show, it's only to make these troublesome things steady and durable. There is not much of form in it."

Perhaps my own thank-offering, small as it is, lies in those few poems or stories in which I have tried to give form to my vision of the stone. For words too can be "hard matter," enduring, fixing somehow the individual's experience. For a thinker, like Jung, his offering had to be forged by his hands. For a woman whose hands anyway are as ineffectual as mine, words can be the defining, enduring thing. Now, since this year, the written word is not "for show" but "only to make these troublesome things steady and durable."

1979

Jung, after this memorial, had ten years ahead in which he worked to interpret those things in the cube stone. Whatever time remains to me belongs to my own particular way of working towards realization in this life that "child and stone," "rose and diamond," "emptiness of heart and compassion," are one.

JUNE 15   ∽

One of those almost imageless dreams visually, but nonetheless most vivid. In this dream I saw, and was in communication with, a woman who was moving on a ground that moved under her. She had no control over the ground, which seemed to carry her around at random and had no meaning, no visible pattern or goal. But she was on the verge of a total choice, a conscious abandonment of her will to the seemingly haphazard movement under her wherever it might take her. I then saw her after this choice, and what before had been an unfocussed drifting here and there had become a controlled and beautiful pattern in which every movement was highly conscious—though the actual motion of the ground remained entirely the same.

The "ground movements" were, of course, her fate, her destiny, and the thought has long been familiar to me. The dream, however, was not just a repeated theme in the head; it was an actual experience, an awareness of that which transcends both active and passive, meaningful and meaningless, in a unity beyond words, although I still—rightly, I think—struggle to express and define as precisely as is possible.

Yesterday's talk with Barbara Mowat about *The Tempest* was behind— or in front of—the dream.

AUGUST 15   ∽

I wonder if length of life depends, for some, on the age at which they started on the individuation process. This of course would not apply to someone like Jung himself, whose calling in this life involved an immensely long labor of thought and writing vital to the world in this century. I suppose all the great ones die when their work is done, which may be at thirty or eighty or ninety. The length is not important. The vital thing, the older one gets, is to *work,* and to be aware of the changes in the way of working which are rising from the unconscious. Such a change has been going on in me and it needs constant attention.

A dream in which Toni was dying. All her friends and pupils were gathered. We were waiting in sorrow as she made her last bequests. At the very last she whispered in Nancy's ear that she was leaving her inmost, "essential" bequest to me—a piece of ground. She then died. Nancy told me this at once quietly. Then people began asking Nancy what Toni's last words had been. Nancy told some of the words, and I waited for her to reveal the bequest—a bit inflated about it. But Nancy said nothing of this, and I recognized that she was entirely right. This was a secret thing.

There was an undefined feeling that I wanted to go to work at once on this plot of ground—or else wait to go and live on it. But at that moment came "the boss." He was very angry with me for something I had done or left undone, and ordered me to type twenty copies of a long page—good, clear copies, he said, obviously gloating that this would mean typing it four or five times. He was, I thought, determined to delay my entry into the new situation, work, or whatever was offered through Toni's bequest. I silently thought I would type it once and xerox the other copies so it would not delay me long. I seemed not to question that I had to obey him.

Yesterday morning early, in the quietness, I had some minutes of—perhaps I should say a foretaste of—the kind of freedom for which I long: the cessation of any kind of demand, even of the demand for that very state of freedom. It was the experience, not the head-knowledge or even heart-knowledge, of that complete acceptance of the waiting for that which can only be *given* by grace, never attained by effort. A most inadequate description, but I remember often in these days the experience of Thomas Aquinas when suddenly all need to write or explain or analyze anything dropped away when the essential dawned.

1979

A lovely letter from Sister Therese has arrived, the core of which is her thought about the "intrusion of the irrelevant" and her saying "yes" to each intrusion when inevitable. It reminded me yet again of Toni's words about "the important and the essential." The vital thing now on a new level is to discriminate between the important things which must nevertheless be sacrificed and those things which must be accepted and then known as yet another revelation of the essential—the Grail.

AUGUST 26

This morning yet again, perhaps for the third time this week, there was that foretaste, that new awareness of what a wholeness beyond the opposites might be—not in visual images, not in words, but in fact. It is as though I enter a region on the very edge of sleep, yet it is not sleep, nor yet the waking state. I am conscious of the breathing, of the "I am" and the "Thou art that," yet no longer through any effort of concentration. This is to me the essence of prayer.

AUGUST 27

Today, my holidays begin—holy days, I trust, empty of obligations and schedules—a whole empty week. I can hardly believe it. Of course there is much to do before leaving for England, but in my own time, at leisure, and I shall enjoy the preparations.

SEPTEMBER 23

IN ENGLAND

A dream image comes back to me. There were, so to speak, several "starting points" for the reaching of higher consciousness, but none of them seemed right for me. I had, as it seemed, already experienced them. For some time I could not see the one I now sought, then suddenly I saw it.

It was a circle of desert, reddish, sandy, and I knew that this was the new starting point I sought.

The desert clearing is surely the piece of ground symbolic of Toni's "essence" left to me by her—the new starting point, the new ground.

∽

SEPTEMBER 27

AT APPLE FARM

An awful day yesterday—jetlag, reaction from all the extraversion in England. . . . Then last night I managed to go back over the dreams with Else and Jane and this morning life is stirring again and a looking toward the change that is essential now. There can be no doubt at all, now that I have truly looked at the series of dreams in the last six weeks. . . . It is abundantly clear. The new starting point is "the desert," the legacy from Toni, her "essence," a piece of empty ground. The cleared sandy place, newly sown, must be protected as the seeds sprout and grow—a strip of bare desert must surround it. And the promise of the healing of the life-long split between inner life, solitude, and outer work, gregariousness, is likewise symbolized in the experience of August 26.

∽

OCTOBER 10

Breathing in the air that gives me life—I am—Breathing out all that I am as I am into the universal air—Thou art. Breathing in that which is one and universal—Thou art—Breathing out that which is uniquely myself— I am.

I have intermittently practiced the simplest prana exercise ever since Toni taught me so long ago. I am ashamed at how intermittently. And yet each time I have come back to it, often after long gaps, I have been aware that somehow or other it has perhaps gone on growing in depth of meaning at the root of my being. This could only be because psychically I have been faithful to the rhythm of breathing in, breathing out, through all the conflicts and evasions.

The breathing in and out of the earth's atmosphere by the body is a symbol of the eternal rhythm of the Self—I and thou, in and out, up and

1979

down, forward and back, systole and diastole in their final unity. The conscious realization and incarnation of this rhythm, balance, unity, in the unique, individual pattern of one's life would lead—so I feel it—to the breathing out of one's last breath in death into that air of eternity, which is the breath of life when the body is left behind.

There is only one "work" now—the finding of that rhythm, that flowing in, flowing out, in the minute particulars of every day.

The feeling of total bankruptcy of the last two weeks was the inevitable result of those three weeks of perpetual "breathing out" with only short gulps of breathing in. This week, I can feel all through my being the "breathing in" restored in the silence and the solitude.

Looking back over my life I remember the major affirmation of my need for this solitude in Los Angeles, after the years of pouring out. Then came the time when I began to feel bankrupt again and realized it was from too long a breathing in. I returned to the breathing out on a new level of consciousness, I think, and haltingly since then have sought the rhythm through so many dangerous conflicts. I was thinking this morning of my enormous debt to Bob for his support in that intensive time of introversion, when everyone whom I knew and loved was prophesying doom. He was like a bulwark, protecting but never emotionally entering my solitude.

That time was a watershed and now as I reach the symbolic moment of the seventy-fifth birthday I feel that a change just as important as that one is due. It is much quieter, less seen in outer changes, but more subtle and deep, if I will attend and accept. As before, I have the great gift of friendship—of two who protect, support, and deeply understand.

OCTOBER 30   ❧

Yesterday baking the Christmas cake with Hope—long, tiring, but pleasant. On Sunday, analytical hours and bulb planting. Both evenings TV. But some reading of von Franz in the night gave me a thought for next Friday's group—and, more important, a thought for much contemplation: that is, how easy it is to leave parts of one's life out of the individuation process. She mentions how she had suddenly discovered after years of inner work that she had entirely left such things as income tax out as being mere matters of common sense! It is easy of course to think about the inner meanings of such things—exchange, real community, and the meaning of law. But only when an image comes from the unconscious does it truly enter the symbolic life. And to me taxpaying came as the image of the pouring of a libation to the god before drinking. For every government is in some sense an image, however imperfect, of the Self. In democracy how vital it is for individuals to preserve and to obey the Royal image behind all effort towards fair exchange, which always carries within it its opposite, corruption.

The impact of the Pope's visit is fascinating. I see it in people's dreams. They don't realize that he is a supreme symbol of the Self incarnate, and what he says is of very little importance. He is *symbolically* infallible—and even more powerful in the unconscious of those who misunderstand and violently reject this image.

1980

JANUARY 2

I am worried about what seems to me an often increased nervous tension, so much at odds with the increased "peace" which I sense down below. It is as though, as soon as an image moves and sparks to life and I enter the symbolic dimension, I come home.

I was thinking this morning that, as T. S. Eliot said, "Only through time, time is conquered." One might also say "only through images may one pass beyond images." This has been universally known in the East and so all their teaching is concerned with transcending the image. Here in the West our job is to enter unreservedly into the world of images; only then shall we be led into that which is both image and non-image. We don't realize how enormously hard it is for a Western consciousness to accept totally the reality of the symbolic life. Many who are rationally sure they "believe in" it haven't come near this acceptance.

FEBRUARY 8

1980

Thoughts about the symbolism of East and West. In the northern hemisphere the North Pole is the center in the mysterious dark North, but East and West have acquired strong political and psychological meanings. The East is the place of passive contemplation, being; the West is constantly active, doing. Nevertheless it is to the further west that the whole mystical tradition of Europe and Britain has always turned: Atlantis, the Isles of the Blest, Avalon under all its many names—they all lie over the sea to the west beyond the setting sun to a new rising in the beyond.

The strange lands to the east were very early known; the unknown lay to the west over the great ocean. The world is now charted, but for those with Celtic blood especially, the well at the world's end and beyond it the dark path to the ocean over which we travel to the beyond lies symbolically in the West where the sun goes down into the dark in this world and rises again in the here and now.

The words at the end of *The Lord of the Rings* have always evoked a strangely powerful, numinous response in me: "And then it seemed to him [i.e., Frodo, sailing west from the Grey Havens] that as in his dream in the house of Bombadil, the grey rain-curtain turned all to silver glass and was rolled back, and he beheld white shores and beyond them a far green country under a swift sunrise."

FEBRUARY 14

The minute one starts trying to be a contemplative, one travels fast in the opposite direction. I so quickly lose touch with the images and then immediately I am caught in ego-improvement. Even the striving to let that go can simply transfer the lust for "achievement" from one level to another, more dangerous one.

I realize more and more clearly how specifically my recent stories (in active imagination) are a response to the threats of unconscious burning, drowning, falling into the abyss. Contemplation is a gift, a grace, realized only when I am true to my own way of goal-less affirmation of images. To envy the way of negation—to feel inferior because it is not mine—is at this stage in my life a suicidal urge, precluding the sacrificial death of all ego-goals. This sacrifice cannot of course be made through conscious willing. It may be given at last if I am true to the love of the Praise-singer within.

In the Hexagram "Holding Together" is the wisdom of recollection inwardly and of communication outwardly, and it teaches the need of a leader, a human individual around whom a group finds its solidarity and meaning. The thought that just came to me was that there can be no realization of holding together that is not rooted and grounded in a union of opposites. Any group trying to hold together for any purpose whatever that tries to achieve a goal not inclusive of its opposite is doomed to the onesidedness that ultimately leads to its splitting apart. Even the goal of finding meaning must include the finding of meaninglessness.

We speak much of finding wholeness, yet drift continually into the denial of the very nature of wholeness by trying to exclude this, that, or the other small thing or event or feeling that is repulsive to us. How I have always yearned to exclude those persistently messy ego-dreams. By so yearning, I am unfaithful to the Praise-singer. I truly know that any one of them, if fully remembered, can lead to new wisdom. I may choose not to explore many of the dreams—that is another thing—leave the muse to digest some of them for me, and to throw up again that which must be transformed in images.

So if I am to "hold to this inwardly" and "hold to this outwardly," it can only be through continual awareness of the conflict of the opposites in every aspect of life, and acceptance of the anguish thereof through the song of praise in the depths. This it is which may bring the *coniunctio* and this alone can make one the kind of mediator that holds others together as well as oneself.

This morning there is an inch or so of fresh snow and every branch, every twig is outlined in white, and the cardinals glow red on feeder and tree.

1980

Now and then a gust of wind sets all the delicate tracery in motion. The sky is overcast, so that there is no color at all except the black of the trees and the pure white of the snow, with here and there in the foreground the flying red of the birds.

How blessed it is to have this wide window onto the woods—and also this warm and comfortable bed in the corner from which to look and to write!

I am reflecting on the truth that every single flake of snow is a separate and perfect mandala which we cannot see with the naked eye. What a miracle! We only see the collective merging of those tiny circles with our natural vision and it is beauty enough, but the microscope has surely brought us the vision of beauties unseen and unsuspected. However, watching the other night a TV program about the passionate search for smaller and smaller particles or bigger and bigger objects in space through the fantastically complicated technology of today, I thought with nostalgia of the Greek maxim, "Nothing too much." There is an analogy in the psychological world, the techniques that uncover the truths of the unconscious degenerating into the hairsplitting and nitpicking of prolonged morbid personal analysis or into scientific generalizations and statistics about the human psyche.

It occurs to me that those ardent scientists are really searching through technology for the "smaller than small, the greater than great"—looking for it in the outer world just as we may search forever for that same reality through intense concentration on ego analysis. However small the entities revealed by the microscope, however great the reach of the telescope, the knowledge of them adds nothing to the vision of that which is "smaller than small *and* greater than great" in one and the same reality.

MARCH 28

Dreams and meditations have taken me back recently to Mary Renault's *The King Must Die,* and this morning I came on a quotation from it: "it is not the bloodletting that calls down power, it is the consenting." "To go consenting" to every smallest necessity, unto death itself—this is the "mindfulness" of every moment, the detachment which is never withdrawal and in which the opposites are fully present and at one.

Sister Therese gave me a card she had made with a quotation from Jung: "Freedom of will is the ability to do gladly that which one must do." Also F. Wickes: "The role is given. It is what one must; but the gladness which makes it freedom is man's own choice."

At last a morning lies before me empty. Many thoughts and images wait to be clarified. First, to record this early morning's image. I had been thinking of the Well—the water from it that Simon (in my dreams and in active imagination) brings to my door—and then I fell asleep and a voice was saying, "Ever since the evening of my birth it has been to me like mother's milk." This linked up with the beginnings of a conversation with Simon the Praise Singer that began recently when in active imagination I asked him when I had first met him, and he replied "I was with you before you were born." I remember now that this came out of some reflections on the fifth line of the sign "Duration" in the *I Ching,* which I had never before really registered. It says "Giving duration to one's character through perseverance. This is good fortune for a woman, misfortune for a man." And the commentary says that a woman should follow one man her whole life long, but for a man to follow a woman brings bad results. The modern woman would react to this with disgust. Hitherto I have just vaguely wondered how to translate it into our terms, but this time the image of my total commitment to Simon in dreams came back to me, and I began to understand. The unwavering commitment of a woman to the singleness of the spirit as he manifests himself to her inwardly is an absolute necessity if she is to come to individuation. If she is not obedient to the single voice, the one word, she will run from opinion to opinion and be lost in a sea of words, dissolved in a multiplicity of false masculine values and unconscious emotional reactions.

1980

There is always a hidden truth in a projected belief strong enough to influence men and women through centuries, and the obedience of woman to man—distorted though it almost universally was—is no exception. For the still semi-unconscious man or woman, the traditional attitudes were a container, a protection for inner truths about the nature of the woman's animus and the man's anima, but the traditional attitudes no longer serve. They are broken open, exploded, and it has become of the utmost urgency to rediscover them within.

When rightly fighting the terrible injustices of the past, without equal attention to the underlying inner truths there will be no transformation, only destruction. Perhaps it is a major life-task for some women to discover and meet before the end her single masculine spirit—to recognize into which of her many relationships she has projected him or aspects of him. I could myself make a long list—with Timmy as the central outer carrier of the inner marriage incarnate in my life. Is "Simon" then for me the "single" one at last who has from my birth been the unseen carrier of the water of life from the Well of the Mother? I glimpse him now, and recognize that from earliest childhood he has been the giver of my laughter and of the happiness that so many have spoken of still showing through me in spite of darkness, weakness, near despair. I glimpse him but so quickly lose the sense of his presence in the ever pressing multiplicity of opinion and desire.

1981

JANUARY 28

I had an experience last night bordering on the inexpressible. I have known about it and, God help me, written about it, but last night I *experienced* it—or rather experienced a hint of it in a new darkness that led to the edge of an unknown joy. I feel that I must try to write something around it, however inadequate.

It was the beginning of an *actual* realization that *my* self in *the* Self is not the ego: it was a disidentification for a moment from all that the ego regards as "I"—from the body, from the emotions, from feeling, from thought, from every so-called achievement or failure of my life. A Zen koan: "Show me your face before you were born."

Yesterday came a real "shock" in the form of a letter from the President of St. Mary's College, asking me to deliver the Commencement address to the class of 1981 in May, and offering me an honorary degree, no less! Couldn't believe my eyes! It is an extraordinarily heartwarming letter saying how much they appreciate my work, my life, my "professional achievements"! The really wonderful thing is that a college is honoring an absolutely nonprofessional kind of work which has been wholly nonacademic.

Of course I am thrilled and excited at being so honored—also of course scared. I feel reasonably sure that I should accept this thing, no matter how alien to my hitherto private way. . . . I have been thinking recently of the way in my past life I have been pitchforked, turned upside down and landed in a new way just when I had thought myself settled in the old way. I thought to myself now that I am old, surely I can prepare for death in more and more seclusion and that those repeated "new lives" are finished outwardly. And now suddenly all this unsought publicity has come upon me. At seventy-six *another* new direction? Only yesterday I was relishing the new sense of emptiness!

Yesterday I drove to Kalamazoo—the library, Gilmore's for underclothes, lunch at Walgreen's where I wrote to Elizabeth H. On the drive, as often happens when I drive alone, there was real meditation, even a bit of "mindfulness." Thoughts came of the extraordinary difficulty of that basic change of attitude from "the old man on the new way" to the "new man on the new way." The ego, through its desires, is forever torn between the opposites, and the more we try to *cure* it, the stronger its desires become. I sometimes feel that never in my whole life have I done a single disinterested thing—even the best has come from feeding an ego-desire to be, and be seen to be, good—and all the disciplines of meditation, etc., then merely strengthen the ego. Only objective love, "objective cognition," is the "new man" who mirrors the Self, who is one's unique self—and we touch this only when we act, feel, think out of "the laughter, the joy, at the heart of things"—which is never "at" anything, always "with" everything.

I remember the moment in *The Place of the Lion* when Anthony let go of the ledge on which he stood, let go of all the projections of the ego that give us an illusion of safety—and after this momentary experience he was free of a central knot of anxiety that had been with him even in his moments of greatest insight and love. (I must read it again!) This is a description of the metanoia from the old man on the new way to the new man on the new way—from ego center to Self center. The ego's desires and fears may remain to the end but no longer in control—at least not all the time!

I wonder if survival of ego consciousness in the beyond means that the ego only survives insofar as it has begun to realize its identity in the Self, whereas the wholly ego-centered fragments of the personality are dissolved, the energy perhaps regrouped into another ego to be reborn in this world or another—individuation therefore the one essential.

Elaine's letter came yesterday and linked with these thoughts. She is awakening to the emptiness of monastic oughts and shoulds and repressive rules in this our time. She has just read a book on Merton's sufferings from this, and it made her immensely sad, and then awoke Homeric laughter. She sent me a very powerful piece of writing in response to the book. In it there is a sentence: "it (as system) has worked and completed its work only for those for whom it can no longer work." Yes, indeed.

But how the "old man" clings to a system, any system, that seems to promise progress on The Way. And this is deadly when the point is reached when *no* system can "work." Remember the Mowgli child, and Hindi.

SEPTEMBER 19   ✍

Last night thoughts of *The Odyssey* began again to burgeon. I have realized for some time that there is just one image in the whole poem that has lit this spark in me—perhaps it is the only thing that I shall write about. It is chronologically the last of all the images in the story, though it occurs in the middle of the poem and is not actually referred to again. But it is nonetheless vivid to someone in old age. Tiresias, meeting Odysseus at the edge of the underworld, prophesies Odysseus's fate and ends by telling Odysseus that after his life's work is over, after the battle with the suitors, he will not yet be able to settle down. There is one more journey to be taken. He is to go this time inland on foot, carrying one of his great oars, and he is to travel until he comes to a country where no man has seen the sea, where no man has tasted salt, and there he is to plant his oar and leave it for men to see, and quietly return home, make sacrifice to all the gods, and live in peace until "death shall come to him gently out of the sea."

This image has always impressed me, but of late it has come alive and brought a depth of meaning and joy that is altogether new. Only today have I rediscovered with a new delight that it was Tiresias the *blind* seer who brought that final wisdom to Odysseus—and it is only since my semi-blindness that the story has hit me with a personal impact that I have yet to explore in depth—a thought that brings joy with it.

Last night I had a dream that somehow connects with it. I was in a treeless countryside of pastureland, like rolling downs, and was walking uphill slowly and alone towards something that was to take place on the crest of the downs—I don't remember, perhaps did not know in the dream, what it was. It seemed that I knew part of the way, had walked there before—fields were divided by wires or fences which were to keep the animals in but which humans could negotiate easily. The way was therefore not straight but zig-zagged to left and right. Once I found myself surrounded by young and strong but not threatening animals—a ram? a steer? The latter, brown and white, was butting me in the center of my back, but I stood still and was quite unafraid and the circle of beasts were soon gone so that I could continue. I found myself now on a well-defined path leading straight and gently up the hill, and I thought: "Someone has altered the fencing so that one no longer has to go from side to side."

Here I woke and lay dozing with the strong feeling that this was my

journey to plant my "oar," which of course is not an oar—but each individual has something symbolizing his/her *active* life which must be planted
and left, so that in God's due time "death may come gently out of the sea."

It is very clear in Tiresias's image that Odysseus on his return will be surrounded by his people, in no way *withdrawn*, as he waits beside the sea for
that which is to come—*after* the journey and the planting.

∽

Saturday and Sunday were very tired days, but on Monday I went to
Dr. S. and was very happy to find that the eye pressure was actually down
with the lower dose of pills. He has now cut down another bit, and yesterday morning and also today I feel a real difference. I have actually begun
to put into words a draft introduction to my thoughts on *The Odyssey*. It
is impossible to describe the joy of that. The weariness in the mornings,
caused by the medication, had been making a block I didn't seem able to
break through between image and ordered expression. It is of course always
a great struggle to get started, but this was something of a different quality. The release is indeed a blessing.

Florence drove me into Kalamazoo and it was such a happy relaxed time
with her. We went shopping after the doctor and bought a blouse for Else's
birthday—and for me a Christmas outfit: black velvet skirt and jacket!

∽

As I was working with a dream, some images took hold with power. I was,
in active imagination, watching a man sharpening knives and scissors and
singing. Then I fell (in actual fact) asleep and dreamed. In my dream I was
still sitting there as in the fantasy, but the people, the houses, the little man
had vanished and there remained in front of me only a whetstone, a flat
table like the stone of a jetty, and in the center of it was a small round
object. Was it a ring, I thought? No, it was round at the bottom but rose
to a height of an inch or so looking more like a rock—a kind of tiny miniature mountain at the top. I knew somehow that this strange object had

been ground by the knife grinder for me alone and that I must reach out and take it and discover its mystery, for it represented that which was my task now, to be performed before I could pass on beyond the mist. And a voice spoke to me (aloud? or in my heart?) saying "This requires of you the hardest *work* you have ever done." And I woke.

There were two—no, three—associations connected with the "object." First is the similarity to the domed container for my contact lens—which however is white, not black. Second is the shape of the small black stone which Jane brought me from that ancient lake in Peru and represents for me something almost beyond time. Third, the round base was smooth and polished, unlike the upper part, and brought to mind the polished black "worry stone" Rose gave me. "Basalt," I thought.

∞   NOVEMBER 24

I have returned every morning to the black object found on the whetstone in my dream. It has become clearly a black, shiny stone ring—basalt—surrounding the black "miniature mountain" stone from the lake in Peru. "Basalt," besides being a dark, shining volcanic rock, is also derived from the word for "touchstone" (stone used to detect the alloys in gold). It is a powerful image that the "worry stone," the shards of the "egg" from which the child emerged, have become the basalt circle, the "touchstone" perhaps of the gold hidden in the mountain which keeps connecting in my mind with Amman Hen, the mount of seeing in *The Lord of the Rings.* I remembered suddenly my first thought on waking from the dream with only an ill-defined image of the "ring" on the whetstone. "It is not a ring to wear. Does it have something to do with the third eye—or perhaps the center of a clock from which the hands have been removed?"

Perhaps it is relevant that a dream of sudden clear vision in the right eye came after a confrontation with an onset of despair over my vision—outer and inner—and not long after the dream of the finding of the black object and the call to the "hardest of work" (which is associated for me with Hannah's words about active imagination).

In active imagination, I stood in the doorway of my cabin home, appreciating the simple comforts, the quiet welcome of the familiar things, and I could not understand why tears came to my eyes and my heart began to ache with a kind of loneliness I had never felt in this place before. I thought, "The room is shaped almost like a cave . . . but it is warm and comfortable and familiar." And yet I stood there plunged into a pit of loneliness, a darkness which surrounded me like an impenetrable fog. I thought of my friends whom I loved, so near, so easily to be called upon, whose love and care for me were constant and true. But this loneliness was something that could not be reached by human friendship. It had been banished earlier by the utter aloneness of the black rock mountain on the Island of Seeing where I had eaten the fruit, digested the husk, endured the storm, been given a glimpse of the Eye—and where I had dreamed of the Great Man—the two-million-year-old man, as Jung calls him, in all of us.

And I knew suddenly as I stood there that this terrible loneliness would be with me to the end, except when I could remain aware that the only true meetings were now the meeting of the Great Man with himself in every human encounter. People would come, people would go, and I would be happy, interested, feel blessed and enriched as always, I would laugh and be sad in all the familiar ways. The loneliness would recede out of emotional range, but the vital thing now was that I remain aware that it could never be done away with, avoided, destroyed, by the old natural, temperamental warmth and affection and the comforting reassurances of others—a thing the ego continually tries to do. These things are rightly sought and enjoyed and loved. Only the Eye, the sacrificial eye of Horus—the *single* eye which is known in *aloneness*—could finally transform this sense of isolated *loneliness,* because the final acceptance of aloneness would bring at last the unity of all the opposites in the Great Man who is also woman, and the fellowship of all men and creation, present or absent in time, in the Self.

The recent dreams of the ego's guilt and weakness are, I believe, stressing my fear of the aloneness in which I might dare to forget all that I (and my mother) have always expected of me, all my need of approval and reassurance from others, without which I have never been able to contemplate living. I don't delude myself into imagining the ego is going to change in this matter, but it is high time for another turn of the spiral way, a much more conscious refusal to fall back into cleaning up the ego, justifying the ego, etc., etc. No more "penetrating" under the bed to fuss about personal darkness. It is there; it will remain. Know it, carry it, and at last the single eye may integrate it.

I dreamed on New Year's morning in the small hours that I was to go through the second initiation ceremony into the Catholic Church, which I was joining. There was no emotional affect in this dream, simply a sense of fulfilling my destiny with entire commitment and detachment. I was accompanied to the place by a man—a totally trusted partner (a husband?)—who seemed to personify all the men whom I have loved and respected in my life, but who was nevertheless uniquely himself. Once he saw me settled to wait, he left me there. There were other people waiting there quietly, but I was nonetheless alone. I had a coat and a jacket with me and had brought certain objects (unspecified in dream) that I had needed for (or received at?) the first initiation, which was baptism. This had taken place some time ago. The coming ritual was "confirmation." We were told that a Mass was going on in the church building, of which I could see an outer wall and light in windows. We were to wait until the Mass was over. I wondered about what would be open to me, expected of me, after the initiation and thought I could receive the Host either standing or kneeling. I realized with some surprise that all that kind of ritual held no mana for me any more, and wondered, that being so, why I *knew* this confirmation was a necessity for me and had no important connection with those rituals which used to carry the mana.

I sat on a green-cushioned bench and waited, relaxed. Then someone came and told me to come with her (him?). I asked if I should bring the baptismal objects. (I have a vague impression of the tongs I use in the kitchen for picking things out of hot water, etc.) The guide said "No"—I needed nothing at all for this ceremony. I was taken to a place on a higher level in the open air and given a seat on a long bench with a line of others on each side of me. Then a woman approached me and I stood up and faced her. She did not speak but held in her hands a pomegranate which she had taken out of a green string bag. The bag disappeared and she made a circle of her fingers and thumbs holding the pomegranate encircled around the middle with the navel upward. Everything now faded out except the vision of her hands and the dance of the pomegranate she held. I noticed there were flaws like light-colored breaks or small clefts in the skin near the center. Nothing had been said to me but I knew that my *whole* attention must be given to the contemplation of those clefts which began to shift and change shape so that it seemed to me they would slowly disappear—that finally I might see the "point" which was the center, or the "pole" point, of this fruit. There was a temptation to use willpower to hasten things, but I knew this must not be. I must do *nothing* inwardly except contemplate exactly what I saw. I became strangely aware of my half-open downward-looking eyes, thinking, "My body is asleep in outer reality but wide awake here," and I entered into a deep, untroubled calm which was nevertheless alert to every tiny change in what I saw. The clefts had all disappeared now and I thought for an instant I glimpsed the central point, but then everything was dark. I did not move in the dream but found myself awake and at peace.

I fell asleep again and returned to the dream, to the darkness and my quiet gazing. And now I saw again not the fruit but the circle of the woman's fingers and thumbs, and it was as though an inner glow in the flesh of her hands shone out of them, revealing their strength and beauty.

(Charles Williams's wonderful prose poetry about the human hand in *The Greater Trumps* came back to me.) Although the pomegranate was now invisible I knew from the motionless hands that she still held its essence within them. I leaned further over, concentrating again on the dark circle where the fruit had been. And suddenly it was as though something gave way and I found myself gazing into a "shaft of darkness" thrusting down from the strong circle defined by the woman's hands, piercing deeper and deeper into the earth beneath us.

"Why does that sound so familiar?" I thought as I woke. Then it broke through to me: that poem long ago, one of the first I ever wrote. It was headed September 11, 1947, the date of my outer confirmation. I have found it, and it begins:

> *The strong slow pressure of a hand*
> *And I become a shaft of darkness*
> *Piercing the silent earth. . . .*

and continues:

> *The clear words sound in heart and mind,*
> *The hidden seed invades the dark.*
> *Passive, the dark receives it.*
> *Seed of the spirit, flame of life,*
> *How will you grow?*

In the days that follow I gaze and gaze into the dark circle formed by the human hands. And then deep down and far away I see the cross-section image of the center of the pomegranate, the six double rays of black seeds embedded in the red juicy pale pulp. The seeds in the shaft of darkness, once more awaiting growth. This time, seeds of the pomegranate. . . .

∞

JANUARY 7

There is a legend that the pomegranate tree grew from the blood of the dismembered Dionysus, the dying and resurrecting god of the vine. Its fruit

1982

is bittersweet, and the seed once "planted" in Persephone made her queen of the underworld (where the seeds of life lie sleeping, guarded by her) and made her the bringer of spring to the earth above when the time for their awakening comes.

At the time of my 1947 outer confirmation—which is the baptism of fire—I was not emotionally exalted. I was going through my first truly conscious acceptance of the dark—hence the image "I become a shaft of darkness." Now, at this 1982 New Year's Day confirmation into a kind of inner "catholic" universal church, I look down into the shaft, not personal as before but defined for me by the Guide, the woman who initiates us, it may be, to a vision of the *pomegranate*—i.e., the "apple" "having many (black) seeds." It comes to me as I see them in the depths that they must be guarded by the women of a future still hidden in the darkness till the time shall be ripe.

For me personally there is a special mana in the fact that the pomegranate is roughly hexagonal and twelve-rayed inside, linking to my mandala (and also to the twelve-sided Round House at the Farm). Likewise, the pomegranate is an annual birthday present from Martha.

FEBRUARY 2

On Monday morning early I had a dream that began with an anxious mess of trying to fulfill a lot of demands before leaving? getting to my own writing? Finally I was outside and saw across an empty field a man arriving with a white horse on a leading rein, and I had an impression of a small brown horse already there. The white horse was full of spirit, pulling on the rein, half rearing up—not a feeling of wildness, just pent-up energy. I began to wake here and thought "Is it the white horse of inspiration again?" But I knew it was not the great white stallion of my old dream. I was approaching them now and thought "It is either a gelding or a mare. I already have my small brown mare. Why another?" Yet somehow I knew it was a mare, and the thought of mare's milk came to me. Had the white mare milk to give? I saw myself reaching out my hands to her ears.

Later in the morning I was looking up something in Jung's letters—a possibility for Friday's group—and I came on one Jung had written in answer to questions about his carvings on the stone tower at Bollingen. It is dated December 1960, one of his last few letters:

> The first thing I saw in the stone was the figure of the worshipping woman, and behind her the silhouette of the old king sitting on his throne. As I was carving her out the old king vanished from view. Instead I suddenly saw that the unworked surface in front of her clearly revealed the hindquarters of a horse, and a mare at that, for whose milk the primitive woman was stretching out her hands. The woman is obviously my anima in the guise of a millennia-old ancestress.
>
> Milk, as *lac virginis*, virgin's milk, is a synonym for the *aqua doctrinae*. [*There's a footnote to the letter: "The water of doctrine, originally a Christian concept for the store of pure wisdom of the church."*]
>
> The mare descending from above reminded me of Pegasus. Pegasus is the constellation above the second fish in Pisces; it precedes Aquarius in the precession of the equinoxes. I have represented it in its feminine aspect, the milk taking the place of the spout of water in the sign for Aquarius. This feminine attribute indicates the unconscious nature of the milk. Evidently the milk has first to come into the hands of the anima, thus charging her with special energy. This afflux of anima energy immediately released in me the image of a she-bear, approaching the back of the anima from the left. The bear stands for the surge of energy and power of Artemis. In front of the bear's forward striding paws I saw, adumbrated in the stone, a ball—obviously this ball is being brought to the worshipping woman as a symbol of individuation. It points to the meaning or content of the milk.
>
> The whole thing, it seems to me, expresses coming events that are still hidden in the archetypal realm. The anima clearly

has her mind on spiritual contents. But the bear . . . sets the ball rolling.

[*There is a picture of the stone on the next page. Next to the female figure there is a carved inscription which translates as "Let the light I have carried in my womb shine forth."*]

I felt almost stunned when I read this—and again this morning, as I write it, I am near to tears at the great mystery of synchronicity. The image in my dream and fantasy about it I could well have dismissed as "nothing but," born of my empty longing for the "spark" as it used to be. But I feel now that my dream is a hint of the archetypal pattern Jung speaks of. He, being a man, experiences it all in the image of the anima, but in the fullness of time the conscious woman must reach out in worship for the lac virginis, the aqua doctrinae, which flows from the feminine aspect of Pegasus and must also turn and accept from the dark she-bear the ball of the totality, the meaning of the light she has carried hidden for so long in her womb.

I remembered that I had a strange intuition of paradox in my own images. I was somehow convinced that the white mare was, as it were, virgin, but told myself that was nonsense as she could not be giving milk if that were so.

What kind of ethical decision does this synchronistic experience require of me? I have just come on the passage in *Memories, Dreams, Reflections* which says that without such a decision all dreams and fantasies lead nowhere.

FEBRUARY 3

I am beginning to emerge from the stunned feeling after the synchronicity experience. I remember a little more of the dream that went before the coming of the white mare. The "obligations" or "concerns" or "demands" that I felt in the dream as so frustrating came from my grandparents—in particular my grandfather, who appeared in this dream in his prime, a man of **great** integrity and strength, upholder of the authority which was his truth in that day and age. I remember thinking in the dream that my mother was not a factor in this dream. The confrontation was with the "grandfathers," not the parents. It therefore goes farther back and deeper. My grandfather (and I write about this in my autobiography), while he embodied the superior male to his wife and daughter, nevertheless did a great deal for the cause of women's education in India. Even at home he went to a woman doctor. Also, while the Victorian narrowness and snobbery held him in his personal life, he risked his whole career by disobeying an unjust order from his superiors during an Indian famine. He would stand in my dream for the best of the patriarchal order (the grandfather equivalent to the old king replaced by the mare in Jung's vision). Perhaps the dream is indicating that my obligations to this value must be paid before moving on to the place where the white mare awaits—the feminine Pegasus with the milk of the new wisdom which alone, when received by the women of our time, can bring the transition to the new age of the next constellation of Aquarius—who also in legend has been seen as woman as well as man.

To Jung his vision expressed coming events still hidden in the archetypal realm.

Mingled with these thoughts came another memory from a few days ago, when, after waking, I experienced a hint of what it actually means to *know* (not just with the head or intuitively) when the center of one's individual being moves from the ego to the Self. It is impossible to put these things into adequate words, but I must try to express something of this experience if it is not to disappear again into the unconscious. It was not at all the same thing as the familiar moments of acceptance of the will of God, of the facts of one's outer and inner life exactly as they are. On the personal level it came, I think, in a moment of recognizing how many of my recent dreams have contained warnings that somewhere in the shadow I still cling to the half hope that the old kind of spark—the writing spark from the great stallion—will return to me once more. And I saw how this has been at the root of the recent meaninglessness and the frustrations in the lesser dreams. And there came a leap of joy. It was not the usual, my thought or feeling which I had expressed in the story called "Inner Truth," * when I gave back to the white stallion that energy spark which he had given me fifteen or more years before. I knew when it passed into me that it was given not to possess but to carry for a time. This present joy was not, as I say, at the thought of it, but at an actual momentary *experience* of that energy flowing back into the Self and leaving the ego not deprived, not empty of meaning, but in a state of peaceful readiness for her new way, however little may be seen manifestations of the Self in this world or the Beyond.

1982

I had already put aside the attempt to write of this as too difficult, and so have half-forgotten it already. Hence perhaps the mystery of the white mare.

FEBRUARY 15

I have been trying to decide whether to ask Dr. Smith to take me off the pills for my eye problems, since the pills are sapping my energy. But this morning I am reconsidering, because I have been suspicious for some time that what the pills are doing to me is in some way a blessing at this period, until the transformation of attitude so constantly prefigured in recent dreams has truly broken through into my life. A return of the old energy could most easily throw me back into an attempt to "ride" the white stallion again, and then I would lose the vision of the white mare and her milk. In the image Jung carved at Bollingen, it is the bear behind the woman which sets the ball rolling towards her, not the white stallion. If it were he, the mare's milk would no longer be the lac virginis—the milk of the Woman who is one-in-herself.

Now, the bear is the heavy shadow thing, the weight of the instinctive mother unconscious which can smother and devour the life of the spirit—and yet it longs for the light which only human consciousness can bring.

---

* Helen refers here to the story she wrote over a several-year period that records her work in active imagination and that includes Simon the Praise Singer, Chung Li, and other figures that also appear in her diary.

Last night's dream contained another phase of the grandfather theme. In it the house next door but one to mine was on fire. I saw the inmates standing on the threshold looking out, outlined against the fierce blaze of the fire. I knew no one was in danger but hoped the fire engines were on the way, as the fire might spread along the line of houses. It was a terrace, no space between them. But no fire engines came, and I realized that the fire seemed wholly contained, limited to the one house which would be completely destroyed. The inmates were sitting around on the front lawn watching it burn without concern. There was a feeling that they were the grandfathers—and I now put into words as far as is possible the images which moved as I watched the dream in a half-waking, dozing state. It seemed to me that these people from the burning house were now free to move on, as it were, to the place where they belonged, and that one or two who had been living in my house, or in the in-between house, now emerged and joined them as they walked slowly away, talking gravely and serenely together. There was also something about Aunt Emmie or Em following them (a widow with a small daughter, Joan, with whom we lived when we were first in London, when I was three to five years old, and who was a somewhat severe mother figure to me). In the dream her name was the important thing, being Em = M, and a comprehensive image it seemed of all the "mothers" in my life.

Fully awake and reflecting, it seems to me that this dream is symbolizing the separation of the grandfather archetype—and subsequently the mother archetype—from the personal level where they attach themselves to our projections onto the people we love or hate. They can now live fully in the Beyond and their wisdom and meaning can flow to us through the pure milk of the virgin, the lac virginis, and through the stream of lifegiving water from the Aquarian jar, undistorted by the projections and by emotional possession. This can come about when the fire of the emotions is allowed to burn objectively, as it were, when it will burn down the old structure which has housed it so long and set free the meaning. Perhaps the three houses in my dream are the three generations on the personal level, the one between the grandfather house and mine being the mother's house. This would fit with the previous dream of having to free myself from the demands of my grandfather in which, though my mother was present, she played no part. Both dreams might therefore be saying that once the authority archetype is truly set free from projection and known in the Self, then the mother is already free to join him. I have to remember that my personal grandfather was the original father image for me, since I never knew my father, as well as being very much the grandfather.

This all seems to me to amplify and deepen many recent dreams. Also the fire now reminds me of the instinctive fire of the bear image.

FEBRUARY 21   ❧

Much dreaming last night and I woke restless, but in my musing time one image from a dream came alive and moved. The dream was about a woman who had been expected to care for her five younger siblings. At the end of the dream a figure appeared—a man dressed in a kind of checkered costume that reminded me of a Fool—who interrupted saying "What about *me?* The family never even looked at me." I thought, "He is the youngest brother," and I said to him "No, but you saw them. You truly looked at each one and at their children." And then for a moment I felt joy and slipped into a half-dream in which perhaps for the first time I allowed myself to *feel*—not just think about—the things I had been told about my father. Especially did I somehow realize the enormous importance of the fact that he and I did *meet* before he died. I have been told he used to carry me (maybe five months old?) in his arms round and round the garden at The Warren. He certainly looked at me and I, as certainly, no matter how young my eyes, at him. The baby's experiences, however unconscious, remain, and may someday be known.

And I suddenly believed that, whatever this "fool" uncle meant, my father had more than a bit of the Fool in his short life. All that I have heard about him—especially the extraordinary quality of his laughter—as well as the joy that sprang up in people's hearts when they were with him, would confirm this.

I passed into sleep and an eye was looking into mine, very close to my own. It was of an extraordinarily limpid aquamarine color, yet colorless—how to describe it? like clear water with the sun on it, not blue, not green, both and neither, transparent, sparkling, still.

I have always had some difficulty with the image of the Eye of God seeing us. Suddenly I have an intuition that this connects with my never having allowed myself full awareness of the fact that my personal father—first image of the Great Father to the child—truly *saw* me, looked into my eyes however briefly. "That never is absent (in the Beyond) which always is beloved."

I am now wondering whether the recent dreams, when the grandfather image has suddenly become so much more objective and his old authority is breaking, perhaps mean that all my long life the personal father image was carried by my grandfather and stood between that one vital unconscious meeting with my true father and my conscious awareness of it.

FEBRUARY 22

To return to the "eye" theme. I remember the ancient greeting of the Bushman, and of his animal images, which is always "I see you." How beautiful and profound that is! Not a question—"How do you *do?*"—or a conventional wish—"Good morning"—but simply a statement that the individual is *seeing* another unique person, seeing his essence, not his qualities good or bad.

I have written a real letter to Laurens van der Post with special gratitude for *The Heart of the Hunter.* There is a beautiful paragraph in the chapter "Homesick for a Story" which I wish I had reread before writing my introduction to *The Inner Story:* "He knew intuitively that without a story one had no clan or family; without a story of one's own, no individual life; without a story of stories no continuity with the beginning and therefore no future. Life for him was living a story."

It occurs to me that the whole vocation of the "analyst" is to listen to the individual story of each person who comes, and thus to *see* him or her and to recognize the connection of each unique story to the "story of stories"—and to recognize moreover its impact on the analyst's own individual story.

1982

FEBRUARY 23   ∞

The greeting "I see you"—if one could use it not only to every person but to every *thing* one meets! This was surely Jung's greeting to his pots and pans in the Bollingen kitchen. Every smallest thing *seen,* and therefore oneself also fully seen. No calculations about "use."

Musing this morning, I'm aware, in the dream of the eye, of a deeper and deeper impact. I have been remembering what I wrote about old age bringing a greater sense of one's own life as a circle and not a straight line. Then the looking back of the old becomes not a regressive nostalgia but a wonderful discovery of unsuspected meanings, a "sniffing out," a "casting about" for new scents of the pattern. My eyes as a small baby, looking up before ego consciousness began into the eyes of my father, looking up through the yet unclouded, clear water of the unconscious—one of the first meetings which all babies must experience, meetings with "the Other" that begin with the emergence of the new person from identity with the mother's body. I know that in my own story I was begotten in love and that my eyes must have met the response of love in his eyes—a meeting reflecting in this world of time the eternal meeting of love between creator and created. Very soon afterwards came the experience of my mother's terrible grief at the loss of her beloved, devoid of meaning for her at that time, and entering into me as a lifelong sense of anguish, fear, and guilt. Somehow she was separated from him because of me—because of me she had left him in India—and the timeless meeting with him sank into the unconscious as though it had never been. But it rises now in the circle of my life as though I clearly remember it, and it carries me beyond itself to The Eye—and the possibility arises of the "seeing as we are seen," "knowing as we are known," as St. Paul said and realized. Perhaps only those few, such as he, could have written such as II Corinthians 13, or Jung's great paragraph on love at the end of "Late Thoughts" in *Memories, Dreams,*

Reflections. (Von Franz, writing on the bonds of relationship in the Self, is with that great company [*Projection and Recollection,* p. 17].)

No dreams remembered in these days, but very briefly there came another experience of the kind I tried to describe on February 3—the momentary release from that lifelong hidden "angst" that obscures and cuts the ego off from the serenity, the deep peace that lies below and above and all around and through it, even including the angst itself in its totality—even *that* a vessel of meaning in the glory of conflict accepted, which is the human condition.

I woke with a musing dream. The theme of seeing—of the greeting "I see you"—was moving below consciousness, and I thought, "What is the first thing to greet with 'I see you' when consciousness returns after sleep?" And I greeted *myself,* "I see you," and looked, wondering just what (not whom) I should see. And what I saw was so astonishing that I tried for a moment to push it away, but then knew I must truly look. It was a small round thing—the size perhaps of a hazel nut, and so light that it was lifted and blown about as though by a light breeze, playing into, it as it were. And when it was still, I saw that it was a tiny *person* curled up in the position of an embryo, head on knees and hands clasping her/his legs. I thought first, "It's a boy," then, "No, it's a girl," then, "No, it is neither or both," and then, "It's like Ariel, who lay in a cowslip's bell." This person whose face now looked up at me had straight fairish hair and was like a most beautiful small boy or girl, and was yet quite certainly not a child. One look and then the little round nut went dancing up into the air and down again, rolling over and over in the wind. It is an embryo, I thought. Must it find a womb in which to be held until the birth into this world? I had forgotten by now that this vision had started with a greeting to myself and was bewildered and a bit frightened to remember it. And now the one thing that repeated itself over and over again in my mind were Hamlet's words, "Oh God, I could be bounded in a nutshell and count myself a king of infinite space, were it not that I have bad dreams." I could absorb no more that day.

Later: It was only this morning that the meaning of the nutshell dream and Shakespeare's words began to expand for me. When I said "I see you" with all the objectivity possible to me, I did indeed see for a moment the embryonic kernel which exists in all of us, which is neither male nor female yet both, which is bounded in the smallest facet of this earth and at the same time a king of infinity, and which so few of us realize because of our "bad" dreams. The very phrase "bad dreams" reveals the answer. There are no such things, there are only dreams, neither good nor bad but *facts* of nature, of the psyche, of the spirit, some of which yield their meaning to us, some of which we cannot decipher. Whenever we touch the true meaning for us individually of an image, we are both bound and set free by it—bound to the conflicts, the obligations, the physical and ethical realities of life in time and set free by a glimpse of eternal meanings.

I realize afresh how vulnerable I still am to the lifelong collective habit of reacting to an often improperly remembered dream with the feeling "what a 'bad' person I must be; no 'good' dreams come to reassure me," and I am caught in the ego's good/bad comparative merit business all over again—*caught*, not *bounded* in the human conflict, and thus enslaved by it instead of being set free into the realm of the creative symbol.

I have another thought—or intuition—this morning, which is born, perhaps, of the foregoing. And it would explain the constant repetition by the *I Ching*, when I have spoken with it, on the necessity of "the small." It comes to me that I so easily forget what my actual gift is. It is a small gift and it expresses itself best in immediate and brief responses to things I love, whether in life or in my reading of the great ones. I have said that this is the feminine creative gift par excellence, and all my fussing about *The Odyssey* work, for example, has come from the animus wanting to produce a long, continuously thought-out "work." There are in these later journals many reflections and responsive thoughts to my reading which I would love, for my own sake, to put into some kind of brief form (a collection of Reflections?) The *King Lear* paper is one of my shortest, and I am sure one of the best, at least it is to me. And it was an intense response to one brief speech, deeply heard and loved.

A dream last night.

I was sitting beside a large trough of water and a woman was in it who had decided in full consciousness to drown herself. (The woman was pale, whitish all over—dress, face—dark hair, and some beads around her neck.) She lay down in the water and submerged her head. Another woman behind me left at this point. I knew I must stay, but that all I could do was pray. I must respect the drowning woman's choice. After a few seconds there was a movement and she sat up in the water. She had changed her mind, but not because she hadn't the courage to go through with it. She climbed out shivering with cold and dripping water. I wanted to wrap her in a towel, filled with relief, compassion, and the desire to warm her. But she thrust the towel aside, and I wondered if she could not bear at this point to feel anything remotely smothering again so soon after emerging from the drowning sensation. At this point she either became Emily, my cat, or was replaced by Emily. I took her to a warm place near my fireplace.

Either immediately before or after this dream I saw an image of a fireplace and down out of the chimney fell some lumps of anthracite coal—fuel for the fire—and immediately after that, numbers of smaller pieces of coal burst as it were "out of" Emily, who was sitting beside the fire. As I woke I thought of the clean burning of anthracite, the often gleaming facets—and the name "black diamonds."

The suicide dream was very disturbing yesterday. This morning I stayed with it awhile. Was the cat a repressive thing? I've had, though, several associations recently with thoughts of the cat as a goddess archetype and of the cat that walks by himself and yet is in close contact with humans.

We cannot possess or control her as we can a dog—yet we can and must care for her in exchange for her gift to us.

Is it possible that this is a dream insisting on the absolute need for me to let go of all perfectionist striving in my inner life—everything now depending on my relatedness to the completeness symbolized by the animal? (I read a day or two ago a passage in Jung's letters referring to this animal wholeness.) The perfectionist shadow—her joyless whiteness reflected in the expression of her face—is in despair and in danger of simply going back into the unconscious, in which case there would have been no instinctively complete image to replace her. The feeling in the dream was that I could give the cat a warm place to dry off without any danger of possessing or smothering her. . . .

The release of the coal, the black diamonds which had got stuck in the chimney (upward thrusting), came when those two white women disappeared and the cat herself brought fuel for the hearth fire, but if I was unconsciously thrusting this fuel, unburned, up the chimney it would constitute a fire hazard.

The *I Ching* and dream after dream, for a long time, have been emphasizing that I must absolutely stop *pushing,* goal seeking, etc., inwardly as well as outwardly.

MARCH 29

I dreamed I had moved house. My new place was a large room on the ground floor of a large house. It felt wholly private and yet in some strange way open to people from another part of the house who cared for my needs. I had slept awhile, tired after the move, and I woke now. Wondering what time it was, I thought I must fetch a clock from my former dwelling, on the same road and owned by my mother. I saw then that someone had brought me a clock and had set it down beside me. My bed was on the floor and the clock likewise. It had a black face and white numerals. It was 6:30 P.M. I also wished I had brought my electric heater. I tried to remember the number of the former house. My part of it had been called "The Annex." Then I saw that in the center of this room was a round brick fireplace with coals, ready to be lit, but there was no chimney over it. However a wide reddish brick channel, more like a pathway, led from the round fireplace sloping steeply upwards with at intervals small neatly piled heaps of coals at one side then the other. I wondered whether somehow or other the smoke would be drawn along this pathway and away from the room.

MARCH 30

❧

Sunday night's dream of the "brick road," the coals, the round fireplace (shaped like a well, by the way), the room absolutely empty except for the bed (or, rather, blankets on the floor) and the clock—it has all become more and more numinous. I sit there behind the central place looking up along the brick way. There is no fire yet, I see, and no kindling to make it possible for me to start it. Someone else must bring a flaming torch, a burning coal to ignite the waiting fuel, the black diamonds.

APRIL I

❧

Talk with Else and Jane on Tuesday was very valuable, and opened up the dreams for me in many ways, especially perhaps Jane's feeling that the last dream connected to American Indian images of the smoke path to the Great Spirit, linking images of Old World and New.

My task seems to be to stay with the waiting fuel, contemplating the black diamonds now freed from being thrust up the chimney, thrust up to heaven unburned. Stay and guard the round fireplace and the fire shall come in its own time. This image is closely linked to the circle of the woman's hands and the dark pomegranate, whose seeds must be guarded by the woman (Persephone) until the time for their sprouting. It is the great transition time from Pisces to Aquarius, the time of the feminine aspect of Pegasus, of the white mare giving her milk. The water from above, the fire from below may not come in my lifetime, but that is no matter for my concern. The conscious women of today must perhaps simply make possible the gathering of the fuel into the circle, by work on their own feminine receptivity to the lac virginis, their own deepest contemplative values.

Tonight I am wakeful and I have touched the edge of a new experience of the opposites, the opposites in God which I hardly dare to attempt to express. Indeed I can't begin to put it into adequate words, yet I must begin.

Something in me has long recognized the identity—the brotherhood—of Satan and Christ, the truths of *Answer to Job*, but the recognition has been somehow remote, only dimly realized through the agelong white veil set up by the Christian one-sided version of the all-goodness of God. But tonight it came to me for an instant that the unswerving love of God for his creation which is Himself must be as ruthlessly self-centered as any of the self-regarding passions of the human ego, and as utterly unconcerned with the appalling sufferings of countless innocent people, who are simply parts of the tremendous and unknowable patterns of the cosmos. It becomes then indubitably clear that it is only through his creation of individual men and women with their capacity for unlimited expansion of consciousness that God can also become conscious of Himself, consent to experience the separation and overwhelming conflict between good and evil by his incarnation in each unique human being, and so reveal the transcendent wholeness which is the meaning of both dark and light.

This has suddenly brought to vivid life the images in recent dreams: the contemplation of the dark pomegranate descending into the earth, and most powerfully the meaning of the cat from whom the black diamonds, the coal from the earth, emerged and lay ready in the round brick fireplace—fuel for the new fire, the new flaming of light and energy from the black fuel. The cat is a marvelous symbol of the beauty and terror of nature in her wholeness—the cat, remote yet related, horribly destructive, full of the grace and beauty of the animal who is always whole, fulfilling that for which it is created. No fuel for the new fire can come to me from that pallid "good" woman who had reached a kind of martyred despair. But having suffered and done her best she brings the cat in her stead, and the cat the fuel. My need is for acceptance of the wild and destructive creative aspect of the Godhead—the things most feared.

As these images flooded into me I felt the beginnings of a great freeing, a new sense of detachment from all the levels of good and evil in the world, which can come only with the glimpses of wholeness that now and then touch us by grace. A strange double thing this detachment can be—all the worldly joys and sorrows, horrors and beauties seen as so trivial, while at the same time they are the essential means leading us to the total commitment of love and compassion in any situation whatsoever.

With this came realization of the utter ruthlessness of the ego's love of herself: "I want what I want and I will have it no matter what it does to others"—the ego is identified with the rejected cat, identified with God's darkness when it is hidden and denied by the phony whiteness of man's exclusive affirmation of the good God. God's answer to Job: "I created Leviathan and all the other horrors. Merit and demerit have nothing to do with it. Yet I too must become man and suffer and make ethical decisions, as you do, in order to know myself."

∽

APRIL 13

The brick fireplace and road of my last big dream have remained vivid through these days, the black shining coals awaiting the fire and myself sitting crosslegged behind the circle of bricks, waiting quiet and still, returning again and again from speculating thoughts.

But also I have been considering other images in that same dream. The woman, black-clothed, meeting my needs, coming and going without need of words between us, I know as the same whom I have met before, notably in the dream, years ago, of the child playing outside the public building where I had business to transact. When I emerged I saw the woman in her "cart," the horse stopped beside the entrance to the building, the woman watching the child for me and ensuring her safety while I was gone. As soon as I appeared she waved to me in recognition and I to her, as a policeman moved her on—at exactly the right moment.

So in this last dream she brought me the clock when I woke on my pallet on the floor and needed to know the time—the clock with black face and white numerals. The time was 6:30. I thought it was 6:30 P.M. I had been resting after the hard work of moving. 6:30 is roughly the beginning

1982

of relaxation in the evening for me. Around that time I undress, turn on the TV (6:30 news), get my supper and eat it while watching. Such programs as I watch are for the most part between then and 9 P.M. Then I read, then sleep. The work day is over, including social meetings. Has this some connection with the emergence of the coal from the cat, which is so lovely an image of complete relaxation when she ceases to move?

I am having some strange thoughts—are they far-fetched? Here goes anyway. In the dream I had been sleeping in exhaustion after the move to this strange new place without furniture—nothing but the pallet and the waiting coals. When I wake, I am tempted to fetch needful things from the mother's house, but my needs are met as they occur, and I see by the clock that (by association) it is the end of my working day, the beginning of relaxing. It comes to me that the feeling of these latter months has been so often of work going on just below consciousness, which I have been too tired to bring up but which nevertheless was a valid work, out of sight below. Now with this dream begins a time of *conscious* contemplative waiting beside the gathered fuel. . . . The same conscious contemplation of the dark was indicated in the pomegranate dream. The "rapt contemplation" of the cat in T. S. Eliot's poem "of his deep and inscrutable singular name" occurs to me suddenly here—so very different from the perfection-striving woman and her despair. Her sudden replacement by the cat bringing the fuel is startling indeed. And now the string of large, dark wooden beads round the woman's neck as she rose out of the water comes back to me and springs to life in association with the gift of the old woman with her sores at the bottom of the pool, the necklace which was the girl's unique identity.*

Rosary-like beads, but unique, each roughly carved. I feel them between my fingers. "There is a providence that shapes our ends, rough hew them how we will." Yet we must hew them, however roughly, joining our best attempts to the flow of our lives from the Self. And so may we come to

---

* Helen's story of the old woman's gift, "An African Tale," appears in her book *Kaleidoscope: The Way of Woman and Other Essays* (PARABOLA Books).

the contemplation of the "deep and inscrutable singular Name" which is One and infinitely many.

Thoughts about atomic power and the symbolism of the Self: split into the Christ and Antichrist it can mean final destruction or the discrimination-bringing conscious wholeness. The *use* of atomic power for personal ends, even for creating the "good" productive energy, means destruction either by war in a few hours or by slow pollution of the earth. The only answer lies in the individuation of enough people who renounce all such use of the power of the Self when faced with the conflicts and tensions of life in time and space, the human condition. Tolkien's images express it as no rational words can. On all the other levels we must fight the evil thing, retaining always our compassion, but ultimate disaster is assured if the wizard—or the King or Beatrice or Galadriel—within us are identified with the Self and possessed by its power. (That way lies Jonestown.) Hence the great danger of even our best-meant efforts to manipulate the images of the unconscious both in ourselves and even more in other people. It is being done in mental healing techniques, in depth psychology, in artificial med-itation and mystical power drives. For the power of atomic energy outwardly is paralleled by the psychic powers which are opening for those who will seize and use them. Therefore, very much more awareness of the nature of group activities, health slogans, fear-breeding propaganda, and collective panaceas is one of the most vital needs of the time. In all these things the sense of individual destiny, the meaning of suffering in each separate life, is swamped and the miraculous cure of the symptom is sought; the true healing through the discovery of individual and community meaning in the Self is deferred and thrust down again and turns negative by the *use* instead of the *recognition* of the mystery of the divine.

I am aware suddenly that, over the years, in so many of my deepest dreams and visions, the insight, the wonder and joy, have been broken into and succeeded by repressive images because at the end of these dreams I have been concerned with the thought of telling others, my friends, about the vision I have had rather than contemplating the image in itself. The right kind of sharing is a lovely thing in a woman, an essential of her being, but it is also her particular danger. This, as I have often said, is the paramount message to women of the Eros-Psyche myth—the fatal turning aside from *the* "one thing needful," as opposed to the willingness to turn aside from all lesser goals in the service of others.

The crudest of the statements of my danger, mentioned in my autobiography, came far back in the early months of work with Toni when I dreamed that I saw a cat and a bird meeting each other in amity, and thought I'd write to the *Times* about so wonderful a thing! Since then there have been many similar hints, the clearest in my memory being the great dream of the cube of stone and light descending beside me and my calling out to those who had taken shelter below to come at once and share this glorious thing. The stone slowly lifted again, changing from square to oblong and then disappearing. This was probably entirely necessary at that time, but of late there have been many indications that the "sharing" is no longer my specific task—that the Rainmaker, contemplative phase, upon the threshold of which I stand, is as yet a looking at the dark (pomegranate, unlit coals), and that the urgency is great for me to let go far more consciously and comprehensively of that seeking for reassurance from others of the validity of my "seeings" and of the usefulness of my life.

JUNE 9   ∞

Last night's dream: I saw as it were an "egg" in my head—pale, cloudy, blue-white with much movement going on inside, the activity in the egg that produces new life—a kind of alchemical vessel, and I knew with certainty that it was the moment when my old kind of thinking must be let go completely to be replaced by a wholly new way of thought represented in the dream by the new life being created in the egg.

I think I half-woke here with the realization that the old way had a constant undercurrent of trying to improve, to reach a goal, and thought how difficult it was to stop this entirely in order to make room for the egg. Then came an association with von Franz's chapter in her *Alchemy* which describes the dangers of overanalysis and the ease with which one can miss the vital moment of change from this to conscious spontaneity.

After this half dreaming I went back into full dream, and it now seemed that the egg, as well as being a wholly new order of thought, was also a new food. It seemed to be based in the mouth and sending fumes up into the brain. I thought with a smile that some people would call it "brandy," but that this image missed the point because although the egg had a fiery quality, like brandy, the latter was something that brought back life, restored the old kind of vitality after a shock, and its effect wears off, whereas the egg brought food for something entirely new and different from all that had gone before.

This takes me back to the cat and the coals dream. Also I see that although I have longed for years to be free of the analytical goal-seeking and felt it to be time—and there have been dreams, often enough, showing me functioning in this way—yet I have never let go of the old—could not perhaps before the time was fully ripe.

Von Franz tells of her patient who dreamed it was time to jump into the water where there was a golden fish. She says he jumped long ago into the unconscious and confronted a long, hard analysis, but this new jump meant it was time to swim there as the fish swims, not to catch it and not to identify with it. (The "purification of the motive" was over.) In the new state one can show anger, happiness, all the impulses of the heart, but always there is present the ability to *choose* in a split second when and how—spontaneity so like the child's innocence but so different.

∾   **AUGUST 14**

I have frequent feelings nowadays of being so near to at least an approximation of that "condition of complete simplicity," the empty sound. And then at others a devastating awareness of the ego's unending demands and laziness. The beautiful thing that I must remember, return to again and again (quoted by Hannah) is Jung's reply to those who said "What do I *do* about it?"—"Nothing. You just *know* it." And he would then quote the Chinese saying: "Indolence of which you are aware and indolence of which you are not aware are a thousand miles apart."

It is the same as Christ's saying "If thou knowest what thou art doing then thou art blessed."

This does not in the least contradict that other teaching of Jung when he insisted that the dreams *must* affect one's outer actions. If we really know, then we shall inevitably take the appropriate actions. I am forever putting the cart before the horse, fussing and struggling to discover the right actions before attending to the images and waiting for the Self to bring the change.

SEPTEMBER 15   ✐

I dreamed that my father had come from India at last to visit. We had been total strangers and I was looking forward now to building a close personal relationship. He approached me courteously and we shook hands and exchanged a few words. Then he said he must leave again and go back to India. There was no emotional involvement, but I was simply astonished that this brief meeting was to be enough.

Then the dream continued on another level, and I was watching some children about to cross a street and knew that they were in danger from a huge snake, half-hidden in the long grass near the curb, of which they were not aware. I was standing some yards away and I suddenly and quite quietly knew that they would be safe because some kind of communication was going on between me and the snake which diverted its attention from the children so that they safely crossed. I knew that this communication with the snake was now possible to me because of that brief meeting with my father. It depended on constant attention and awareness of the snake's hidden presence.

The main association is a passage from Jung's *Mysterium Coniunctionis* which I discovered over the weekend:

> The dark sun of feminine psychology is connected with the
> father-imago, since the father is the first carrier of the animus-

image. He endows this virtual image with substance and form, for on account of his Logos he is the source of "spirit" for the daughter. Unfortunately this source is often sullied just where we would expect clean water. . . . These hints may suffice to make clear what kind of spirit it is that the daughter needs. They are the truths which speak to the soul, which are not too loud and do not insist too much, but reach the individual in still-ness—the individual who constitutes the meaning of the world. It is this knowledge that the daughter needs, in order to pass it on to her son. (pp. 182–183)

I think that all the recent animus dreams have led up to this glimpse of resolution. They have shown the falsity of the "good boy" animus, my yearning back to the Timmy and Bob images. I have projected the father onto many men, but most especially onto Timmy and Bob, and in one recent dream I am positively running after Bob, who is the "ideal" spiritual image whose critical disapproval I still fear and resent. But in this last dream I finally meet my own actual and natural father, and his extraordinary gift to me is something far beyond any personal projection or emotion—the possibility of a relatedness to that great symbol, two-natured, healing-destructive, which is in a woman the masculine archetype of the spirit, and whose truths reach her "in stillness" and are passed on to others without words.

◦∕◦

SEPTEMBER 16

Last night a visionary experience about which it is not possible to find adequate words. It was preceded by a dream in which someone had a huge projection onto me and was following me around starry-eyed. I was afraid she was in danger of being swallowed by the image she had been projecting onto me. I felt great compassion for her, but knew that I could not do anything to help. I simply remained aware. After a while the woman turned to me again and I knew she was now free and had shed the projection.

I woke and lay reflecting on the dream. My own shadow projecting the Self onto my ego? I felt the dream was somehow a continuation of the ser-

pent dream—the simple, compassionate awareness of danger again bringing freedom to the other.

Then came the vision. I was contemplating my own lily pool with one
tall "Blue Star" in full bloom standing high above the water and several
other strong buds of different heights and fullness, and the clear dark water
with the vivid green pads, but I was not looking *at* it, I now realized. I was
somehow at one with it, as though seeing it for the first time both from
within and from without—experiencing the whole plant, the roots thrusting down into soil and manure, the new shoots and young curled leaves,
the spreading pads and the frogs upon them, the strength of living growth
in the thrusting stems and buds and the glory of the blue star flower with
its golden center. But this does not describe the core of the experience at
all. For simultaneously with this completely relaxed at-one-ness with the
vision I was not withdrawn at all from the ordinary concerns of my mind
or heart on other levels, but they were all in an indescribable way also at
one with the life of the plant. It was in me and everything around me and
I was in it together with everything that could ever happen in the universe.
The extraordinary thing was that the thinking *about* the experience and the
experience itself had become one thing. I don't know how to express it. I
was fully awake and conscious throughout. It lasted well over an hour, I
think.

SEPTEMBER 18

One thing not clearly expressed in my writing of the vision is that I was
not looking down from above on the lily. It was as though I saw it all from
the level of the stem and saw the intense blue of the flower from just below
its spreading petals, the light of the sun shining through it and the dark
but clear water below. It feels as though my ego *was* the stem. . . .

The image of the Buddha sitting in the lotus, the jewel in the lotus,
came to me. And I remembered Jung's words in *Mysterium Coniunctionis:*
"God cannot be experienced at all unless this futile and ridiculous ego
offers a modest vessel in which to catch the effluence of the Most High
and name it with his name." Leading up to this Jung had written that the

inner peregrination must embrace every aspect of existence. "Nothing may be 'disregarded'. . . . Not a turning away from its empirical 'so-ness', but the fullest possible experience of the ego as reflected in the 'ten thousand things'—that is the goal of the peregrination." (p. 215)

This now is strongly associated with the experience I had in the vision, when all the manifold thoughts and distractions were a part of the one-ness with the lotus—and with the feeling that the ego was somehow the strong and essential stem holding up the cup, the vessel of the flower itself in the center of which is the jewel of the Self—and the ego names it with *His* name, not its own.

I have delightedly realized the full meaning of the word *interest*. It derives of course from the Latin *inter esse*, "to be between or among," to be between the subject and the object, between the I and the me. And the word *between* itself is from the root *twine*—two separate threads woven together into twine (not merged). To be *interested* is then to be between one's own sub-jective ego and the other person or object—and it involves a complete awareness of the present moment—the moment of meeting, or seeing, or hearing. Worry about or desire for what is to come, regret for or clinging to the past, destroy true *interest*, the moment by moment experience of the opposites from the point *between* the two in which they are both in and outside time in the Self. (The Germanic root of *between* is given in the *American Heritage Dictionary* as meaning "at the middle point of two.") *Between* of course always implies only two persons or things—therefore, an individual meeting. "Inter-" can mean either "between" or "among," and it is a matter of "the many, the crowd." The *interest* which is simply existing among the ten thousand things or part of the mass, and the *interest* which is between, meeting each separately and consciously, are poles apart. *Conscious* interest implies between, not among. It begins with the meetings between one's ego and single figures of the unconscious and ends when that which is between is known as the Self.

1983

JANUARY 3

It came to me this morning that only when one can realize that it is in fact *impossible* for anything, anyone, any "distraction" whatever to "interrupt" the Self—only then does one know the freedom of the spirit.

The meaning of the word *interrupt* is "to break between." Since in the wholeness of being nothing is excluded, when we feel interrupted it hides a refusal of the "so-ness" of life. The memory of the vision of the blue star lily and of that intense experience of oneness, in which I was aware of all the usual distractions of the ten thousand things, is a benediction to me, even just in memory. In that moment there was no need to *escape* them to reach the inner stillness: they were "just so" and were included in that quiet, unconditional "yes" of which Jung speaks, and they did not cloud the sense of oneness for a second. To have been given that experience once (as old Father Robson said to me) is blessing enough in time. It is enough to enable one to imagine the life of eternity—to know that it *is*.

JANUARY 10

A haiku!

> *On my face*
> *The soft paw of my cat—*
> *A new day.*

JANUARY 17

"Winston Churchill: The Wilderness Years" began on *Masterpiece Theatre* last night. I am reminded of R. H. Blyth's definition of the Zen man: the whole, individuated person. He is, as I have often thought, one who does *everything* with his whole heart, with complete commitment and devotion—or, in Jung's words, one who lives his hypothesis to the bitter end, to the death if need be. That is why Hannah called Winston individuated. He committed himself with utter devotion to all his activities, and moreover he neglected none of the functions—brick-laying, painting, his love for Clemmie, his thoughts, his political beliefs, his gambling "risks," his intuitions. We are so conditioned that we are always mixing up wholeness with being "good" and "right." It is the devotion that matters—the conscious devotion with which we are willing to risk all kinds of mistakes and willing to pay the price if we are wrong. "That which your hand findeth to do, do it with all thy might."

I am not clear at all yet as to what it means in my life to set free the Ariel within, to let go entirely of that spirit, that spark, that produced my writings and attracted people to me. I know very well, of course, the periodic darkness and emptiness that comes to everyone who does creative work. But the final letting go requires quite a different kind of emptiness, which would be quite free of any thought of being deserted by the spirit or of hope for its return. Until the final freeing, Ariel was held in the service of the ego—however beneficent that service, however "unselfish" the ego might become.

Once completely free, Ariel would be known not as going or coming, but as the objective everpresent reality of joy, never again to be a "spell" operating through a specific kind of work or activity or through personal emotion but present in every smallest thing when we are aware enough to recognize it, even in our stumblings and mistakes and "dryness."

∽ JANUARY 30

I cannot concentrate, cannot pray or hold an image just now. Last night's dream states the danger. I dreamed I was in a large, high-ceilinged, empty room, which was mine, and there were a lot of flies, mostly playing around in the upper lefthand corner of the room. I had a can of fly spray in my hand and was preparing to eliminate the flies when I saw an enormous black beetle walking about. I was horrified, calling it a cockroach to myself, though I knew at once on waking that it was a scarab beetle. I had seen its shape very clearly. In the dream I thought, "The spray won't kill it," with a kind of double reaction of relief and dismay. Then I thought that it could be crushed if one stepped on it, but couldn't bear to do that, and wondered if I should ask for help in coping with it—and I woke.

Many associations. The flies, the fragmented thoughts and dreams that I have been longing to get rid of—an attitude that at once obscures the meaning of this time of my life, which lies above all in the "unconditional yes" to every inner and outer fact. I even had the conscious thought yesterday, "How, oh how can I finally be rid of these wandering distractions?" The dream comments in no uncertain terms, "If you try to kill or repress these tiresome flies, you will be in danger of trying to kill that great symbol of resurrection, of the rising sun, which is the scarab." I now think of—see clearly—the Renaissance picture of the Madonna and Child (was it by Correggio?) in which a fly has settled on the Virgin's cloak and the baby sitting on her knee is wholly absorbed in watching it with that total attention of the small child. I have always loved that picture—no gazing up in a holy way to heaven, but whole contemplation of a most despised and tiresome insect. For me, no destruction by collective means of collective invasions, but a singling out of one "fly" at a time, with love and kinship. If I fall now into the destructive attitude even briefly, I am in danger of rejecting that possibility of new life which, like the scarab, is born fully formed from the egg laid in the dung.

JANUARY 31   ❧

The red-bellied woodpecker has just come to the bird feeder. Each year there is just one who comes each day briefly. I think this is what makes them so numinous to me, so that my heart lifts each time I see them. This year it is a male, last year a female, never both. Do they have very distinct territories even in winter—and is perhaps each bird alone except when nesting? Anyway, when it comes it is like a visit from a known individual, not one of a flock. This year for some reason my visitor has taken to feeding on the ground, not, as usual, on the feeder. I have never seen a woodpecker do that before. He also perches on the ginkgo from time to time, which gives me a beautiful view of him.

❧

The red-bellied woodpecker
Sits on my ginkgo
And jerks his red head
This cold morning.

❧

It came to me recently, more powerfully than ever, how there is no delight in the true sense of the word that does not contain in the midst of the glory of meaning the awareness of total meaninglessness. We continually seek delight by banishing despair. What we find then is perhaps an intuition of the glory of meaning, but never the experience of translucency that unites both poles of reality in one ultimate and unshakable delight.

❧

Awake after a strong dream with much affect. I was visiting Paris with two or three friends (Else and Jane?). We were looking for a hotel, and I wondered if I could find the quiet one I had stayed in before. We were talking about what to see in Paris. The friends were new to the city. I felt I could not do much sightseeing, but would go to the Louvre and sit in front of just one picture. I mentioned the Frenchman whom I had met and got to know on my holidays last summer. He was, I knew, an eminent person—doctor, professor, statesman?—and would open doors to interesting places.

The level of the dream changed here and deepened. Suddenly I saw a line of people waiting, I thought, to book into a hotel, and I thought it looked familiar, or at any rate very pleasant. The line of people was then dispersed. I saw the woman in front of me step across a kind of cleft to the left and I was alone. Now I knew that the greatly loved Prime Minister of France had just died and that the whole city was utterly silent in mourning for him. I found myself inside the hotel talking to the manageress, and I knew that the man who had become a friend last summer was indeed this Prime Minister. And I said to the woman, "I met him and his wife last summer and he was a wonderful person." Then I realized that this wasn't so—that his wife had not been there. I wondered why I had unconsciously made that mistake, and thought it was probably because I had met his inner feminine side. I thought too of the difference his death would make to our visit—the sadness, the black everywhere, the funeral. But the atmosphere would be one of love and solemnity and beauty. And the ancient buildings and the pictures would still be there.

I also seemed to know that Winston Churchill had been with him from England when he died—a strange sense of Winston having already had his extremely moving funeral as well as being alive (as an image perhaps) to make this visit.

The essence of this impressive Frenchman was very clear to me as I woke. It had a resemblance to the memory of Professor Foligno and his looks and voice when he spoke about Dante. Also he reminded me of the gentle and intelligent Alsatian whom I met in the Jura in the early 1920s. *"Il faut toujours planter des pommes-de-terre"*: no end to conflict. Also out of the past came the memory of that intense moment in the sixth-form room at school when I suddenly *saw* Rex Warner as he sat with a Greek text. He was not actually reading but his deep-set eyes below the high forehead were turned, I somehow knew, to an inner vision, and I had a kind of intuitive flash of recognition—of seeing for an instant a person of high intellect whose thought was illuminated by the imagination. Of course none of these words came to me then—we were both about seventeen years old. It was an intuition of the mind of a scholar-poet (as Rex indeed later became.) In the dream the Frenchman was of this kind, but he had also a doctor-healer aspect, and he was also a statesman-ruler who was greatly beloved. And with all this I had known him as a simple, humble human being.

What does it mean that he is dead? I feel a great sadness and also a fear. Whither now? He is my poet-healer-guide, and ruling influence in the unconscious—for France is in a very particular way the "other side," across the water, to me. In spite of my love of Italy in those years of study, she was never a home from home as France was, for I had first known France at four or five years of age and loved her ever since, and Paris was really the first place in which I consciously faced the pains and fears of loneliness and found, I believe, as I look back, the support that enabled me to endure this loneliness through a kind of love affair with the city itself— its streets, its buses, its shops, its churches and galleries, and its theaters to which I went alone. I was then nineteen, terribly shy, my French not yet fluent though I could understand well. (France is also the place where feelings are very rarely sentimental.)

Winston would be symbolically the ruler of all my outer life, and if France stands for my inner life, Winston's image in the dream beside the dream image of the ruler of France at his death would somehow connect, I feel, with the coming together of inner and outer worlds. The death of both aspects of the guiding animus leaves the ego alone to make the sacrifice which accepts the sole guidance of the Self—or else regresses to meaninglessness.

∽

FEBRUARY 25

Here are some of my gropings since Tuesday towards the meanings of the dream. The death of the "heroes," "great leaders": it has happened collectively in our age in the outer world, and is, I believe, both the great danger of chaos and destruction in which we find ourselves and also the inevitable, inexorable condition for a new birth, the birth of the leadership of the Self in the lives of individuals—which produces also groups of people on the way to individuation such as von Franz describes, whose bonds are created by the Self. Such groups may start—perhaps inevitably so—from a spark from the Self manifested through one individual; but, if they are to survive, this projection onto a leader must gradually be withdrawn and the Self be known inwardly in each separate member of the group. In my own life I have tried at least to be aware of the moments for withdrawal, of the necessity of accepting projections which must nevertheless be known as such and refused when the right time comes, of the dangers of my own counter-projections, and so on. So I have come to this time of retirement which, I am now certain, is not just another degree of the often-repeated transitions involving smaller deaths and rebirths of greater consciousness.

It is a revolutionary thing. It is a moment when, in terms of the dream, the time has come to accept the final death of that animus and wise old man, that guide in my psyche through whom I have been able to produce all my writings and mediate some healing and creative support to the many people who have come here.

This is why the end of *The Tempest*—Prospero's freeing of Ariel and the return from the numinous island to the everyday life of Milan without any power to rule—is so extremely moving and full of meaning for me. The dreams have shown clearly the danger for me now of failing to make the conscious sacrifice, of any fruitless searching for long-abandoned support in old ways and for new kinds of (unsuitable) persona images. Yet there are moments when I know the new freedom, when I let go of any idea that I ought to write as before—*ought* to do anything but attend to every actual moment—attend to the beauty, ugliness, boredom, futility, splendor, pain, and joy present in the simple ordinary facts of every day.

MAY 4   ✍

A dream about being taken to visit the planet Jupiter. Two friends had established a sort of pied-a-terre in the rocks (which resembled pictures of Mars). Each had brought one or two pieces of furniture—and each had brought a photograph of his father. Jupiter, of course, is the beneficent Father-archetype planet. The two explorers had evidently brought some things to keep them rooted to the human realm, to protect them from the power of the place. This I felt *in* the dream. The sun was shining brightly, and one had to walk very carefully on the whitish bare rocks where nothing grew. One of the photograph-frames resembled a little clock-frame. I wondered if we would see any of Jupiter's moons.

I had been thinking this week of my whole "father" experience, and remembering the recent dream of my actual father coming from India to shake hands with the adult me and then immediately returning. I had the intuition that I could not have visited the place of the Great Father safely if that "meeting," that "joining of hands" had not taken place. Also there was a questioning image in the dream, that of the explorer's photograph of his father. It was seen by me in the dream as a print so faded as actually to have become merely some dark and light. There was also the question: had it been a clock? This would link with my readings in Larry Dossey's *Space, Time & Medicine* about the non-existence of linear time—and with Eliot's words, "Only though time Time is conquered." Dossey's explanation of the necessity of linear time for "survival of the species" is superficial if taken materialistically but accurate if it applies to individual consciousness. No "Fall," no consciousness of the opposites, without which no *conscious* unity.

I have offered to have a group on Saturday June 11, as I feel moved to share some of Dossey's *Space, Time & Medicine* and Jung on the *unus mundus*. I don't think I have yet written anything here of the extraordinary beauty of this book, in which Dossey really makes clear in language comprehensible to the ordinary person what a tremendous revolution has taken place in the realm of physics and how out of date all our cause and effect thinking is. Dossey's chapter headings are almost all from mystics or poets, and he finally states that the new "physical" facts of the universe can only be expressed in this kind of language.

Jung, writing of the *unus mundus* of the alchemists, foretells these things, and indeed for Gerhard Dorn the final unity, beyond wholeness of psyche, was in the marriage of psyche and matter.

What Dossey does not even hint at is the fact that the new understandings of the physical universe can only have *meaning* in the consciousness of individuals who have first confronted their shadow and come to Dorn's first stage of unity. "Only through time Time is conquered." The great temptation today when these tremendous insights are breaking through to so many is that they too will be *used* by fallen man to inflate his ego and to escape from instead of integrate the dark.

There are moments when I experience briefly the certainty that whatever is to happen *is*, just as everything that has happened *is*—one's whole life simply *is*, and is at one with the One, so that anxiety as to what may happen or desire for a particular thing simply dissolves. But this does not mean that in the linear life of time we are set free from hope and fear—or indeed that we should seek such freedom. We can only increase our detachment from *both*, from pleasure as well as pain, which means the continual alert state of contemplation which all religions have taught through their mystics.

✐

I have just remembered a dream which came perhaps a week ago. I was standing outside a country house on a bright, sunny day. It was empty and had been completely repainted—a creamy white, inside and out. The doors stood wide. Someone who was showing it to me suggested I go over it. I said, "I don't need to do that. I remember it very clearly, every room in it." Then I remembered that this house (which was a small Georgian type, very gracious) was joined at the back to a much older, dark building; a corridor from the white house's upper story led to a series of rooms, also on two stories, almost like a warren—perhaps stables underneath. It was dark, Tudor-feeling—oak beams, etc. I thought to myself, "I used to know those dark rooms too," but I could not remember them so clearly as the "white" house in the front, and I wondered if I should go through the latter and explore again those other rooms behind it. I seemed to know they were all clean and empty too, the whole place, front and back, awaiting a new tenant.

When I woke I had a strong feeling of having known this place, both the light and the dark, very well at some time in my life. The only association—and it may be relevant—is the Oast House at Sparks Hall. It was not a bit like the beautiful Georgian house of the dream, but the dark rooms behind remind me of the barnlike rooms to which the Oast House was attached—and so the hay loft where Paul first kissed me and the ensuing guilt when my mother found out. (One did not kiss in those days unless engaged to marry!) Yet the feeling persists of a far more direct recognition—an old dream, I feel sure, that hovers on the edge of memory.

But the obvious and frightening association is from Matthew 12: "When the unclean spirit is gone out of a man, he [i.e., the spirit] walketh through dry places, seeking rest, and findeth none. Then he saith I will return into my house from whence I came out; and when he is come he findeth it empty, swept, and garnished. Then goeth he, and taketh with himself seven other spirits more wicked than himself, and they enter in and dwell there: and the last state of that man is worse than the first."

Some thoughts about the dream: The house is the structure of my personal life—the front part where the conscious ego has lived (culture, home, family, friends, gracious living) and behind it such dark places of the unconscious as I have known and explored and loved. (For that was clear in the dream: I remembered my joy in leaving the white house and finding unknown places in the dark rooms.)

In the dream, I have been brought to see this place again—now newly cleaned, painted, ready to welcome a new tenant—or perhaps the "agent" who brought me was hoping I would return to it. I am glad that in the dream I was not tempted even to enter that open door. My only interest was in the dark places behind, which I did not fully remember. I sense that this too is to be resisted. No need to go over again or "remember" the old complexes in the personal unconscious behind the house. All that past structure has been cleaned out, swept, and garnished. If I were to return to that way of life, that structure, thus identifying with it, the "unclean spirit" which has left me would quickly repossess me with sevenfold strength.

Others may take over that pleasant house—its garden, its farm. The "unclean spirit" is not seeking to reenter the house as such. I, my *ego*, is its house, and in the old structure it would indeed find it easy to possess me again, sevenfold. But if I have moved on to a new dwelling where I am not "swept and garnished" and open to unconscious invasion, then that unclean spirit who has been wandering restless in the dry places may *meet* me now and find rest. So I hope and pray.

MAY 20

1983

Trees in full leaf everywhere
And now, at last, on the gingko tree
A frill of green.

I did not imagine, when writing yesterday, that the nameless fear, the exhaustion, the darkness would leave me—perhaps ever in this life. The serenity beyond it is a joy to be "kissed as it flies." But I do feel nearer to a deeper recognition that my suffering of this kind of fear during the whole of my life from babyhood to old age is a destiny which contains perhaps the deepest meaning of my individual journey in the world.

I believe that my latest fantasy images have brought me nearer to the possibility of embracing in love the lifelong fact of my constant fear—of recognizing it as an essential strand in the web of my individual pattern without which that pattern could not be woven. This is why the experience of Pauline in *Descent into Hell* has always been to me an image of such power and beauty—I mean the moment when she faced and accepted her ancestor's fear and found instead her radiant Doppelgänger who had been at the root of her long neurotic terror, and she knew those old fears as completely valid, as the bearing of another's fear.

JUNE 21

No clear dreaming for the past few nights, but last night images connecting with Charles Williams's *Many Dimensions*, which I am now reading. I had forgotten its power, and the relevance to the *unus mundus* is startling. When Williams evokes the simultaneity of time, it truly lives for me. *Many Dimensions* at the same time makes clear the validity of linear time for mortal man and the extreme danger of trying to escape it before it has been fully accepted.

AUGUST 10

Books proliferate—and talk, talk—about how to die, how to help people to die. There is surely only one way to prepare for death—by learning to *live* in every smallest *fact* of the moment. Jung said somewhere we should simply go on living to the end as though there were no end—which of course is only possible when one is constantly aware of the eternity of every moment.

A half-dream this morning in which someone was describing how he had been among many who were striving for knowledge and enlightenment, when suddenly he fell down to another level of the earth, and once there he just went on tumbling around and realized with joy and wonder that he was tumbling "to the music of God." (I saw this in images, too, the tumbler curled like an embryo, wearing a striped rose and grey robe.)

I woke delighted, and remembered the old story von Franz tells (in *Shadow and Evil in Fairy Tales*) about St. Anthony who, after all his fasting and praying in the desert, was very jealous when an angel told him there was a man in the city who was much holier than he. So St. Anthony sought out his man, who turned out to be a shoemaker living in a very poor street. St. Anthony questioned him as to his life and religious practices, and the shoemaker replied, "All I do is work hard to keep my family fed and housed—nothing else." So St. Anthony was humbled and learned his lesson.

Last night I was awake in the small hours and the dream of two weeks ago came back to me with numinous power—the dream of the person who had been striving for knowledge now "tumbling to the music of God"—discovering the music of God when he tumbled off his high place. I had not before remembered the phrase "to tumble to the meaning of something." That's a delight.

Nancy's birthday yesterday. Gardening, cleaning—blessedly cool. Barbara M. called last night to talk about a dream whose main theme was music—its use or misuse and ultimate healing power. It was a bit of synchronicity for me. I have been remembering the sequence of "music" dreams that have preceded this last one of the music of God. And yesterday I was reading Mary Stewart's last Merlin book about his final hearing of the music of the stars—the single note of the unplucked harp string. How dulled are our ears! The Bushmen still hear that music of the spheres.

I thought regretfully of how I cannot even see the stars, the constellations, clearly any more—but then closing my eyes I suddenly realized with what wonderful clarity I could see them within, shining in the dark sky. Sirius blazing in the east above the horizon; then Orion with every star distinct; and above and to the west the Pleiades—all my favorites through the years—the great Bear turning around the pole star, fixed and unmoving, with the lovely Casseopeia nearby.

One day perhaps I may catch their song—but if not with the ears of earth, no matter. It is contained in every daily hint of the music of God. I look out this morning at my late summer garden—the golden and orange balls of the giant marigolds, the delicate pinks of the tall cosmos. They are tumbled about by the wind and rain, lean over, stand up again. There is one huge weed that has grown taller than them all and somehow adds to the joy of the tumbling.

SEPTEMBER 26

I am thinking that music is *disciplined* feeling, sound given form and pattern through number and rhythm—the single sound of the universe bringing consciousness through incarnation in music to the inner ear of the soul. Since I am a woman with a major feeling function, it is the "animus," the masculine creative spirit within, who brings to me the sound of the music of God—not as in man, who hears it through the "siren," the numinous feminine within. God's music unites all. Blake sang when he knew he was dying.

SEPTEMBER 27

I am thinking that the *Tempest* writing is no longer a matter of completing a project—it is concerned with the *living* of such insights as are arising in me from it—and any pressure (as distinguished from discipline) kills this.

I begin to understand that the setting free of Ariel—of the imagination—means the absolute withdrawal of every hidden *use* of it by the ego—for prestige, power, achievement, or for the saving of either oneself or anyone else—motives that have thousands of ways of hiding themselves.

As Jung has pointed out, there is no action, thought, feeling, nothing at all, that does not emerge from the images in the unconscious. Men have called these "airy nothings," and only the poetic vision (which is religious contemplation) can give them a local habitation and a name—conscious incarnation. Without this, the images live us unconsciously and we delude ourselves by thinking we are in control of them.

When Prospero gave up his control of Ariel, he felt the emptiness which can bring despair—but knew also that the answer lay in prayer, which is the opposite of this control. It is an end of all ego-power and an opening of the soul to the inpouring of the Self into whose reality Ariel has now passed into new life. "Merrily, merrily shall I live now." But for Prospero there is a time of dark meaninglessness, and I find the appeal to the "audience," to the human "others," intensely moving. Prospero, having won through to forgiveness, says "Let me not . . . dwell in this bare island by your spell," but let me return to the mainland. To stay on the enchanted island after the "letting go"—what would that mean? Perhaps it would be to isolate oneself from the ordinary human condition after tremendous experiences of the unconscious, to refuse to descend to the ordinary day-to-day conflicts of life on earth—and in Prospero's case it would have been a deadly regressive return to his youthful refusal of the responsibilities of his dukedom, his duties in this world.

He cannot even set himself free from this danger. He has the humility to recognize that only through "prayer" and the "Mercy" of God will the Self, working through those ordinary "others" to whom he had felt himself superior, set him free. Then indeed he may know that Ariel is not lost but found in the thoughts and imagination of death.

More thoughts about the changes going on in old age—and they connect to Prospero's epilogue and to Odysseus. One of the great dangers of the old is to succumb to boredom, as the oar slips from the hand and the "oar" is planted and left behind, and one feels so denuded of energy for *anything*. Imagine the excitement of Prospero's life—raising storms, casting spells, producing pageants of the gods, ruling men and circumstances. No wonder he says, "Now I want [i.e., lack] / Spirits to enforce, art to enchant, / And my ending is despair / Unless I be relieved by prayer"—because he knows he faces the possibility of unbearable boredom, and his thoughts of death (every third thought, he says) will be utterly negative and unimaginative, *unless*. . . . So many old people (and they are often encouraged by all those well-meaning people who want to help them) meet the boredom by a busyness that gives them a frail illusion of their youth—keeping boredom at bay and turning from the thoughts of death—just filling in time. This would be to stay on the enchanted island, isolated in unconsciousness, without Ariel, or even any valid projection of him.

I am becoming more and more aware of boredom in myself creeping into the places where I have never felt it in any of the past thirty-five years or so since I began working with people. Of course I have known for some time that peoples' personal problems have become less and less my business, but to be bored by them as I have felt now and then of late must mean that in some way I am clinging to them in the wrong way— that is, filling time with them. Suddenly I will feel (after a group such as yesterday's, or even after a real talk with someone) that I have only been saying the right *words*, repeating the things I know to be true but without the old imaginative spark.

I have not felt this at all (yet?) in the occasional big groups of Apple Farm people, because there the subject-matter has been based on recent explorations of my own, or sharing of response to images that are moving in me nowadays.

Those few I still work with regularly do not engender the boredom because their day-to-day problems are now just the occasional stepping stones to the realization of "the new man." To be a channel for whatever little I have experienced of this newness of life is perhaps the only "teaching" that is my job. I am now quite clear that any sort of ongoing problem work with anyone is not to be undertaken, and I think this week's hints of boredom with the work have come from a threat of slipping back into looking for "results" of work of a personal nature.

I have been thinking this morning of von Franz's words about Jung in his last years—of how no one, even his closest pupils, took personal questions to him any more. He just talked of what interested him, and whenever they were with him they felt their personal questions answered.

I am not claiming to have reached this level—but I do know that the thing that rings truest to me is when, after a group that has been full of meaning for me myself, some individuals say to me, "It seemed that you were talking especially to me individually and answering my questions"— and I know that if I were trying to do this is would indeed be as boring to the hearer as to me.

I am remembering the dream of a few years ago of seeing the calendar of my life and each square filled with this and that until the last eight or ten squares which were entirely empty except for the words clearly written in each: "Of the Mercy." And I suddenly realize why the words of Prospero's epilogue:

> Unless I be relieved by prayer
> Which pierces so, that it assaults
> Mercy itself, *and frees all faults (emphasis mine)*

are so numinous to me. The imaginative contemplation—the "objective cognition" which is prayer—releases one from despair, from boredom, from the barren island where one may be confined by mass thinking. It releases one with the compassion, the Mercy, which frees all faults, resolves all problems, and may bring at death the light of freedom.

∾

NOVEMBER 2

I have had some moments of realizing that prayer is *serenity*—serenity surrounds it (overarching, Sister Therese says), encircling everyone and everything one remembers in this state of prayer and setting them free. I have so often remembered the words of old Father Robson so many years ago when he said that serenity was *the* divine condition, the love of God realized.

The derivation of "serenity" involves "brightness," "clarity," a natural state of calm that cannot be shaken. It does not spring from the disciplined composure of the will.

NOVEMBER 7

I have looked more carefully than ever before at the inner pattern of the stem of the blue star water lily. To my wonder and delight I see it is a mandala of the number eight—eight spokes to the center, eight hollow circles, then sixteen, then thirty-two tiny holes on the outer rim—the water drawn up through all these. This gives more profound and vivid meaning to the fact that in my vision experience of last year I felt—and still can feel—myself to be one with the *stalk* of the lily in particular, my eyes just below the open flower.

Thus the ego would be the channel through which the water from below flows to the lotus flower opening in the light and warmth of the sun, with its golden center. As long as one's attention remains there, the ten thousand things are all included in the circle of eternity—the circle of the pool—with all the conflicts, mistakes, joys, and griefs known as the "pattern of the glory" here on earth and in heaven; and this "futile and ridiculous ego," in Jung's words, would indeed be experienced as a "vessel" receiving the "effluence of the most High" and naming it "with his name."

Well, to have been given this in one moment is a fact in eternity. For the rest, in this world of linear time there is always the swing between the opposites, the human condition of "divine conflict" (Jung), but also the memory, the gratitude, the acceptance of all that is because "it is so and not otherwise" (Charles Williams, *Place of the Lion*)—the "just so," however painful the regressions.

The thought is with me of how the "letting go" of the ten thousand things, the detachment, is paradoxically one with the ceasing to *exclude* anything at all from the affirmation and acceptance of what is—the horrors of the nuclear threat included. You or I may be the "makeweight that tips the scales" (Jung, *Undiscovered Self*) through this daily, moment-by-moment work of non-exclusion. Watching, I realize how constant is the slipping into tenseness in case this or that small thing happens which may interfere with my plans or expectations. It is a humbling thing, bringing one down again and again to the "humus," the earth of the smallest things in life.

There is a passage in a story by Amanda Cross which I find beautiful (*In the Last Analysis*, pp. 67–68, which I was reading last night). She quotes from George Eliot's *Middlemarch:* "Strange that some of us, with quick alternate vision, see beyond our infatuations, and even while we rave on the heights, behold the wide plain where our persistent self pauses and awaits us." Kate Fansler, the English professor caught in, and obsessed by, fears for her friend accused of murder, and occupied rightly with plans for saving him, reflects that "while she had discussed *Middlemarch* she had been incapable of thinking of anything else. The persistent self lived, she thought, in that work where one's attention was wholly caught. It occurred to Kate that few people possessed 'persistent selves.'"

I find this intensely beautiful. It is probable that only this "persistent self" survives individually, in whatever unknown dimension, after death. Hence the immense importance of finding and committing oneself to work where one's "attention" (and therefore one's love) is wholly caught. It is the "sphere of being on which the mind is set" which alone bears fruit in the lives of others (T. S. Eliot, "Four Quartets"). Perhaps it doesn't matter what kind of work it is. It is the intensity of the attention, the devotion that matters, attention free of all desire for ego-achievement.

DECEMBER 3

1983

Amanda Cross also writes (p. 67) "Did anything after all matter beside the fact that imagination might create worlds like *Middlemarch*, that we might learn to perceive these worlds and the structures that maintained them?" I think the imagination is always at work when the attention is whole, when we are not just possessed by hidden drives for power, success, greed.

DECEMBER 11 It came to me with power this morning that the "work" lies now in one thing only—the removal of attention to the ego—and so the "will" may be "pacified" and the Self can enter in. Concentration on the "small," on the "just so" of the moment, is the way to this, insisted on for so long by the *I Ching*. It is appalling to realize how much of the time the state of the ego is my preoccupation still. Those moments of strange happiness come only when this preoccupation disappears. The tension, the blood-pressure problem, etc., come from the deep instinctive level where rejection of the just so still lies hidden. The growth of the awareness of Inner Truth, as the *I Ching* says, is the only thing that could finally reach the "pig and fish" level.

DECEMBER 31

The last day of the year, and this morning just before dawn I saw the slim crescent of the waning moon above the first light on the horizon—and above the moon was the brilliant morning star, Venus the beautiful. I put on my heavy glasses and could see them very clearly. The horizon turned to pale gold and still the moon crescent shone. Tomorrow I suppose will begin the dark of the moon—until the first evening crescent of the new year. The beauty of this cold, clear morning brought back to me most vividly the memory of that glorious sky—the sun just set, the moon—full moon—just rising on that evening when I left my mother for the last time, knowing her near death—deep grieving but an extraordinary joy in the awareness of her setting me free into a new life.

FEBRUARY 10

To return to the whole matter of inner disciplines: I need to remember every time I read of either Western or Eastern ways—or even Jungian ways—the fact that the tremendously urgent task of individuation means that each one's discipline is unique—and, I believe, changes its form at different stages of a human life. If all one can do is to sit alone and intend concentration—and fail—then, in Charles Williams's image, the patterns of exchange with friends will bring that which is needed—the *temenos*, the protected place of the "Mercy."

FEBRUARY 14

In the midst of my continuing messy, unremembered dreams, the image of my blue star lily vision returns every day as a point of rest—and two days ago I had a brief recurrence of the *experience*. This time the vision was more powerfully centered on the interior of the stem, the eightfold mandala of holes through which the water flows up to the flower. I was briefly those holes—quite simply and in utter content the channel for the water.

FEBRUARY 15

A dream last night that ended with a large, irregular lump of coal—anthracite, with shining surfaces, indeed like a black diamond. It was lying on an oval Chinese dish (a little like my own Chinese dishes but paler colors) on a low table beside me. I did not feel a sense of ownership but watched, perhaps wondering how it could start burning, when suddenly it burst into flames, giving out a wonderful white light. But then I thought: that is quite the wrong place for it, it will simply break the dish and the fire be uncontained—and immediately someone (unseen) poured water over it and the fire went out. Then I said, "It needs to be in a fireplace or in some place where it can ignite other fuel, give warmth and light."

There was something powerfully numinous in the white fire. Is it some new blaze of consciousness rising from the depths, reaching into daily life in the "black diamond" fuel but as yet without my having found the right "container"—the place where it can serve instead of just being kept on a dish to be looked at? Yet I have a feeling that it was the "looking" that, so to speak, generated the fire and that the dream is saying it is time—for what? the work of writing? the groups to come? yes, but no, just for the daily living of whatever comes. In the words of Charles Williams about the creative life: "To be, ever new, the thing expressed; to live, in fact, the life of glory. It is, however, to the liver largely dull—but I have no doubt that it exists everywhere and at all times." All this with a joyful sense of one's own superfluity.

FEBRUARY 18

Waiting for Spring—
Not—waiting for God.
Dull green, dull white, dull sky.
Thou art that. Just so.

The vision of the star lily—the stem with its eightfold channels—the momentary experience of oneness. But to try to hold it is the temptation always. I reach toward oneness with the dead grass, the muddy snow, the grey sky. That too is "the life of glory—the 'pattern of the glory.'"

APRIL 15

So often have I talked of self-knowledge, of knowing the Shadow, for example, but the experience which comes now in old age of the need for "total surrender to the truth of oneself" (van der Post?) is something hitherto unknown. It is this "recognition" of the all-pervasiveness of one's ego's self-interest that is the terrifying "judgment" without which "Eunoe" cannot be passed. (I think of that terrible judgment scene in *Till We Have Faces*.) Only passing through the near despair of this recognition can the self-knowledge come that reveals the City of God. . . . Perhaps the only thing that keeps me from the despair Prospero talks of is the pride of my ego—and that is a mere cover-up. Only "prayer" can save—not the ego's prayer but the prayer of the "other," the "exchange" of the crucified Self.

Last evening St. Gregory's had invited us to a "play" about Dame Julian of Norwich, a one-woman performance by Roberta Nobleman. She was really wonderful—though the play did not include some of my favorite "shew-ings." Afterwards I met her and was of course delighted when she said she had read my books and loved them, and she was sure Julian did too! She gave the character just the flavor I am sure she must have had, utterly down-to-earth and full of humor.

Julian lived through three epidemics of the plague (the Black Death), which eliminated half the population of England. R. N. conveyed the hor-ror of it with great power, and it made me think of how we forget the terrible fears and sufferings of earlier ages in our obsession with our own, how we forget the kinds of suffering and misery from which we are freed. It does not change, really—the terror in the single individual. Only because of the media—instant news of everything all round the globe—does it seem so much worse. "God's peace—I think I have felt it; God's voice—I think I have heard it," says Julian. It is the answer which only an individual can give in any age.

I am reminded again of Jung in his 1939 lecture "The Symbolic Life," saying that he is not concerned with the historic future at all, not at all. He is concerned only with those individuals who are going to fulfill their hypotheses, who are going, like the true Pueblo, to "do today everything that is necessary so that my Father can rise over the horizon." And earlier: "If anyone lives his hypothesis to the bitter end (and pays with his death, perhaps), he knows that Christ is his brother."

He repeats that faith toward the end of his life in *The Undiscovered Self*, saying he is concerned only "with the fate of the individual human being—that infinitesimal unit on whom a world depends, and in whom, if we read the meaning of the Christian message aright, even God seeks his goal." Lady Julian in the language of her own time spoke and lived this same truth.

I am beginning to feel more deeply the truth behind the insistence, in Christianity particularly, on God's love for us. This truth has been so debased and sentimentalized by superficial projections onto an anthropomorphic (as opposed to an incarnated) image of God that it is repeated and repeated without meaning. But Julian, in the performance last night, saying it again in the image of one woman's love for her child, suddenly linked in my heart with that great paragraph in Jung's *Memories, Dreams, Reflections* about love, that mystery that cannot be defined. He quotes II Corinthians 13, St. Paul's great words: "Love beareth all things, endureth all things," and then goes on to say that this is all there is to be said. "For we are in the deepest sense the victims and the instruments of cosmogonic 'love,'" love not in any of the "desiring" meanings but as "something superior to the individual, a unified and undivided whole." We can consent to our total dependence and containment in this "Mercy" or rebel against it, but we are still there—and our freedom to choose is part of it.

&

More and more frequently, it seems, I enter those very dark places where I know how easy it could be to give up completely, to turn one's face to the wall and sink into oblivion. I even long for that, and then I wonder if the only thing that keeps me going is the ego's pride. It is not an emotional thing—entirely different from a state of depression. It is rather a brush with complete meaninglessness (Prospero's despair). And yet as I write, I realize how the very words which describe this state are defining what is necessary if ever one is to be empty enough to know the eternity. It is indeed a matter of "giving up completely," of becoming detached from every desire for anything to be other than it is. In the East devotees often sit to meditate facing a wall—cut off from distractions in the outer world, so that the third eye may open to that "something other" in the emptiness.

Last night I dreamed that the rain came pouring down bringing enormous relief and joy. I was looking out of my big window but in place of my garden there was a shallow ravine with the ground covered in big stones, now wet and shining with rivulets of water running between them. I was thinking of what a wonderful blessing this breaking of the drought was, and especially I rejoiced for the farmers everywhere.

I had actually been thinking yesterday morning of the Hexagram "Deliverance"—"Thunder and Rain set in," and the release of tension. The weather forecast was no rain in the foreseeable future, and I thought it was really becoming a serious drought. I was certainly caught in one psychically this last week!

A lovely letter from Laurens. He has found a London bookshop that stocks all my things, and said how delighted he was. Also he wrote of his own problems with writing and interruptions. So like mine.

It had been months since I felt that rare "empty" delight that came to me at intervals last winter. But it has returned several times since "the rain came" in the dream last week. The image of the dark stones shining in the water has been vividly with me, and the water beginning to rise and become a running stream reminds me of the beautiful photograph that hangs beside my bed. Water and stone—and the running horses—the images that came from Jung to Miguel Serrano when Jung died. The recent dream of the white horse comes back to me.

This morning, as I breathed, an image came from the past. It was the memory of that dream twenty years ago or so, when the great cube of stone which was also pure light, apricot-colored dawn light, came crashing through the roof of a great barn, and a small chip from the stone had flown off and into me unseen. I was so excited by its beauty that I called urgently to Else to come and see it—whereupon immediately the stone began to rise again and disappeared through the roof.

1984

When the image came back to me this morning I found that instead of running to spread the news to the others I simply stood still in awe, and the cube did not move upward or lose its shape but the light in it gently faded and darkened and I was only aware of the form, the outside of the cube, in the dimness. And I knew that though the light may be invisible so much of the time in this world, yet always it is there as long as one is still and not caught in the ego's desire to *do* something, to show it to others.

This immediately led in my musings to the other great dream of that period, the great white horse rearing up and passing his power, his inspiration, into my cupped hands held out to him—and then my sitting beside a milestone and knowing that this gift was a responsibility I must carry for a time, but that it was not mine to possess but must be given up, handed on, when the time should come.

It seems to me today that these two dreams have much to do with my *Tempest* writing, and of what may follow now, whether to be shared outwardly or not.

1985

MARCH 4   I dreamed I was recovering from a serious illness but there remained something embedded in my left wrist. I went with Jane to see someone who knew how to cut it out (not an ordinary doctor). He (or she?) gave no anaesthetic. I braced myself. There was something almost numinous about the "hole" in which this object was. It was square and I had the feeling it was also round (a clear association with the powerful Zurich dream of Mephistopheles piercing my thigh with a rod, making the same kind of square-round hole—the test of bearing the pain). That which filled the hole in my wrist had a kind of knob at the top—two square bubble-shaped spheres of skin which seemed tied at the bottom and inflated. The healer took up an instrument and cut these in some way—I didn't see exactly how or what—and then immediately he was holding up something that had long white roots. I knew the roots of this bulb-like thing had been embedded in the wrist and now the hole was empty except for a few severed small roots which I was told would wither and could be easily removed. The hole was clean flesh, I think—no blood. I thought about the expected acute pain, but all I felt was a faint soreness, which was somehow reflected in a momentary "answering" twinge in my left foot.

Associations, besides the Zurich one mentioned, are, first, with the breaking of the left wrist, which was indeed a watershed for me, a new beginning, just as was my illness in Zurich in late 1948. That marked my great temptation to run away from the "career" ahead of me in the psychological world. The dream was my refusal to do so.

Exactly thirty-five years later (at the end of 1983)—half a lifetime—came the broken wrist and the first experiences which produced the *Tempest* writing (*Old Age*): both the darkness and the "cool delight" in the midst of it all, the entry into the later stage of old age. The same mark of the squared circle was evidently made this time in my arm. But something has been filling that hole for the year and a half since then, held there by strong roots, and I have not been aware of it. Strangely, the cutting off of those two small spheres immediately releases all those roots and the mark of Lucifer can be consciously seen and accepted in my arm, as it was earlier accepted in my thigh. That Zurich illness was in my *right* arm—the fear of going out into life. This last was my left arm—the fear of letting go.

I have a fantasy that the two spheres that must be cut out are the two aspects of the work I still do—the hours with people and the writing. I am still often torn between them. I do not think the dream means it is time to give up working at either or both, but rather it could mean that it is high time to let go of the delusion that it is important which I do and when, and simply respond to the immediate moment in either kind of work. It is the piercing consciousness that Lucifer brings with his "laming" wound that "squares the circle."

It has been with me over and again these last weeks—that deep recognition of the necessity to let go more steadily of the feeling of conflict between various kinds of "doing," when I know that it is only *being* that matters—being incarnate in action, in work, as long as one is still given strength and joy in the doing—the kind of doing in which "nothing is done." "The agony of the immediate fact" that brings the "laughter at the heart of things."

1985

MARCH 14

The wind blew through my hair
This morning
As I walked past the bare trees
Leaning on my stick.

APRIL 11

I know that the true experience of joy lies in those unsought, unexpected moments when one becomes aware of it in the midst of unhappiness, pain, or even fear. It does not *take away* the unhappiness or the pain—it is most certainly not a "way out"—because of course joy excludes nothing. We probably lose it most easily when we are happy for exterior reasons. Joy is causeless, in the fullest sense.

MAY 7

The last part of D. H. Lawrence's poem "Shadows" stays with me. It is a time when indeed so often the "heart seems dead and strength is gone, and my life is only the leavings of a life." Yet there are those "odd wintry flowers" very occasionally and the necessity to realize how utterly helpless one is—until "the unknown god" shall have broken one down and the ego can only wait at last with empty hands.

The dream of the kneeling, the letting go even of that small "sin" of my life—that is the image of these latter weeks. So only will the water still flow through the empty stem to the lotus above as in that vision of nearly three years ago.

The extraordinarily *different* kind of loneliness of old age—in the midst of so much friendship and warmth of exchange.

It seems in these days that the opposites become more and more intensely known—and yet at the same time there is less and less personal emotion.

I am wondering whether the many incoherent dreams not fully remembered, but disturbing when I try to relate them to my life now, are for the most part images picked up from the collective conflicts—often through those I talk with or the TV. I have always been wary of this explanation as a possible evasion of shadow things that are my own business to remember and work on, but I have noticed in recent months how detached, though not indifferent, my ego image remains in most of them. I am aware of what is going on, involved to some extent, but there is rarely a feeling of any necessity or even possibility of my interfering.

I have thought often, since getting Janet Baker's letter, of her perfect description of the sudden experience of joy in the most "ordinary" moments. I have noticed in recent weeks a new aspect of this which comes to me now and then—or rather the same experience but coming in smaller and smaller contexts, set off by something so infinitesimally small as to elude definition. It has nothing to do with cause and effect, or with beauty in the ordinary sense either. Rather it is a kind of "bliss" (to use Janet's word), of *recognition*—of some tiny thing: a pinhead, a fly, a pricked finger, a spent match, some such seemingly "irrelevant" detail—a recognition of the totality breaking through to consciousness in the most "useless" trivia, as it were. I would not exchange such moments for all the great visions and ecstasies.

Another new thing—"odd flower on the withered stem"—is an extraordinary feeling of not knowing who I am or where to find myself anymore, of knowing nothing, yet feeling at the same time more at one and free and more alive and aware of little things than ever before. This comes also unsought at odd moments.

Russell Lockhart was here on Saturday. He and his wife have an old hand-printing press and have produced two books already. He gave me the second—a poem by Marc Hudson, "Journal for an Injured Son," very beautiful. It has brought powerful images to me, especially some words in the preface by Lockhart. Lockhart writes that Marc had just received a lot of recognition—a big prize—when his brain-damaged baby was born.

> Marc asked "What are poets for in a dark time?" Calling upon . . . the poet's last hope—language—Marc began to find his answer, giving voice to the profound experience of tending the fragile yet stalwart spirit of his injured son. . . . These poems are not only a father's gift to his son; they are a gift to the injured spirit in each of us.

The image came to me suddenly, the memory which has remained vividly alive in me all through the seventy-five years since that day when I must have been about six years old. I am standing again in the small sitting room of our flat in St. John's Wood and my mother is telling me—probably in response to my questioning—about my father's death. I had known of course the fact that my father had died in India when I was eight months old, and that was why I had no Daddy like other children. One day some children had come to visit us with their parents, and I remember that I went up to the father and said shyly, "May I please sit on your knees, because you see I don't have a Daddy," and he lifted me onto his lap. It is likely that this growing awareness in me of loss led to that talk with my mother. I remember none of her words but her voice broke as she told of how he had come to England on leave during those first months after my birth and had spent much time carrying me round the garden of his parents' house where I was born. My mother had come back to England before her confinement because of delicate health. We were about to go out to Bombay to join him when the news came of his sudden illness and death. They had been intensely happy in their marriage;

my mother and others who knew him told me in later years of the extraordinary joy that he radiated to those close to him, so that their angry
moods or resentments somehow dissolved in his presence. When he died
while she was so far away, my mother told me, she too came near to death
and cursed God, and only the fact that I was there kept her alive.

Of course, I do not know how much she actually said on *that* day. The
thing that happened to me at that moment when her voice broke was my
first and extraordinarily intense *experience* of grief, of the wound that still
bled in her. I do not think I spoke. I am sure I did not cry. The hurts and
losses and injuries of a child may have deep effects on the psyche, but this
was something other. It was, I could almost say, my first conscious and
objective experience of compassion—that is, of "suffering with" another—
and therefore, as Lockhart says, it must have brought with it an intuition
of the "injured spirit" in myself. Not till many years had passed—not till
I reached the dark wood *"in mezzo del camino di nostra vita"*—could I begin
to understand these things, but the memory of the power of that moment
never left me, and now in old age it expands into new dimensions.

When I read Marc Hudson's poems and Lockhart's words—"These
poems are not only a father's gift to his injured son; they are a gift to the
injured spirit in each one of us"—there came to me a yearning to make "a
daughter's gift to an injured mother." If only I could write of that experience in poetry, I thought. Some single lines even formed in me.

Anyone who has read Charles Williams's *Descent into Hell* and has
allowed the profundity of the images of "exchange" with an ancestor to
enter into his or her soul, will know that a "daughter's gift to an injured
mother" through language, even many years after the mother's death, may
be valid. I do not think I could write an actual poem—I am no poet—but
sometimes, now and then, the spirit of poetry has entered into my prose
writing, and that spirit springs out of the images themselves.

One early morning this week I lay dozing, half dreaming, with a
feeling of being in search of an image for that experience of my childhood—and suddenly the image was there and I realized that all my life I
had somehow been waiting for it to become visible. It is very simple: I saw

that at that moment, young as I was, I had become a *vessel*—and my very body I saw as a dark, empty vase into which the grief of my mother was poured and contained. Through the years, whenever the memory returned, I felt again the almost unbearable pain of loss which entered into me, and was somehow aware of an extraordinary stillness beyond tears; but never until now have I seen myself in that moment of time as a vessel, or known that I would feel that she had poured into that vessel a *gift* from her inmost being, something that was mine to carry, something that would give meaning to so much of my life.

Perhaps that experience was the beginning of the myth behind my life. It was the first real experience, in the deep sense of the word, that I had known. For an "experience" is not a mere outer happening or emotional reaction. It is something that an individual passes through consciously and learns from: "ex" means "out of" and "per" is also the root of "peril" and implies the presence of danger. An experience is born of a perilous happening which touches both conscious and unconscious and does not come to fruition without work and imagination. Perhaps all true experiences must be carried in the vessel of our being, sometimes for a lifetime, before they are born again in new creation. And during their sojourn in that womb they will grow stronger both in light and shadow, yielding new growth or spreading poison.

The initial dream of my inner life began at just about that same time, and it was recurrent for what I remember as a considerable period of time. This was the dream in which the hard-faced woman was driving me out onto a dark and lonely road. I was greatly afraid, but found strength in the milestone I was sitting on as I gathered courage to set out alone.

The fear of losing my mother was strong in me all through my childhood and school days. I had to face many separations—boarding school, my mother's illnesses, her work—but it was not until my late twenties that I began to be aware of my inner clinging to her, my fear of the lonely road within. I was forty when, discovering Jung, I began analysis and the confrontation with the great mother.

One of the greatest insights in *Descent into Hell* is that, as soon as a burden of suffering is consciously accepted—as Pauline consented to carry her ancestor's fear of the fire—then the years of unconscious suffering, neurotic suffering, become at once valid, and the consciously lifted burden is suddenly light and felt as a release. "*My* yoke is easy, *my* burden is light." It is now carried by the Self, and the ego is released from the crushing weight that is too great for it to bear. But the ego must be willing to carry it, to face the danger, to *experience* it, before this release comes. Even a young child such as I was must open herself as an empty vessel to receive another's pain, even if it be only for a few seconds—as when it reached me through the break in my mother's voice. It was perhaps the first conscious "yes" of my life to the "way of individuation." The word "conscious" for such a thing may sound strange, but it is I believe accurate. The pain had undoubtedly had a deep impact on me from babyhood, but it remained a happening, showing itself in my fear of strangers; and later in analysis it became clear I had suffered always from unconscious guilt for my father's death. These things are one's destiny from the beginning to be lived either as an outer meaningless fate—inevitable happenings—or as experiences known and integrated into the myth behind one's life.

I had one more dream of the lonely road—I do not know how long after the first, but still when very young. I was walking in darkness along the road of my earlier dream when I saw to the left below the level of the road my mother bound to a stake and fire burning all around her. What she carried for me is incalculable and not for me to probe. There is only the grateful heart. The impact of Marc Hudson's poem has evoked all this, and writing it has been part of what I have been discovering about the *re-creation* of memories as a major part of the work of the old.

I was remembering this morning the beginning of this regular diary-writing, with the dream of a voice saying "Keep a diary of vowels." And I

1985

looked up "vowel" again in the dictionary. Vowels are the sounds made by unhindered breath—the "unstruck sound"—the essence of all life. "Diary" is a much more personal word than "journal." It's a private reflection, having no association with such things as newspapers.

AUGUST 7   ∽

Yesterday morning I dreamed that someone (unseen) was asking another (also unseen) a question about his or her work—something like "What or who are you?"—and I heard a voice reply in tones of great beauty and power, filling as it were the whole universe, "I am no-thing and no-one." It filled me with joy, and I looked out over a great expanse of very still water with dark, surrounding cliffs, rocks, trees. It was night but the sky was pale with light like moonlight. I awoke.

The words spoken in such peace remind me of my recent vivid memories of Jung's words: "The older I grow the less I know and understand about myself," and Lao Tzu too: "All is clear, only I am clouded." And D. H. Lawrence of the Unknown God: "He is breaking me down to his own oblivion to send me forth on a new morning, a new man." Also, the universal mystical experience of the disappearance of the ego in the old sense. The words "I am no-thing and no-one" are the necessary experience which gives birth to "I am everything and everyone"—the "co-inherence" of eternity.

OCTOBER 15   ∽

The thought of death is with me very often of late, as is indeed right—the natural fear not rejected but also the anticipation (to use Charles Williams's words of Margaret Anstruther, in *Descent into Hell*, when she waited for death), the anticipation of "discovering the joy of death." Margaret had indeed lived in the "joy" of every *fact* for so long, and the facts can be—must be, indeed—at the last so very small, even to the irritation of my gums, or the experience, if one will be still, of the "music" of the pain.

Last night there was a persistent image of myself carrying a deep bowl—the shape of my tiny silver bowl, but about six inches high (and across, perhaps). It was two-thirds full of water which was in the dream an essential element in the sacramental meaning of a whole house (or way of life). It was my responsibility to carry it as I walked around, taking great care that it should not spill. Others were moving in a similar slow and quiet way. A sacramental consecration was going on not in an outward ritual but within the whole situation.

I wonder if this dream reflects Jung's words that I remember so often from *The Undiscovered Self* (I had done so particularly the day before the dream), that the individual's mite, if he or she carries his or her own small responsibility, may be that which tips the scales in the world situation today.

Last night the image was with me clearly. In the dream I walked slowly and carefully, my attention centered on the bowl, and was aware of the others moving slowly also. There seemed no danger of collision—it was more like a patterned dance, perhaps, though I could not see the whole but rather instinctively moved on my own path and knew they did so too, and there was harmony.

I had had a beautiful letter from Janet Baker in which she spoke of the peace and joy of Apple Farm, and of how it was made by the "weaving" of our individual lives here. That is an association behind the dream, the "house" being consecrated sacramentally—the Farm and the world too.

My own part to carry the bowl of water? The bowl is like the little silver bowl which has played so frequent a part in my active imagination over the years. (In the dream it was a dark bowl.) I was trying last night to imagine what I was to do with the bowl of water—give it to people to drink from? Or put it down somewhere? Then I thought, "I can't put it down because of the rounded base"—and saw myself for a moment in my own living room sitting on the little ancient "nursing chair" and holding the bowl quietly on my knees. Actually I do not think I should be *active* about this dream even in imagination. The task was clearly to trust the "dance" movements, simply making sure the water was preserved and did not spill. If I do this, my movements will be in Tao—in the oneness of the sacramental life. The "why?" is not the ego's business.

1985

The glorious autumn weather continues, a true Indian summer. Today warmer even, though not so crystal clear at sunrise. The leaves are falling fast, but the colors, though muted, continue to be a splendor in the sunlight. My little ginkgo tree is pure gold and only just beginning to lose its leaves. Rosebuds still open one by one.

Another association comes to the dream: T. S. Eliot (in "Little Gidding") on the only redemption from the guilts of old age being the fire in which we learn "to move in measure like a dance."

NOVEMBER 13

I dreamed last night that I had been on a long journey underground. A number of individuals were on the same way. There was no sense of underground trains, just empty dark ground on which we had walked. Now after a last stretch we were moving towards the surface at the exit nearest to "home," which was our goal. A brief last bit of rising ground was ahead. I was waiting, however, before going on because I thought my mother— who had not traveled with me for the last part of the journey, having chosen another way—would want to be reassured that I had arrived safely at this point where the alternative ways met. It felt as though many traveled on this underground way, but each was alone—though there was a sense of comradeship. I waited awhile and then I saw my "mother" arriving. She was slender, dark-haired, middle-aged—she recognized me and nodded a greeting and walked on. I was relieved and released to continue my way to the exit. She was wearing a trim suit of natural-colored moire silk or perhaps linen. All the others I had seen were in darkish dress. She did not physically resemble my memories of my mother.

This must surely be a death dream. The rising ground ahead leading to the exit and thence home was bare and empty of people. The other few people around were also halted at this pre-exit point—except my mother, who disappeared after passing me. I have a vague impression of a serene, seated woman who was a sort of guardian of this otherwise unmarked "gateway" to the last climb.

Does the separation of our ways on the previous part of the journey refer to the last thirty-six years since she died? There was a momentary happy but detached contact in the dream before she, in that beautiful natural clothing, went on her way, leaving me content to follow mine. The "mother" in me?

There is an association with my saying yesterday there were still a few things I would like to do in this world—such as re-reading the diaries, making extracts perhaps. I was reminded of the "Of the Mercy" squares. They feel remote, but I do touch now and then an intuition of "holy indifference" to the ego's fate.

∽

NOVEMBER 18

Before I woke this morning a dream image of my lily pool as it is now, almost all leaves and buds gone as winter comes. But in the dream at the exact center of it a fire was rising out of the water and in the midst of the fire a blackened, bent-over stalk. The fire was not leaping flames but an intense glow, a "pillar of fire" rising out of the water.

There is an association with Shakespeare's sonnet which begins:

> *That time of year thou mayst in me behold*
> *When yellow leaves, or none, or few, do hang*
> *Upon those boughs which shake against the cold,*

and which includes:

> *In me thou see'st the glowing of such fire*
> *That on the ashes of his youth doth lie,*
> *As the death-bed whereon it must expire*
> *Consum'd with that which it was nourished by.*

In the dream, fire out of water, burning in water.

∽

NOVEMBER 25

Old Age arrived from the printers in time for Alison to take inscribed copies to St. Julian friends. It is really beautifully done.

As to my inner state, I know nothing. The ego still fusses around, but

I sense that somewhere deep down there is a growing sense of the immense difference between the longing to grow and the true darkness of letting it go—of dying to the ego center while still in this world. The dream of the fire rising in the center of the lily pond and burning the last blackened stalk of the lily as winter comes is very powerful. Even that great symbol—the lotus—and my experience of oneness with the stem must pass through the fire. I think too of how even the joy of the ego in that kind of vision and in the work that has flowed through me must pass through the fire before we can "move in measure like a dancer" in the Dance of the totality.

NOVEMBER 28

It is Thanksgiving Day. I am to go up to the Farm House for dinner—about fourteen people! I miss Alison—and today a piercing pain of loneliness for Else. No one here now at all from the Old World—and perhaps I feel it even more today when my genuine gratitude to the New World rises. It is the anniversary of my first day in L.A.

1986

JANUARY 4

I have been reading Borges' "Conversations At Eighty" and was greatly moved by the following:

> A poet should think of all things as being given him, even misfortune. Misfortune, defeat, humiliation, failure, those are our tools—we are given mistakes, we are given nightmares—and our task is to turn them into poetry. And were I truly a poet I would feel that every moment of my life is poetic, every moment of my life is a kind of clay I have to mould, I have to shape, to lick into poetry. So that I don't think I should apologize for my mistakes. These mistakes were given me—in order that I might turn them into poetry. (p. 6)

I was re-reading this yesterday and thinking of how the turning of experience into "poetry" could of course happen in so many ways which were not actually poetry. That which Borges says of the actual poet's task is true for the poetic spirit in everyone—the work of giving form, expression, to everything that happens, thus discovering and revealing meaning, "the pattern of the glory," discovering that all experiences, light or dark, are stars and take their place in the constellation of wholeness.

∞

The lovely feeling of "space" as my two "empty" days begin. Chores finished, I sat down and was still this morning. I have thought recently of Toni's answer to me when I asked the question which I hear so often from others now, and I have remembered her answer, *the* answer: "stop thinking." It does not of course mean in the ordinary sense that thought must be abandoned, but that all cause and effect reasoning must be suspended if the transformation of action and attitude is to come. As I sat this morning I was, as usual, aware of the weight (and lightness) of my feet on the floor—on the earth itself—and the image returned, still as vivid as it was almost forty years ago, of that first experience of the Self that came to me in the midst of the greatest sorrow of my life, in the most unlikely of places, as I waited alone for a bus late at night at Notting Hill Gate with its sordid buildings, watching the traffic lights change. As I described in my autobiography, my feet were suddenly rooted in the earth and yet at the same time the orderly changes of the green, yellow, and red in the silence of the traffic-free roads became a dance of joy—and Notting Hill Gate became the gate to a new life. Here was born the blue and white mandala which is peculiarly mine. Toni asked me what I called the mandala, and when I replied without hesitating "Notting Hill Gate" she seemed to brush that aside as foolish. But though it may have come from the Fool within, it was not foolish. When I have been given the rare experiences of the life outside time, they have come (except once) in the midst of the ten thousand things. They have included, not excluded, the world.

Together with the Notting Hill Gate memory came the thought of Lorraine Kisly's mention of the *Parabola* issues ahead. There was one title that lit a spark in me ("Sadness") and I felt an urge to write something about this. I also read this week somewhere of someone saying that there is always sadness in Heaven. And the Notting Hill experience was deep sadness purged of bitterness, transmuted into joy.

Perhaps I shall write of this, and it is well as long as I am acutely aware of the danger from the ego's lurking desire still to achieve "publication."

I think of the dream of the black and white bird that fell into the water and that I lifted out in time to save it—finding it had been weighted with desert sand. In the months since Else died all my energy has gone to talk with people. That other side, the writing side, is perhaps forcing itself on my attention now. The conflict goes on, as Jung says, to the very end. One cannot lie back and rest on one side of it and neglect the other. The tension alone brings the next transformation.

JANUARY 24   ∽

I was thinking this morning of how the wounds of one's early life are the "stuff" of one's whole journey in time. "Stuff" means, among other things, "the basic substance or essential elements of anything; essence" (*American Heritage Dictionary*). If we remember childhood dreams, they express this essence. "We are such *stuff* as dreams are made on." Shakespeare's words hint also at the truth that the poet in us *makes* dreams from this essence, the dreams created through the divine gift of imagination, actively—in other words, active imagination. As Borges says, every smallest thing in life, including mistakes, misfortunes, nightmares—every moment—is a tool given to the poetic imagination to be worked on like clay.

My own childhood dreams grow more vivid with the years. This morning the first of all (when I was carried helpless and terrified on the great curve of the rainbow) came back with new power and meaning as I lay in bed looking at the flame of my candle. I closed my right eye (unfocussed without its lens) and saw that the left eye with its cataract produced a most beautiful circle of light around the flame (which the cataract makes seem many instead of one). This rayed circle is of all the colors of the rainbow against the dark background—as though the half circle of the rainbow that we see in daylight were completed in the dark around the individual candle flame, symbol of the tiny human consciousness of the individual human being.

I thought of the total helplessness when I was carried in that immense rainbow, moving at great speed, terrified yet aware of the glory of the colors. But, however helpless, I was still an embryonic human being, aware of myself—able to feel fear of the living God, so to speak. And "the fear of the Lord is the beginning of wisdom."

The message of this morning's vision of the tiny rainbow rays of a completed circle was that it was the "wound," the cataract dimming my outer sight, that enabled me to see it. Perhaps in these images are mirrored the meaning of our individual lives as we awaken to consciousness of ourselves and of life in time and the terror of the opposites. The white light of eternity is split into many colors, and if, as we grow and plant our feet on the earth, we will confront our fears with courage, then indeed we shall glimpse the rainbow circle within. The outer rainbow lifts the hearts of all with its mythical promise—it is born of sunlight shining through rain, of the final unity of fire and water, light and dark, conscious and unconscious; it is a half circle disappearing on the horizon of this world. But through the darkness of our wounds, if we never cease to tend that small individual flame, we may come at last to a glimpse of the circle, completed in the darkness under the earth, that is the certainty of wholeness, the many colors and the one.

It is a fact that from babyhood I suffered from all kinds of irrational fears—and yet there was always a spring of delight and happiness in me. It occurs to me that this too was foreshadowed in the rainbow dream— and that it enabled me to face the awful loneliness of the milestone dream, the second childhood vision of the stuff of my individual life.

∽   **MAY 22**

On Tuesday night a dream of great power. I was walking up a hillside in twilight. I had come to the bottom of the hill in my VW, bringing with me a small suitcase, since I was, I thought, going to stay overnight in a house which I was now looking for, knowing it was on the top of this hill and that one could not approach it by road. I was being "led," as it were, by a black dog (a border collie?) which ran ahead. My heart was light as I walked on the springy turf like that of the South Downs. There were dark bushes around. The sun had set and the light was going, and I wondered if I would be able to return to the car to fetch the suitcase as I had no flashlight, but thought perhaps someone from the house would come with me to help. Anyway, it did not seem very important, and as I walked on and up my body felt lighter, stronger, and the air grew fresher, cooler. I drew deep breaths and my spirit rejoiced. I could scarcely believe in the extraordinary life-giving quality of that cold, invigorating air and the lightness of my body moving steadily without effort and without haste up the steep hill on the firm and quiet turf. It was sheer wonder.

Then I saw without surprise the outline of a large house ahead against the darkening sky. The bushes and some trees near the house were black now. The dog still ran ahead towards it. The house itself was square, I thought, and several stories high—almost a cube. It was not a stone "keep" as in a castle, but an old house, I guessed (perhaps a sort of gate house) of dark and weathered brick, and I came now in near darkness to the door. Then I heard voices coming from inside, from the depths of the house. They were deep but somehow musical voices—I "saw" as well as heard them in a strange way (but not strange to me in the dream itself)—and these voices brought to me still greater joy and delight and spoke to me of welcome. I stood on the threshold and woke. There was nothing in the least eerie in this dream and absolutely no anxiety.

I lay for a long time content. It was surely a death dream. The black dog (reminiscent of Mephistopheles and his dog in *Faust Part II* leading into the darkness below) was a "border" collie—a shepherd dog. There are associations to von Franz telling of the companion animal on the path to death, to the lovely story of the Indian hero who would not enter Heaven without his dog, to Jung and the guidance of instinct in confrontation with the unconscious, and to Sister Therese's dream of her ever-lightening steps on her journey into spring through the dark to light.

However, in my dream the emphasis was all on the darkness, the *black-*

ness that became increasingly the center of my deepening wonder and joy. Blackness of the dog, then of the bushes, then of the interior of the house, and then of the voices themselves. I thought of the black holes in space which are in fact black to our eyes because of the tremendous intensity of their light, and remembered the woman's dream, before Jung died, of his disappearing into a black hole—but she saw also the green of his coat.

∽

MAY 29

I have been reading T. S. Eliot's introduction to *All Hallow's Eve,* and it is interesting to see that he speaks of Charles Williams's writings in exactly the same terms as Hannah writes of Jung. Neither Williams nor Jung wrote anything that had not been experienced. That's why I feel they are so alike. It is what sets them apart from so many others. Williams's experience of "the essence of Evil," in Eliot's phrase, is exactly the same as Jung's confrontation with the deep unconscious.

Eliot ends this introduction with the words, "For the reader who can appreciate them, there are terrors in the pit of darkness into which he can make us look; but in the end we are brought nearer to what another modern explorer of the darkness has called 'the laughter at the heart of things.'"

This laughter was also at the heart of Jung, as those who were closest to him have testified. Both Hannah and van der Post have told of the extraordinary effect on them of hearing his deep "belly" laughter ring out.

∽

JULY 6

My dreams are showing my unconscious resistance to letting go of my need for people to depend on me. I could not expect it to be easy after all the years of being sought after. The central meaning of my long life is the sacrifice of being needed, as for so many women. How marvelously, as I look back, I see the steps in time of this sacrifice—the weaving of the pattern through my losses, the way the need for reassurance was transferred from one of projection to becoming less and less personal and demanding, I believe, through suffering, more and more inward and more dangerous, and coming near in these latter days to the meaning of Christ's ultimate humanity in the words, "My God, my God, why hast thou forsaken me," which are a necessity of wholeness.

1986

The deep roots of the ego's clinging to its need to be the center engender the nameless fears I have suffered and have recognized much more objectively of late. Nevertheless they still threaten in times of great weariness. It helped to read Hannah's words about how in old age one is so tired all the time.

JULY 8

⚬

Last night I came on a quotation from Jung: "The creative activity of imagination frees a man from his bondage to the 'nothing but' and raises him to the status of one who plays. As Schiller says, man is completely human only when he is at play."

That hit me like a sudden flash of lightning. *That* is what I so easily lose touch with in these days of weariness. I have had more than a touch of the "air-lock" indigestion this last week, which is always the warning sign to me of a psychic block. I have been caught in a certainty that the images would never really come alive again, a prison of ego-consciousness, an acceptance of the ineptitude of my trembling hands. (I had seen Nancy's clay work on Sunday and had a vague notion I might try this, but it's hopeless.) But I can indeed return to "play" with images, remember the play attitude, however inept and distracted I am.

1987

JUNE 14

Near the beginning of last week there was a fragment of dream that remains with me in which I felt I was on the way into the Beyond, through death, and took someone's hand who would be my guide. But at that moment I was called back. There was a need behind me and I must return. This is the third such dream in the last year or so. In the first a little boat took me, but it was turned back. In the second the black dog led me to the gateway and I heard the music, but there was unfinished "business" I could not take with me. And now there is a human hand ready to guide me but my choice was to stay yet awhile.

As I stay with this last dream I realize that I did not let go of the companion's hand as I turned back, and it seemed that she was entirely willing to stay with me in this world. There was a sense of ease about it all.

∽

Last night (not sleeping till 5:30 or so) I read the *Inferno* and came to the canto about the Wood of the Suicides. What a tremendous image it is! Charlie Taylor's suggestion about "the symbolic aptness of the Wood of Circle 7 and how it relates to the Wood of the beginning" drew my particular attention. Yes, indeed . . . when we enter the dark wood at the turning point, the midpoint of our lifetime, we do not know, as Dante says, how we got there since we are so "full of sleep," sinking into the unconscious, into fear and the bitterness of near-death. And the danger then of refusing to open our eyes to "the good I found there" is very great. If one does so refuse, it is exactly like a spiritual suicide. I still think with a shiver of how near I came in Zurich, in that darkest wood of 1948, to giving up entirely and going home (in the warning words of my horoscope, settling for "sickness" instead of "work"). Dante by the mercy did not turn from the hidden good—he glimpsed the sun on the mountain peak, *tried* to climb, and there met the guide who would take him on the long journey of self-knowledge, down into the depths and *then* up the mountain of purging to the stars.

The Wood of the Suicides in the Circle of the Violent is the same wood where the one who refuses the conscious journey chooses to stay. He or she has done violence to his or her true self, "murdered" the life within, and is thrown into the wood at random by the Minotaur, mindless offspring of devouring sensual instinct to which the anima has offered herself, and there in that wood when he has taken root is devoured by Harpies— birds of prey with human faces—another form of deadly mixture, this time *intuitive* thought turned utterly destructive when identified with negative anima. These human trees and branches still put out leaves of growth, which are immediately devoured, and their life blood pours out through broken twigs. What a picture of neurosis, of refusal of consciousness.

There is an extremely moving passage in which Dante, in his ignorance of what these trees are, breaks off a branch and the tortured soul whiningly accuses him of heartless cruelty as the blood pours out, so that deep compassion enters the poet's heart again. The soul who speaks to him had fallen into despair when wrongfully accused by others of treachery to the one he served, and had killed himself.

How often do we experience in lesser ways all through our lives that temptation to incite the harpies within to tear away the new growth. We call it "nothing but," try to possess it, demand the constant reassurance of others that the ego is right, pouring out our life blood in useless striving or supine demand to be the "victim" of others, of circumstances, and so on. Every time we must once again pass through a part of the dark wood wherein alone we may find the "good in it," the new guide or attitude at each stage of the journey.

The image of the wood in the tremendous and unforgettable first lines of the *Commedia* is powerfully enhanced when the image of the wood of the suicides is also in our minds. Do not ever put down roots when this darkness is upon us—move through it with our *feet* on the earth. Remember the sun and the stars, and simply go on to meet the guide who is always there if we don't sink into the sleep of the unconscious.

I am reminded of George MacDonald's words about the "spiritual murder" that "kills the image of the hated" (the refusal to forgive oneself).

1988

JANUARY 8

I've been experiencing some dark times at night and in the mornings, but when I return to Sri Ramana's words I am at peace again. He said: "We think that there is something hiding our reality and that it must be destroyed before the reality is gained. It is ridiculous. A day will dawn when you will yourself laugh at your past efforts. That which will be on the day you laugh is also here and now."

I think it is this that has revived in me a memory from my childhood which has remained vivid all through my life, but that I don't think I have ever written down—nor even spoken of to anyone—simply because I could not find any words to express it. But now I begin to recognize its nature.

I was about eleven or twelve years old, I think, and was at school, St. George's, walking alone close to the wall near the headmaster's wing and going, I imagine, towards the back door into the girls' changing rooms. Suddenly I stood still and out of the blue came an extraordinarily new experience of "being," beyond any identification with my ego's wants and dislikes. I think the question really took hold of me, the question "Who am I?" and for the first time for a few seconds I consciously knew myself as part of the universe. The sun was shining, I stood on the earth. Who was this "I" whom I had never really looked at?

Perhaps it was in that brief moment that the quest began—and perhaps that was why at my first reading of Jung in my late thirties I had so certain a sense of recognizing what I already "knew" in my heart but not in my head.

⌒

NOVEMBER 3

A moment of great beauty last weekend. The rising sun was not yet shining above the horizon of my hollow when I glanced out of my living room's northern window and saw the golden maple tree near the Farm House blazing in the newly risen sun. Some days later a similar moment, looking out of my morning room window as the last rays of the setting sun lit up the dark rich red of the flowering crabapple tree's berries. I have never seen it so loaded with rich fruit as this year—or so it seems. As in the vision of the maple in the early morning, so in this evening moment the sun's rays seemed to be wholly gathered in the single tree, and the land around it was the dark silence without which the light could not be seen.

Then the night before last there was a dream which again was an image of glowing color. I have remembered vividly one of the final pictures we chose for the new edition of *Dark Wood*—the petals of the white rose behind images of Our Lady and Dante. I don't see the details, but the petals of the circle of the rose reminded me of some of Georgia O'Keeffe's miraculous flower paintings. My dream was simply an image of such petals, and they were of that incredibly intense blue of the small delphiniums and (to me) the even more moving blue of the scilla blooming before all other flowers in the early spring in my garden. (I had just been planting a few more of those miraculous little bulbs.) In the dream the petals formed an opened flower bigger than myself—and I stood simply gazing into the intensity of the blue which had the numinous indescribable quality of color in some dreams.

I remember my poem "In praise of blue" that I wrote a year or two ago in a mood of lightness. Gold, red, and the blue I most love, all in one week.

I have a notion that as I woke—or perhaps even in the dream itself— a part of my mind was not content with just *seeing*, was bothered about "meaning" and troubled by seeking it. But only the depth of the color now remains.

1989

JANUARY 20

I read some pages from *Be As You Are,* a book about the teaching of Ramana Maharshi, during a wakeful hour in the night, the chapter about the Guru, with Sri Ramana's answer to the often-repeated question about the necessity for finding one. He insists on the *inner* guru; the outer guru is at one with the inner, and indeed may be found in all our true meetings with outer experience. But the outer sage who *has* achieved unity with the Self may be a particularly needed channel of grace to others. It was so lovely recently to come on a passage in a book of extracts from Thomas Merton's journals (1964–65) in which he expresses his deep response to Ramana Maharshi—to his *real experience* of "God as the ultimate Self, who is the Self of every self," of Grace, incarnation. "The impact of Maharshi's experience awakens in us the real depth of this truth and the love that springs from it."

Soon after this I came across in Jung's *Letters* a reply to "N," who had asked if there was some place he could go to help the world with his knowledge. "I should give you the same answer as Shri Ramana Maharshi," Jung wrote. (In answer to the same question, Shri Ramana had told N: "Help yourself and you help the world, for you are the world.") Jung went on: "If you want to do something useful, it can only be there where you live, where you know the people and circumstances. . . . Not rarely the unconscious blindfolds you, because it does not want you to find an application of your energies to external circumstances. The reason for such a resistance lies in the fact that you need some reconstruction in yourself which you would gladly apply to others. Many things should be put right in oneself first, before we apply our imperfections to our fellow beings."

∽

FEBRUARY 2

Last night I dreamed (in images I can barely remember enough to describe) that I had been directed to light a fire in a small, contained place of stone, a fire which would burn its core. Outside it there was left a single tulip dying from the heat, bent over, which was strongly associated with the picture of one of Vita Sackville-West's sink gardens in which there was a single yellow and reddish tulip.

(I have been reading with great delight a book about her and Harold Nicolson's long and beautiful love of gardens, of every growing thing, and also the beauty of their marriage growing and deepening with this love of the land. Maintained by the National Trust, Vita's great garden at Sissinghurst gives pleasure and awakens love in thousands of people, even now, long after her death. She herself often wondered whether she was selfish, giving her energies to this work of creation she loved best. Here is a great example: the true "influence" is never consciously directed. It springs from love of one's work.)

Then I half woke and dreamed again that a voice said something like "Now you will be able to hear the music of 'salt' as long as you remain here." I knew this meant that because of the unseen burning of the "core" of whatever it was, this music could sound for me as long as I was alive in this world.

1989

FEBRUARY 3

The symbolism of salt in *Mysterium Coniunctionis* is most fascinating. Like so many of the essential images, it is "arcane substance" (*nigredo*) and the transformed, coagulated, whitened *albedo* and finally the lapis itself—the aqua permanens, the Wisdom of God. The emphasis of salt is on the feminine wisdom, moist yet dry, lunar.

The question for me about the dream is what is the "core" that must burn before the music is heard?

I find that the small garden with the single tulip at Sissinghurst is not in fact a sink garden but is a small inset on the paved walk of the Lime Walk—Harold's creation, with every kind of spring flower at the base of the trees. However, it has in fact as in my dream the feeling of the sink gardens, and in the dream it was lifted above the ground at about knee height, close up against the blocks of stone surrounding and hiding a hollow center where I had lit the unseen fire. It had somewhat of the feeling of an oven (perhaps for the heating and drying of the too-moist salt).

Another association: Vita created sink gardens for the old or infirm who could no longer manage ordinary gardening.

FEBRUARY 7

Early on Monday morning came a dream in which I saw a man lying on a stone and I knew that he had been dead. A glowing light as of fire or flames was all around him; he was beginning to sit up and looked at me with eyes full of life, of recognition, of joy. I did not know his face and yet I deeply knew that he carried in some mysterious and beautiful way the essence of every man who had been important in my life—ancestors, lovers, sons, and guides. And I knew that this image linked with the burning of the fire in the core of the stone in my dream last Thursday—that it had to do with a deep transformation perhaps of the creative masculine spirit

through the fire which is finally kindled and shines in the center of the
Self, the stone, and which at the same time releases the aqua permanens
of the moon, the shining "salt" of Sophia, so that the sound of the music
of the feminine Wisdom of God can "play" and be heard in this world,
and the fire of consciousness burning in the hidden core of the stone is
one with the water of life.

The image of the ancient blocks of stone which Vita and Harold found
at Sissinghurst and used in uneven "walls" as rock gardens are vivid in my
heart.

∽

I find it increasingly difficult to separate my inner life from simply staying
with "the next necessary thing," in Jung's words. I have been aware fairly
frequently of what I call "working nights"—waking with a feeling that
inner work has gone on and on in the night but has left no visual images
behind. I think often of the last canto of the *Paradiso* in which the geome-
ter works endlessly to fit the circle to the square and can't because it is
impossible, but he must work and then wait and the impossible comes in
"God's good time."

∽

I had a dream earlier last week of a house in which I was living, with other
people living in other rooms of it. There was a fire in adjacent property
and the firemen were at work, but it began to look as though our house
was threatened. I was talking to a fireman and he asked whose house it
was. I suddenly realized that it was not a place I had rented temporarily
but my *own* house. I said so clearly, yet at the same time felt a kind of
clarity and release, as though if it burned down no one but myself would
be the loser, and it didn't matter to me much. There was no sense of danger to anyone's life in the dream, only to possessions. (The person's house
is often his or her ego-structure.)

After waking, the memory of words from a Psalm came strongly into
my mind: "Except the Lord build the house they labor in vain that build

it: except the Lord keep the city the watchman waketh but in vain" (Psalm 127). The next verse too is a delight: "It is vain for you to rise up early, to sit up late, to eat the bread of sorrows: for so he giveth his beloved sleep." (The Jerusalem Bible translates this as "In vain you get up earlier, and put off going to bed, sweating to make a living, since he provides for his beloved as they sleep.")

1990

NOVEMBER 16

Over three weeks since I wrote here, probably the longest gap yet since starting the "Diary of Vowels"! There seems less need for any words—few dreams that I remember, though occasionally an image speaks clearly and is gone. Yet the great images of my life speak with increasing power and beauty, and when I live with them I feel no need to ask for more. I remember old Father Robson's words: "*Once* the heavens opened for me. How could anyone ask for more?"

The continually present image is the vision of the blue star lily—my oneness with the stem, all without losing the other level of conscious daily life. I looked it up where I had recorded it in September 1982, and began to read what came before that experience. I had entirely forgotten that it followed the often-remembered dream of my adult meeting with my father—that this brief meeting was followed, without waking, by the dream, long forgotten, of the dangerous snake with whom I had some kind of wordless communication which made it harmless to the passing children. Following this I had copied a very fine passage from Jung about the father image and the gift of Logos, Spirit, to the daughter.

How astonishing to have forgotten such a dream, which seems now such a lovely image of what I have tried to express in my writing about "intercession"—the wordless, goalless, yielding *between*.

The gaps in this diary seem to get longer as energy wanes for everything but the exchanges with people, exchanges that include the "center" level. I remember, however, how Hannah replied to someone who asked what her remaining wishes were in her extreme old age. She said her first wish was to be freed from *laziness.* And I am not at all sure that this is not also my major sin—that in the tiredness, I waste my remaining energy on "inferior people and things," in the *I Ching's* language. It has told me to beware of this recently when I asked a question.

I have three recent images from dreams in the last two weeks. First a dream inspired by John Dunne's image, taken from his experience as a child, of being in the eye of the storm during a hurricane on the east coast. He writes, in *Peace of the Present,* of the goal of living always in that inner center that is everywhere and has its circumference nowhere, moving always in and with the center while the storms of life in time and space rage around us. My dream image was like that. I was standing in a sphere, colorless, empty, and moving slowly and calmly from side to side. I was holding out my cupped hand, into which a succession of small spheres, each representing my next task or the next small necessity of my life, was gently put by an unseen giver hidden in the storm clouds surrounding the eye, the calm center. This center space itself moved, as I moved within it, with the movement of the clouds or unseen forces around it—the eye of the storm. Again when I woke I was struck by the "matter of factness" which seems to characterize many of the deepest and biggest dreams I remember in my life.

1993

JULY 31

There was a dream last week in which I was visiting the house of my grandmother Reinold and my Aunt Beryl. Someone pushed in a stretcher on which my grandmother lay, having just died in her old age. (She was nearly one hundred when she actually died.) The person said I would probably like to look at her. I didn't want to, but I pulled back the cloth that covered her. I had always loved her—her simplicity and warmth—but had never been really close to her. As soon as the cover was pulled back, she sat up and began talking. I thought what a mercy it was that had brought her to me and revealed that she wasn't dead before burial. I talked to her gently because she was speaking incoherently about the past and I felt she had not yet realized what had happened after her experience of death. I hoped to help her come to herself as we waited for her daughter to appear. She had immediately been sent for. I thought, "I will wait with her until her family appears and then go to my own house."

This dream came shortly after my week off, towards the end of which I wrote and revised the promised article for Father Bede's book, which Beatrice Bruteau had asked for. Jane and the others I shared it with liked it, so I felt good to have written again. I am wondering whether this dream is connected with the other one in which I was trying to avoid extreme old age and the failure of possibility of new writing and other kinds of effort as energy goes and the darkness of the world deepens. However, there was my Reinold grandmother whose extreme old age was, I believe, as simple and accepting of everything as she had always been, and that side of me had still something to do or be in this world.

Then last night came another very powerful dream. I was working slowly and carefully on a task which involved emptying a living thing, to which I was attending with intense concentration, thinking it to be the process of my own death. Its shape was egglike—or perhaps more like a mandala—and it was dark with narrow white stripes. In this dream the mandala had become a large living thing, and I was to empty it of the fluid that filled it so that it would gradually come to its end. I was sad because I knew it had been a thing of much beauty, but as it grew empty I realized that the joy in its beauty did not disappear but somehow became a great sense of freedom and content within myself.

There was one moment in the dream when I thought how much easier it would be to set off an explosion that would end the whole long-drawn-out process immediately—get it over—but then realized that the explosion would destroy a whole lot of things, even people, around the mandala, and so absolutely dismissed that possibility and continued the slow but joyful work.

SEPTEMBER 13

An even longer gap, but very little clear dreaming during these weeks, though it seems to me that of late I have woken from essentially the same dream almost nightly. Last night an image was clearer. The ongoing message of the dreams has been that there is one more experience to be gone through, one step in consciousness to be made, before it would be time for me to die. Then last night I dreamed that I saw three (or perhaps four) tall containers of plain glass—too tall for even the tallest flowers, not tall enough to be holders of umbrellas. They were of slightly varying heights but all were of clear white, smooth, transparent glass. They were *empty*, and all shiningly *clean*, and I felt they were standing there waiting to be filled with that for which they were made. And again as I watched I felt they were a part of my life ready now to receive their meaning, their truth, and I was grieving that I did not know how to fill them or with what, but somehow knew, in T. S. Eliot's words from "Four Quartets," that "the faith and the love and the hope are all in the *waiting*, / Wait without thought, for you are not ready for thought: / So the darkness shall be the light and the stillness the dancing."

1994

Yesterday was Good Friday. I dreamed about two nurses who were caring for a newborn child. This child, according to the doctors, was mortally sick and unlikely to live. The child was also exceedingly ugly. I felt respect and gratitude to the nurses, who were like my own splendid Nurse Campbell in Jerusalem who had literally saved my life, and also like Lauren's description of a true nurse in his last letter. (I had been talking of this recently, and it was a numinous memory.) I myself in the dream did not want to look at the child, doomed as he or she seemed to be. But I looked all the same, and saw the ugly face. I then seemed to know that the child's name was Theraphene—and at once, as I half woke, associations crowded into my mind. First of course the derivation. The meaning of therapy—treatment with intent to heal either the body or the psyche—and then "phene," phenomenon, an immediate object of perception, strange and often mysterious, a *happening*.

Following this there was a much clearer vision of the face of the child and the likeness to Janet Adam Smith at Oxford, a "*belle laide*" of great intelligence, a philosopher, a mountaineer, second year at Somerville when I was a Freshman. For some reason I never understood she asked me to one of her highly individual parties. I was so scared, feeling totally ignorant and incapable of joining in the conversation of the men and women present. I don't think I once spoke! After Oxford she married a poet, climbed the great peaks in Switzerland, had several children. I met her once or twice at that time (still feeling terribly infantile). But I have never forgotten her ugly-beautiful face. A descendant of Adam Smith, the eighteenth-century economist and philosopher—a true individual wholeness in her even as a young student.

After lying awake for a time I slept again and was aware of the same ugly child, but this time not a baby. She or he had not died but grown and neared adolescence. Then it was as though at intervals through the night the child grew into adolescence, passed through it, and just before I finally woke in the morning the image was fully adult. But the face remained the same as when I first saw the baby—the mature and wise belle-laide. Theraphene from her beginning.

I woke yesterday morning with a fragment of a dream in which I was with two or three Apple Farm friends, and we had met in order to read a book together. We had not decided on what book, but suddenly the title came to me with certainty and I said I would like to read Charles Williams's *Many Dimensions* aloud—and then I woke. So I have started to read it again. I have always felt it to be one of the most powerful stories I know in its message about the dangers of the manifestations of the Self whenever we *use* that unnamable mystery for attaining what we see as "good" on the levels of the opposites, when it inevitably constellates the dark side of its destructive opposite. Williams's story of the stone in the context of twentieth-century life has an unparalleled impact on the Imagination (in Blake's sense, and Shakespeare's).

Perhaps, it now occurs to me, I should be reading it actually out loud (perhaps to Daniel, like Quilleran reading to Koko and YumYum).

A new Common Reader catalogue came yesterday, subtitled "a selection of books for readers with imagination." It is truly exciting. I am even filled with an urge to revive my learning of ancient Greek—that which began with that great teacher of the classics at St. George's, Mr. Howe, who awaked in me the first touch of a true love of learning, a love of the beauty of words, a deep intuition of the life-long pursuit of the white bird of Truth. My love for languages was transferred later to French and Italian, but it began with that small class, four boys and myself, to whom Howe first opened the wonder of Greek. There is a book in the catalogue which tempts me to return to it.

Or, with my small energies, would this be an evasion?

I had a dream about ten days ago, at the end of my "quiet" week, but though each day I thought of it and wanted to write it down, there was so much going on that I put if off—though I did tell it to Jane.

It was like the dream (perhaps two years ago?) when I dreamed I was dying, having a heart attack, and, in the dream, thought that I should be telephoning to tell Jane about it. (I think my heart must have missed a beat or two.) In that dream I decided there was no point in waking Jane at 3 A.M. or so, and disturbing her sleep, when I didn't want her to do anything about it anyway!

In this recent dream I had the same feeling—this time more severe, including the sense of a process, a change in consciousness that seemed to be going on as I died; and the same thought about calling Jane came to me. But this time the reason I refrained from doing so was because I felt it was of vital importance for me to remain totally aware of this process, this experience of dying, and if I moved to pick up the telephone my attention would be broken. I was aware of a slight apprehension about this passage into the unknown, but the fear was, I knew, unimportant compared with the intense *interest* I felt. There was darkness around me, and on the edges of the dark I thought for a moment some images were moving, but they were gone when I made any effort to see them more clearly. So the darkness returned, but my consciousness was even more alert and clear as I waited and watched—and then woke with a normally beating heart!

I had been talking to someone the day before about Dame Julian of Norwich's lovely words, "I saw God in a point," and also of *Mr. God, This is Anna* and Anna's discovery not long before she died of the "I am" name of God—the "I am" at the center of every thing, animal, and person—and of her last words of joy, "I am inside out," which echo, says Flyn, the last words of a simple old woman dying in her eighties ("I feel as though I were being turned inside out"). The discovery that outer and inner are one—not split apart anymore. These are the thoughts that came to me immediately on waking from the dream, especially thoughts of "the point."

I have remembered with much joy this week the "point" as I experienced it in the blade of grass on my first visit to the little walled garden after my hysterectomy in the old hospital in 1952.

I dreamed that I held a bowl or a sack of golden yellow flower heads and I knew that they were about to transform one by one into small golden yellow birds and fly up into the clear air. I had been talking that evening with someone about my melon-lemon, squeezed-out lemon dream that came to me in Zurich and which I told to Jung in my hour with him, and remembering his reply to me, "You identify with the husk." Associations: the clinging to the "old skin" in the story Mark Nepo tells in the essay he sent me on "Terrible Knowledge"; a photograph of Ellis Peters with a sack of seed pods on the cover of *Brother Cadfael's Penance*. She is holding a single pod up to her face, the face of old age with calm joy in her eyes.

In a second dream, I was dancing down a long empty corridor, feeling free and happy, when I turned and, looking back, saw a man whom I knew to be a famous music teacher, and then found myself in a room talking to him and feeling both astonished and very grateful to find that he would accept me as a pupil, in spite of my ignorance of music. (This is a feeling very familiar to me, beginning with my stunned astonishment when our headmaster at St. George's School spoke in glowing terms of me at the Assembly meeting on the last day before my leaving school, and continuing when Toni accepted me as a student, and on into my eighties now whenever I think of the great people of the spirit who have become friends outside time and space, as it were, and of the extraordinary number of beautiful people who come here and give or write wonderful responses to my writings.)

Now this last dream shows me interrupting my totally unself-conscious dancing. Ever since the time at school when dance became the one performing art which I loved and longed to study and somehow knew was my one inborn art, I longed to make dancing my life, but the collective pattern was already set for me. Yet here I am so near the end of my life still bound to the need of my ego for dependence on a teacher, this time for something which is not my inborn gift. (Indeed in the last two years or more I have dreamed several times of hearing and responding to the music of God, clearly heard, and even the "unstruck sound" of the blue Vishuddha chakra of the throat.)

But I have not yet recorded the end of this latest dream.

1994

I was thanking the famous music teacher for his willingness to teach one so ignorant when I noticed that he was in fact a man much younger than myself with black curly hair, good-looking, but I suddenly realized with revulsion that he was wearing a fur coat of black Persian lambskins. I remembered how in the thirties, when there was little collective objection to furs, all of us who loved animals were fiercely horrified at the use of unborn lambskins for fur coats. And as I woke I was thinking, "There can be no *kindness* in a man who will wear such a coat—and no matter how brilliant a musician I do not think I could learn music from such a one."

Fully awake, the associations came. The Dalai Lama: "My religion is simply *kindness*"; Jung: "In the abysmal darkness of the unknown God I found a great *kindness.*"

Is the Guru now to be found inside and outside, beyond duality?

∽

EDITOR'S NOTE: When Helen died in January of 1995, she had not written in her *Diary of Vowels* since September 23, 1994, when, on the final page of her fifty-fourth journal, she recorded her intention of beginning a new volume soon. While she did not begin a new journal, we found among her papers a few sheets written in the spring of 1994, which reflect on her inner life in a way that seems almost a summary of the writing in her autobiography and her diary. At the end of this fragment is a brief quotation from a poem she had written many years before. We include the poem itself, since it, too, seems to reprise her inner story. She headed these reflections with the title "Memories, Dreams . . . New and Old."]

MAY 9

∽

The initial dream of my life—carried by wind on the lower half of a rainbow circle. My fear was intense as I was blown upwards from the lowest point along the bow-like cradle of color towards, as it seems to me now, the lowest point of the rainbow visible on earth—in other words towards my birth as a conscious human being.

Now, as I approach the rainbow's end after the long journey of life in time, I recognize the basic fears of my infancy, my childhood, my youth— the fear of the wind that "bloweth where it listeth" and over which no rational consciousness has control. But I know now, though I could not have put it into words until the approach of old age, that I was from an early age intensely if obscurely aware that the meaning of life lies in the small choices by which one confronts this fear. I may have been three or four when the dream came (I remember it as recurrent) and perhaps I was about twelve when I had the experience of consciously knowing myself as part of the universe. Although I recorded it in these pages, I never told this latter experience to *anyone*—not even to Toni—since I could find no words for it. Yet now I recognize it as a major leap in consciousness which continued to live in me throughout my life, unconsciously active until the great change of my entry into the second half of my years, with the discovery of Jung and the revelation of the way of the dream. I had at that point remembered *no* dreams clearly since the two major dreams of my childhood, and they returned to me on the threshold of my recognition of Jung as my outer guide to the inner world.

It is a month since I wrote the above, but it seems much longer. There have been so many wonderful times in these weeks, as also so many hours of darkness and tears, with tinges of self-pity and therefore of inflation, I suspect, hidden in those fears of the ego that every beautiful tribute I get must be invited by a lie, a dishonesty, in my whole life. Well, I know very well that the Self does not lie, and that the ego's ups and downs are all part of the ultimate pattern, the dance of dark and light which one can only know through the uttermost weakness accepted and suffered in life and in death.

But to return to what I was writing last month: I wrote most of the important dreams I remember, plus the bare facts of my outer life, in "Such

Stuff As Dreams Are Made On," the autobiography written in my early seventies. Since then about twenty years have passed and there have not been many "outer" facts to record; but there have been many dreams, making, it seems to me, a pattern of "return" to the beginnings of my life in time and connecting the major inner facts, dreams, and experiences of my whole life into a circle, small and unique, yet one with the final unity. And I have begun to realize that the black holes of the past month are a kind of agony, born of the need to clarify this pattern as death draws nearer, and born of a new "fact." Since my dreams first hinted at this work as a "legacy," I have repeatedly been told, in various ways, that it was not time to do this. But now the dreams have a different trend. It *is* time and I am agonizing about the delays—about the "laziness" that blocks me, and what seem endless obligations that take all my energy on this deep level. But now, Jane having helped me by implementing the new schedule of weeks without appointments, and more help, physical and practical, I truly can, if I will do my part of finding the new thread in the timing of the Spirit, at least begin to listen and record the dance as it comes to me on that wind that blew me in the colors of the rainbow when I was born. I remember the last words of the small attempt at a poem written in the early years at Apple Farm, beginning with the memory of that first dream: "The rainbow's end is in the rainbow's source." Looking this up, I read the whole poem. It hit me as of immense meaning for *this* moment in time. I am no poet in the literal sense, only in a degree of the poetic mind, the poetic heart, which has been, as it is for all mankind, a gift which is ours to bring to conscious life through incarnation.

A child dreamed long ago; in panic woke.
She dreamed she lay in a great arc of cloud
Like an inverted rainbow; helpless, alone.
Around her as she crouched, the colors glowed,
Driven by a mighty wind and she with them
Circling forever in the inhuman void.

The child has grown and lived, suffered and sinned;
She stands now on the earth feeling the weight of years.
Once more she sees the spectrum of that bow
Which springs from fire seen through the mists of tears.
The glowing colors swirl in that same wind—
The far off rushing sound is in her ears.

There comes upon her now a quaking fear,
The fear that was a panic in the child.
Once more will come that overwhelming force,
Sweeping away all that seemed reconciled
After long strife, and in the imprisoning cloud
Her peace will fall apart in tatters wild.

She gathers courage. "I am no infant now,"
She tells herself; "let the winds do their worst,
I will stand firm upon my mother earth."
But, as she speaks, the rainbow is reversed.
Images rise within and move without,
Piercing her through and leaving her accursed.

Red rage blinding, fierce claws rending,
Red fire burning, wild flames roaring,
Red blood flowing to a violent ending.

Red spark glowing, heart and body warming,
Red fire purging, into vision leaping,
Red blood giving life unto the dying.

Yellow is the fear of the coward at bay,
Yellow is the bile of the sick man's way,
Yellow is the creeping of loathsome decay.

Yellow is the ray of the brave sun rising,
Yellow is the spark of light in the gloaming,
Yellow is the gold of truth never ending.

Green malice hiding in the jungles of the mind,
Green envy brooding, stealing from the blind,
Green snake creeping, poison from behind.

Green trees growing, leaves replacing loss,
Green shoots leaping, smooth green moss,
Green snake healing, lifted on the cross.

Blue are the thoughts of failure after revel,
Blue is the freezing of talk that is sterile,
Blue is the color of the little cold devil.

Blue is the cool in the heart of the flame,
Blue is the flower of the Virgin's name,
Blue is the mystery banishing shame.

Now as she fights, opposing dark with light,
Swings to and fro between each hostile pair,
Weak grow her limbs; the rising sound of wind

Beats on her ears—soon she will cease to care.
Red anger hovers, creeping yellow fear,
Green snake will bite, blue darken to despair.

How foolish now it seems to trust in strength
Of human good; her life work crumbles, falls
In broken shards, and soon she will be caught
By that dire wind razing the strongest walls
And tossing her upon the ruthless wheel
Till colors fade in dark satanic halls.

What is the rainbow but an endless hope,
Pursued by men who seek with anxious care
For that immortal gold which lies at rainbow's end,
An end which is not and yet seems so fair?
None at the last can stand against the wind
That blows them, hopeless, on the colored air.

She lies now on the earth in the black dark
Of the eleventh hour. Her heart is cowed.
The first breeze touches her; a spark of light
Gleams and is gone but pierces through her shroud,
Leaving a thought alive. What of the point
Round which is blown the arching colored cloud?

What if the turning wheel were found to speed
Inward to that still point where in white light
All colors meet in unity at last?
The choice is there before her clear and bright.
She will go with the mighty winds of God,
Whither no man can tell with mortal sight.

She stands upon her feet, her human feet,
But this time turns to welcome the great wind.
She will go with it where it wills to blow
Because she chooses; asking not to find,
Only to go now with no yellow cringe
But in the fear of God, no longer blind.

Then for an instant as that glorious wind
Enters her spirit, and her feet stand fast,
She sees with springing joy the diamond point,
The pure white stone, and in its depths at last
The eternal prism from which all colors leap
Into the dance of time, future and past.

Blow then, ye winds, the colors on their course,
The rainbow's end is in the rainbow's source.

AFTERWORD

ON OCTOBER 15, 1994, during the months between her final writing in the "Diary of Vowels" and her death, Helen celebrated her ninetieth birthday. At the celebration in the Apple Farm Round House, friends performed a play that she greatly loved, Sophocles' *Oedipus at Colonus,* and Helen herself told a story that she had read recently and that had dominated her thoughts during her last few months. The story was about a man who confronted a monster and who, through his courage and his courtesy in the face of evil and danger, saved himself and rescued others. This story has much in common with Helen's own powerful dream, told in her autobiography, of confronting the hideous monster and defeating it through courage, kindness, and courtesy; it also gives narrative form to the two statements she recalls at the end of her July 17, 1994 entry ("The Dalai Lama: 'My religion is simply *kindness*'; Jung: 'In the abysmal darkness of the unknown God I found a great *kindness.*'")

In December, Helen discussed her approaching death with her beloved Dr. Smith. She then said goodbye to those she loved (by phone or in brief visits), requested of the Apple Farm Community that she not be distracted from this final stage of her journey by visits or calls even from those dear to her, and began her long final journey lying in the bed where many pages of her "Diary of Vowels" had been written. During these last days, she was not so much in a coma as in her own private space. She emerged from that space occasionally to speak. Of her reported words, I myself most treasure her question to Jane Bishop: "Do I have to tell anyone where I'm going?" Others are especially moved by the dream or vision she reported in which she was travelling with the Three Wise Men. This image is a reminder of the centrality of the Wise Man in Helen's journey toward individuation, and it suggests that, at the end, the way was not the lonely journey predicted by her milestone dream and experienced through so much of her life. And for those of us still experiencing our "life in time," as Helen would put it, it is pleasing to think of the Three Wise Men being accompanied by such a Wise Woman.

Helen died on January 6, 1995, on the Feast of the Epiphany—the Feast that celebrates the arrival of the Three Wise Men at the cradle in Bethlehem.

BARBARA A. MOWAT

HELEN M. LUKE was born in England in 1904. She received a master's degree in French and Italian literature from Somerville College, Oxford. Twenty years later she became interested in the work of C. G. Jung and studied at the Jung Institute in Zurich. After moving to the United States in 1949, she established an analytical practice with Robert Johnson in Los Angeles. In 1962 she founded the Apple Farm Community in Three Rivers, Michigan, "a center for people seeking to discover and appropriate the transforming power of symbols in their lives." She died at Apple Farm in 1995.

CHARLES H. TAYLOR is a Jungian analyst in Milford, Connecticut. He is editorial chair of the *Archive for Research in Archetypal Symbolism* and, with Patricia Finley, is author of *Images of a Journey in Dante's* Divine Comedy.

BARBARA A. MOWAT is Director of Academic Programs at the Folger Shakespeare Library, Senior Editor of *Shakespeare Quarterly*, Chair of the Folger Institute, and author of *The Dramaturgy of Shakespeare's Romances*. She is currently editing for the New Folger Library Shakespeare series.

OLD AGE: JOURNEY INTO SIMPLICITY

by Helen M. Luke

In this remarkably penetrative book, Luke offers five essays on the spiritual possibilities of old age. Reflecting upon passages from four classics—*The Odyssey, King Lear, The Tempest,* and *Four Quartets*—Luke imagines old age not as a decline but as a culminating stage of life. A fifth essay examines suffering as the redemptive fire that can incinerate the ego, releasing the phoenix of the real self.

FROM "KING LEAR"—

"Here are the proper occupations of old age: prayer, which is the quickening of the mind, the rooting of the attention in the ground of being; song, which is the expression of spontaneous joy in the harmony of the chaos; the 'telling of old tales,' which among all primitives was the supreme function of the old, who passed on the wisdom of the ancestor through the symbol, through the understanding of the dreams of the race that their long experience has taught them. In our days how sadly lost, despised even, is the function of the old! Wisdom being identified with knowledge, the 'old tale' has become the subject of learned historical research, and only for the few does it remain the carrier of true wisdom of heart and mind, of body and spirit. When the old cease to 'dream dreams,' to be 'tellers of old tales,' the time must come of which the Book of Proverbs speaks: 'Where there is no vision, the people perish.'

"And laughter! Surely laughter of a certain kind springs from the heart of those who have truly grown old. It is the laughter of pure delight in beauty—beauty of which the golden butterfly is the perfect symbol—a fleeting, ephemeral thing, passing on the wind, eternally reborn from the earthbound worm, the fragile yet omnipotent beauty of the present moment."

OLD AGE: JOURNEY INTO SIMPLICITY
Paperback; 144 pages; $11.00; 0-609-80590-8
A Bell Tower Book